Praise for *Bridge E*

"The evolution of our species asks for us to build bridges beyond narrowed identities and discover the dimensional wholeness that is our true nature. In this evocative depiction of her own journey, Hala Buck shows us how each of our lives can be an unfolding — from woundedness to healing, and from separation to belonging."

—Tara Brach, Author of *Radical Acceptance and Radical Compassion* (Viking, 2020)

"Hala Buck rightfully sums herself up in the title of her book *Bridge Between Worlds: A Lebanese-Arab-American Woman's Journey*, and what a journey it has been! Mrs. Buck takes the reader on a fascinating and complex worldwide journey, rich in details of the tapestry of her experiences. One cannot help but conclude that there is a need for more Hala Bucks in these very divisive times. We could all learn from her."

—Johnny Young, U.S. Career Ambassador (ret.) and Angelena V. Young U.S. Protocol Officer (Ret.)

"This memoir is a profound, poignant, and personable account of an Arab woman born across faiths, married to an American diplomat, mother to a bicultural daughter. Hala's stories are filled with candor, humor, struggles, and insights as a bridge builder, a peacemaker, a model of an Arab-American woman. All readers will be gripped and moved by this memoir that connects us across cultures!"

—Luby Ismail, Intercultural trainer, Founder and President of Connecting Cultures

Bridge Between Worlds

ADST MEMOIRS AND OCCASIONAL PAPERS SERIES
Series Editors: LISA TERRY *and* MARGERY THOMPSON

In 2003, the Association for Diplomatic Studies and Training (ADST), a nonprofit organization founded in 1986, created the Memoirs and Occasional Papers Series to preserve firsthand accounts and other informed observations on foreign affairs for scholars, journalists, and the general public. Through its book series, its Foreign Affairs Oral History program, and its support for the training of foreign affairs personnel at the State Department's Foreign Service Institute, ADST seeks to promote understanding of American diplomacy and those who conduct it. As a Lebanese-born Foreign Service spouse, Hala Buck shines a cross-cultural light on the important work of our diplomats and the challenges their families confront.

RELATED TITLES FROM ADST SERIES

MARGARET BENDER, *Foreign at Home and Away: Foreign-born Wives in the U.S. Foreign Service*

PRUDENCE BUSHNELL, *Terrorism, Betrayal, and Resilience: My Story of the 1998 US Embassy Bombings*

CHARLES T. CROSS, *Born a Foreigner: A Memoir of the American Presence in Asia*

HERMANN F. EILTS, *Early American Diplomacy in the Near and Far East: The Diplomatic and Personal History of Edmund Q. Roberts (1784–1836)*

PARKER T. HART, *Saudi Arabia and the United States: Birth of a Security Partnership*

JUDITH M. HEIMANN, *Paying Calls in Shangri-La: Scenes from a Woman's Life in American Diplomacy*

JOANNE HUSKEY, *The Unofficial Diplomat*

RICHARD L. JACKSON, *The Incidental Oriental Secretary and Other Tales of Foreign Service*

ROGER KIRK, ed., *Distinguished Service: Lydia Chapin Kirk, Partner in Diplomacy, 1896–1984*

For a complete list of series titles, visit <adst.org/publications>

Bridge Between Worlds

A Lebanese-Arab-American Woman's Journey

Hala Lababidi Buck

Memoirs and Occasional Papers
Association for Diplomatic Studies and Training

Washington, DC

Library of Congress Control Number: 2019908162

ISBN 978-1-7326988-7-1 paperback (alk. paper)

 An imprint of New Academia Publishing

 New Academia Publishing
4401-A Connecticut Ave. NW, #236 - Washington, DC 20008
info@newacademia.com - www.newacademia.com

*I dedicate this book to my parents,
Kamal and Jeannette (Jan) Lababidi,
whose love, guidance, modeling, and safety net
made this journey possible, and
to all the "human bridges" in the world striving for
Peace.*

Contents

Acknowledgments

I want to thank my husband Steve for his continuous support and countless readings of my manuscript and for being my love, my best friend, and fellow journeyer.

My daughter Katie Leila for her encouragement, enthusiasm, edits and invaluable advice, who, together with her husband Adam, continue building our intergenerational bridge.

Adam for his patience and technical support in getting the images for this book in the required format.

My family in Lebanon for providing love, hospitality, and an anchor for my nuclear family here and in Lebanon.

Matthew Perry, whose astute and sensitive line editing respected my voice while improving the manuscript.

And finally, the ADST series editors Margery Thompson and Lisa Terry, whose patience and hard work helped launch "Bridge Between Worlds."

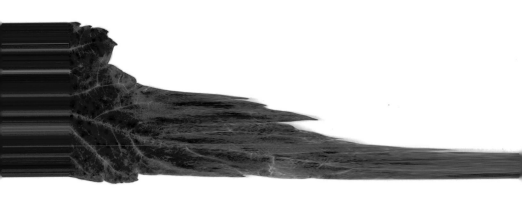

Prologue

The longest journey is the journey inwards...for he who has started upon his quest for the source of his being.
— Dag Hammarskjöld [1]

The first crossing I ever made was in the womb. I was born in Beirut, Lebanon, to a Sunni Muslim father and a Maronite Catholic mother. Twenty-three years later I married Steve, an American, Anglo-Saxon Protestant, Foreign Service Officer. Together, we spent thirty-one years moving around the world from one diplomatic assignment to another, mostly in the Arab world.

I started out writing this book as a journey of self-discovery and something to leave for my daughter and, *inshallah* (God willing), grandchildren. It has become a memoir exploring experiences, cultures and religions that I have navigated. I offer my story in the hope that it will provide readers with an intimate portrait of life and the overarching culture in seven different Arab and Muslim countries. Along the way, perhaps readers may discover more about themselves, and the complexities and richness of living in and between worlds.

As I recalled the past—my child self, the adolescent, and the immigrant—I came to recognize the vulnerability I had held at bay, the loneliness that came from feeling that others didn't understand me, and that I didn't fully belong. This is a story about discovering the gift that the pain had wrapped so well.

In the years after 9/11 for the first time I felt a growing need to present my personal story as a Lebanese-American woman of mixed Christian and Muslim heritage as a counterbalance to the idea that somehow those parts of me are inherently opposed. As the perception in the United States of Arabs and Muslims became even more distorted, prejudicial and threatening, I decided to hyphenate myself further and added "Arab" to Lebanese-American in the subtitle of my book. Those three words define who I am. I was born and raised in Lebanon and I am first and foremost Lebanese. On the other hand, I am also an Arab by virtue of speaking Arabic and sharing such cultural values as hospitality and centrality of family. And as an American I feel enriched by my mixed identity.

Over several years, this book took me on a voyage that not only recaptured memories of my life, but also became an inner pilgrimage of sorts. As my journey back into the past unfolded and poured onto these pages, so did insights and a growing awareness of what belonging means—where I belonged, who I am, and what my life's purpose has been all along. Living the transient life of the U.S. Foreign Service added to the complexity of my identity. Memories that bubbled up triggered more memories, long forgotten and filtered through my inner child's eyes. They appeared as fragments hidden in my heart, body and mind. I have shared my story as best as I can recall. My intent from the beginning has been to present my life as I experienced it, and to do so with respect and compassion for my family. I have therefore changed some names when requested.

Painful experiences influenced my professional work as a Licensed Clinical Professional Counselor, Board Certified Counselor, integrative Adlerian art therapist, and cross-cultural educator. I am also a visual artist and have exhibited in many different countries. Art, my constant guide and companion, showed me the way. It helped me heal, enabled me to help clients and students gain an understanding of self and the "other," and find compassion for the humanness we all share.

I believe that images from within us have a healing and often predictive quality. The first nudge to write this book began with a simple random collage I made in 2004 in response to a question I posed to myself and the Universe: "What's next on my journey?"

At the time I did not fully comprehend its message. It had elements from my life: a photo of myself in front of a cedar tree in Lebanon at age five or six, a ladder connecting me with a blank open book, a bear, eagles, and the sea. I felt them all beckoning me to reach into my past to receive a story.[2] And these words emerged:

1. "Waiting to dip my pen." Collage: ©Hala Buck

"Waiting to dip my pen"

Eagle flying, eagle landing,
bridging earth and sky.
Bear waiting to take me inward,
to dip my pen in that.

Rungs of ladder
in different shades of growth,
enable me to bridge who I was
and who I now am.

Past roles are gone,
the child in the shade of cedar,
the mother watching over her nest.

The old, frames the new
a pair of fruits
waiting to be savored

My pen is poised
waiting for eagle to land.
But she needs still to fly and soar.
That is her destiny, as it is mine.

I finally dip my pen
deep into my life,
as the moon keeps watch
even in daylight.

The past fits into frames
that reach down towards my pen.
A pristine page awaits,
chapters of my life, as yet unwritten,
but nevertheless lived.

The ocean will help support
 this new adventure,
as bear keeps watch
at the entrance to my soul.

Each time my pen lifts up,
it soars with the wings of eagle,
only to descend once more
and create the words I need to write.

It all has been "written"
"*maktoob*"
now it needs to be shared.

"The essence of grace is homecoming to who we are."

— Tara Brach[3]

1

Growing Up in Lebanon

Sometimes it's impossible to know what your story really is until you have written it.

— Tristine Rainer[4]

So, what is home for people of mixed cultures, for immigrants who leave one for another? Is it a house, a place, a country? Is it where you feel you can find your dreams?

For the first twenty-three years of my life, home was Beirut, Lebanon, during what some would call its "Golden Years." The country had found and reveled in its pluralistic identity and as a blend of East and West—as a center for banking, higher learning, tourism, and a publishing mecca.

Lebanon is situated on the most Eastern shore of the Mediterranean Sea, north of Israel and the occupied Palestinian territories, and west and south of Syria. Because of its unique location, its fertile land, rivers, and wells, and safe port, at different periods of its history Lebanon has come under the domination of foreign rulers from all directions, among them Mongols, Assyrians, Babylonians, Persians, Greeks, Romans, Byzantines, Arabs, Mamluks, Crusaders, Ottomans, and the French.[5] Lebanon is the land that the Caananites and Phoenicians inhabited as far back as the Bronze Age around 3,000 B.C.[6]

Despite—or perhaps because of—that, Lebanon is a culturally rich place where many ethnic and religious sects occupy a very small land, sometimes with discord and surprisingly, more often than not in harmony.

I was born when newly independent Lebanon was searching

for an identity that brought together people of various political leanings and nineteen different religious sects. Among them Sunni Muslims (like my father's family), Shiā Muslims, the Druze, and some Alawites. Among the Christian sects are the Roman Catholics, Greek Catholics, Greek Orthodox, Syriac Catholics (like my maternal grandfather), Maronite Catholic (like my maternal grandmother's family), Syriac Orthodox, Armenian Orthodox, Armenian Catholics, Kildan, Latin, Melkite, Baptist, and Protestants, including Quakers. Before the creation of Israel, there was also a sizable and well-established Eastern Jewish population that included landlords (including my grandmother's, Teta Habouba), the head of Beirut's municipality, and others. A large number of Lebanese Jews eventually emigrated, mostly to Israel in 1948, when that state was created in what was then British-occupied Palestine.

Recently, while researching the history of Beirut, I discovered there was a Jewish College as well: Grand Collège Israélite Universel (Great Israelite Universal College). There was even a photo of it dating back to 1900.[7] In 2014, Grand Collège Israélite Universel became the inter-denominational Alliance, and later Besançon, a French-speaking Catholic nuns' boarding school.

2. Collège Israélite Universel–Beirut.

In addition to food, Lebanese Christians and Muslims share the same Arabic word for God, "*Allah.*" God is important both in Muslim and Christian daily life. I remember how, like the majority of Lebanese, my family on both sides routinely uses expressions such as *Allah ma'kun* (God be with you), *mitl ma Allah beereed* (As God wills), or *inshallah* (God willing). And it is the same one God for all.

During my childhood, Lebanon was a place of relatively peaceful co-existence and seemingly an idyllic place for someone like me who reflected the diversity the country embodied. I grew up weaving between my two families and, just as bilingual children instinctively know which language to use with whom, I came out of the womb with an unconscious ability to navigate between my Muslim and Christian families.

Nowadays, when I tell people I was born and raised in Lebanon, many sadly shake their heads in pity. For them, the name Lebanon conjures up a long civil war, conflict, incomprehensible politics, and shifting alliances. For those who truly know Lebanon, however, there are also beautiful vistas of a peninsula going out to meet the Mediterranean Sea; green mountains rising from the coast—some clad in snow; blue skies; rivers, fruit orchards, and vineyards; delicious and healthy food (this is the proud birthplace of *hummos, tabbouleh, baba ghanouj, and kibbeh*); and friendly, hospitable people. "*Ahlan wa sahlan!*" is the typical enthusiastic warm greeting you hear everywhere; the nickname, "Paris of the Middle East" or "Switzerland on the Mediterranean,"[8] and its recognition as a place where East and West meet. Lebanon packs all that into an area four-fifths the size of the state of Connecticut.

In order to understand Lebanon and its current politics, one needs to go back to its creation and the secret Sykes-Picot Agreement of 1916 between Britain and France, which carved modern-day Lebanon out of Greater Syria and handed it over to the French as the spoils of World War I. During the Ottoman era Greater Syria included a large part of the Levant Countries located in the Eastern Mediterranean. It comprised present-day Syria, Lebanon, Israel, Palestine, Jordan, Cyprus, part of Iraq, and Sinai. This haphazard and self-serving division of the Middle East by the colonial powers set in motion problems that continue to plague the region even today.[9]

3. Mount Sannine and village – Lebanon.

4. Jounieh Bay – Lebanon.

5. The Cedars of Lebanon.

Because of its location and distinctive, complex pluralistic culture, Lebanon has always been buffeted by regional political winds, as well as by divided loyalties within the country itself. Its people have navigated through difficult times, compromise, negotiations, and much finger pointing. Despite the fact that Lebanon is often the battleground for regional and international proxy wars, it has somehow managed to rise from the ashes. After the civil war (1975–1990), the Lebanese may have been less tolerant of each other along political, religious, and ideological lines; but paradoxically they also have become more adept at forging political alliances across religious lines.[10]

Up into the 1960s and early 1970s, there was less antagonism between the different religions and sects than today, although, as in most countries, of course it existed. But there were many families like mine, for whom religion was not the central defining factor. Growing up, I was not aware of any problem being the offspring of a mixed marriage. As a child I moved seamlessly between my loving Muslim and Christian families, unaware of the unusual circumstances of my birth and a deep family secret, one I would only discover five decades later.

My Parents

I write about my family in some detail below because the extended family is the backbone of society in Lebanon and the rest of the Arab World. And writing about it gave me insights about the beliefs I absorbed growing up and how that influenced my worldview.

My parents met in the late 1930s while working for the French colonial administration, or "Mandate" that governed occupied Lebanon from 1920 to 1943. My dad, Kamal Lababidi, "Papi," as I called him, at twenty-nine-years old had annulled an arranged *kitab* (marriage contract) with a Muslim woman whom his mother had promoted. My mother, Jeanette Boushkhanji, "Mami," was eighteen. She had recently broken off her engagement with a Christian Lebanese-Brazilian émigré. Even though two of my father's cousins had married outside their faith (one to a Spanish Catholic from Madrid, and one to a Lebanese Jew), at that time an interfaith marriage such as theirs was uncommon, and so was the product of such a union. As in most countries, people tended to marry within their own religious group—and not just the general "Muslim" and,"Christian" groups, but within the smaller denominations (i.e., Catholic, Orthodox Christians and Protestants). The Catholic bishop with whom my mother had grown up threatened to excommunicate her if she did not commit to raising her children as Catholics. Mom refused and announced, "Well then, I'll go to the Protestants!" And she did. Papi went to the *shaykh*, who tried to dissuade him. The story goes that Papi's brother, Khaled, was a good friend of the *shaykh*, who ultimately relented and agreed to draw up the *Kitab*. My parents then presented this *fait accompli* to the family. As a child, and for many years as an adult, I was unaware of the courageous leap my parents had taken. Civil marriage law still does not exist in Lebanon despite ongoing attempts to institute it. However the country recognizes civil marriage that has taken place outside the Lebanese territory.

The Muslim *Kitab* is similar to the Jewish *Ketubah*. The *Kitab* is a prenuptial legal document drawn up by the religious leader that outlines rights and responsibilities of the groom towards the bride; it is traditionally agreed upon by the two families. In modern practice, the *Kitab* spells out promises made by the couple where the bride, for example, might assert that she also holds the right to divorce, or require that her future husband fund her college education, or even take her to Europe every summer. Usually, it has the support of both families.

I was born prematurely at home after Lebanon's quasi-independence. There were no incubators at the time. Under the guidance of our Greek-Lebanese doctor, my dad fashioned one at home with an electric coil heater maintaining the necessary temperature. My mom tells me I was all legs and weighed two kilos (five pounds). Knowing about perinatal and prenatal psychology, I believe that this tenuous and tenacious beginning most probably contributed to my rebellious fighting spirit.

Religion was never a source of conflict or disagreement between my parents. Each followed their faith the way they wanted to. Neither felt the need to convert the other or impose their own religious views on each other. Their conflicts were centered on other differences. Papi was a punctual man, and Mami, well, she was never on time. Sitting in the back seat of our old 1936 convertible Ford with a rumble seat waiting for mom, I could sense and hear Papi's mounting impatience: "*Yalla ya* Jeanne, *lahh nitāayoa*" (Come on, Jeanne, we're going to be late!). I guess that's why I have always been on time.

Papi liked practical furniture; mom liked elegant, more ornate things. Papi never raised his voice; silence was how he contained his anger. I remember after a fight that Papi would withdraw and refuse to eat what mom had cooked. The way it seemed to resolve was with mom telling him, "Kamal, I prepared the frying pan and the eggs," which was the only thing he could cook for himself. That broke the ice and ended the cold war between them—which, as an only child, was a huge relief for me. As for many only children, parent-mediator was a role I took on. From a young age, I became a bridge between them when they fought, which is an easy role for an only child to slip into, but something that no child should be burdened with.

I remember that my mom and I sometimes went to church, especially at Christmas and Easter. My dad, who was never too fond of organized religions and dogmas, had no problem with that. His faith was grounded in the moral tenets and ethical belief of Islam–that one should be generous, kind, and supportive, especially to those less fortunate. I remember Mom being upset when he generously tipped the garbage collectors and others who provided services. His answer always was, "Jeanne, these people don't have much money but they do have their dignity. We need to help them feel that their jobs are worthwhile and appreciated." Decades later, when I mentioned this recollection, Mom would say, even through the haze of dementia, *"Papi avait un grand coeur"* (Papi had a big heart). He always followed the courage of his own convictions, even when they went against the grain of society. I believe I inherited that from him. Above all, Papi was the one I went to for comfort and guidance. Super logical as he was, he was also loving and nurturing; he was my rock.

At the time, perhaps even now, Papi was the only forensic science expert in Lebanon. I remember overhearing family and friends quote a judge or other government official who had expressed admiration for my dad's independent and honest dealings. He was often called in to solve delicate cases that required his non-partisan, and delicate expertise. Papi was a government employee, so we were not rich, but we never lacked anything. Mom wanted more children, but Papi felt that in order to give me everything I wanted, they could not afford more children. I remember how every month Mom and Dad would sit down at the dining room table. Laid out in front of them were envelopes labeled in my dad's firm and elegant handwriting for all the basic expenses: rent, utilities, food, telephone, and my piano and ballet lessons. Sitting next to each other at the table, they would divide the money and place it in the envelopes. Dad always used to quote an Arabic proverb, *"Ad bsatak midd ijreyk"* (Stretch your legs only as far as your mat). He disapproved of people living beyond their means. Nevertheless, my parents also had fun. Whatever was left over after the bills were paid was for fun and unexpected expenses. On most Saturday nights, they went to the Caves Des Rois club with four other couples and danced the tango, Paso Doble, and the waltz late into the night.

5. Mami and Papi dancing at the Caves des Rois.

6. Papi and I at the Corniche.

7. Mami and I at the beach.

When I was seven years old, Papi asked me to choose a lottery ticket from a passing vendor. I picked half a ticket, which won the national lottery. That money paid for my college education, a second bathroom, and probably the first dishwasher in Beirut; I recall it would pop open at the end of the wash cycle to allow the steam to escape, so as to naturally dry the contents.

Papi was a tall, handsome man—"dashing" my mom would add—with white skin, curly black hair, and an unmistakably Semitic nose. When I was born, his first worry was, "Does she have a nose like mine?" Dad walked proud, his head erect and squarely lined up with his back. He always clutched a pipe between his teeth. He was very meticulous about cleaning his pipes and I have fond memories of talking with him as he scraped them clean. He had a large collection of pipes and used Three Nuns tobacco. Even now, whenever I smell that brand, it reminds me of my dad. He had kind, hazel eyes that nevertheless demanded that you be truthful. There was such a sense of authority about him that people always assumed he must be a doctor, the most respected profession at the time. One of his best friends was Agop Chaghlassian, an Armenian-Lebanese pharmacist. Every morning before work, Papi would meet his friend at the latter's pharmacy in *Bab Edriss*, for their morning *sobhieh* coffee and chat.

Papi was renowned in the family for picking the best fruits. He, like most Arab men of the time, did most of the food shopping. The rest we bought from the local grocer or from passing vendors. Papi would buy us exotic fruits like mangos, papayas, *ashta* or cherimoya (also known as custard apples), and persimmons from a specialty store in *Bab Edriss*—the center of downtown Beirut—that imported them. My dad taught me how to squeeze and smell fruits. They had to be neither too soft nor too firm, and there were other subtle evaluations of scent and feel. Today when I test fruit at the grocery store, people often are shocked and intrigued by this ritual—until I explain that if you cannot smell a peach you will not have a tasty one, and if the lemon's skin is too thick it will not give you enough juice. After I move on with my shopping cart I often spy them trying it out themselves.

Papi was a great *bricoleur* (handyman) who would tackle anything—electricity, reupholstering a sofa, rigging wires all around the house— to create more comfort and practical access to anything and everything: the fans, the heaters, even the telephones. I learned a lot helping him out. Now when we have a handyman come to the house, Steve, my husband, immediately informs him, "My wife is the mechanical one in the family. Talk to her." This comes much to the surprise and sometimes chauvinism of many American contractors who come to work on our house.

Mami was a petite brunette with olive skin and silky, wavy brown hair I used to envy. When I was young, I always wished I had inherited her hair instead of my dad's, although now I am grateful for my thick curls. I learned recently that my maternal grandfather's family, the Boushkhanjis, all had Russian names like Olga, Catherine, and Eugenie. Decades later mom met a Ukrainian lady in the United States with the similar family name of Buchkanzi. Knowing that her father, my Jeddo Rizhallah, had immigrated to Lebanon from Aleppo, my mom thought that perhaps her own paternal family had at some point fled the Ukraine and sought refuge in Aleppo in what was then part of Greater Syria. In her latest book *Syria: The Making and Unmaking of a Refuge State*, Dawn Chatty chronicles the history of such migration.[11]

Lebanon itself has also been a bridge and a haven for people seeking asylum and a new life. As imperfect and small as it is, Lebanon has always been a place where people could take refuge, thanks to its pluralism and its unique diversity in the region.

Even after Steve and I left Lebanon, I remember our Foreign Service friends in Beirut telling us how my parents had maintained an open house policy for all of them. My mom and dad represented to me how the world should be. Their mutual respect for each other's beliefs and ability to find the common ground extended beyond their marriage. I absorbed that love and acceptance of differences. From them I learned early on that "differentness" was not something to be feared; it was a celebration and enrichment of our shared humanity.

Into her late eighties, Mom walked with a lot of energy and determination. She was always curious, always focusing on the positive, and always elegantly dressed. I coveted her red, dressy high-heeled sandals that matched her red crêpe dress with large, bold white flowers. "Mami," I'd say, "please don't wear them too often or they'll wear out." I was ten years old. She made her own clothes as well as the ones I designed for myself.

"When you were a little girl," she would tell me, "you would get upset if your hair ribbon did not match your dress." So, something must have rubbed off.

Her pastries, especially her moist chocolate cakes imbued with a little Cointreau, were famous in the family. Besides being a gracious hostess, she always had what in Arabic is called *lisan Hhiloo*, literally, "a sweet tongue." In Lebanese culture, this denotes someone who is courteous, knows how to talk nicely with people, in Arabic *"bit saayir,"* and how to put them at ease. Her *joie de vivre* manifested in her cheerfulness, her singing along with Fairuz, Edith Piaf, and Yves Montand, her love for dancing, laughing, and joking as well as making fun of her own foibles. She liked to recount how one day in Beirut she drove to a big supermarket and emerged laden with shopping bags. Standing at the door, she scolded herself for not having driven her VW bug. So she flagged a car *servees*—like a taxi but it picks up several passengers and has a set route, dropping off people along the way—and got in. A few blocks later, caught in traffic behind a VW Bug, she remembered she had brought the car and had the driver take her back to it.

Mami's Family

Growing up, I was surrounded by a loving extended family. I never thought in terms of who was Christian and who was Muslim. As far as I knew, the difference in religion was not an issue; much later, I learned the story was more complex. Both families got together at birthdays and other occasions. I don't remember any dissent or intentional separation between them.

As far as I knew, my mother's Christian family consisted of my maternal grandmother, Teta Habouba; her sister, Tante (Aunt) Georgette and her husband, Joseph; their three daughters, Nado, Mona, and Rita, who were my playmates and cousins; and Tante Paulette and her family.

Paulette, Mom's youngest sister, went to *Al-Ahliyeh*, a Lebanese school in Beirut whose principal was a Lebanese Quaker. Tante Paulette would later marry a Muslim man, a well-known sportsman and sculptor. She gets along very well with her in-laws who, as it was for my mom in Papi's family, love her as a daughter. The rest of Teta Habouba's family died during the end of Ottoman rule, although two of her brothers emigrated to South America.

It wasn't until I was in my fifties, in a casual conversation with my aunt, that I found out that the paternal side of my mother's extended Syriac Catholic (or perhaps Syriac Orthodox family—we're not sure), the Bouchkhanjis, had disowned her when she married my dad. They simply disappeared from her life—and mine. My parents never told me about that deep rejection. Both of my grandfathers died long before I was born. My maternal grandfather, Jeddo Rizkallah died when mom was just fourteen years old; it never dawned on me that his entire family was absent from my life. Finding out the full story in midlife was a shock. But it helped me to understand why, for practically all of my life, I had felt like an outsider, not fully belonging.

When members of my paternal grandfather's family visited

mom's sister, Georgette, they would ask, "How is the one whose name we cannot mention?" Once the secret was out, Tante Georgette also revealed I had met one of those great-aunts; her name was Tante Eugenie. I did recall a petite woman, always elegantly dressed, with a fancy cane, a distinctive brooch on her well-tailored jacket, a noticeable perfume, and a smile. Something about her had stuck in my mind. I remembered occasionally seeing her at Tante Georgette's when I was visiting my cousins. Since we called so many different people *tante*, I never gave it a second thought until I started writing about my family. As a child, I remained unaware of the drama my parents' marriage had created. To my knowledge no one ever talked about the secret. Not then, not ever, until that day when a single, casual comment changed everything I thought I knew.

When my parents emigrated to the United States in 1975, my mom searched for a church that she felt comfortable in and decided on Bradley Hills Presbyterian Church, even though she had to drive there. When she moved into her retirement apartment and could no longer drive, I asked her, "Mami, why won't you go the Catholic Church next door? It's so easy for you to just walk across the garden to it." Flicking her hand backwards in anger, she said in French *"Ouf! Ils sont tèllement compliqués."* (Ouf! They're so complicated.) I wished I had taken that earlier opportunity to talk with Mom about the devastating price she paid for marrying the man she loved. But once she began her journey into dementia, it seemed cruel to stir things up. Plus, by that point, she would make up stories to cover for the fact she could no longer remember as she once did.

My maternal grandmother, Teta Habouba, was a second mother to me. I remember her as a soft-spoken woman who emanated gentle strength. She always wore her frizzy grey hair in a bun. As a child, I was fascinated by her large, U-shaped bobby pins, marveling how they held her chignon in place. She always wore black or grey clothes, traditional colors of mourning, probably donned after she lost a boy of eighteen months to typhoid. Decades later, she would lose her husband. I have often wondered about these traditions, such as wearing black, sometimes for a year or more, which both Christians and Muslim women observed. A Muslim aunt of mine wore black for the rest of her life after losing her adult daughter. Her remaining children tried to coax her to wear colors, but the most she would do was wear grey.

I understood that better after my dad died. I didn't feel like wearing the bright colors I loved. They did not match the grief I felt. It took quite a few months before I could start adding colors again. I also realized that, in Lebanon, black signals to friends and even casual acquaintances or random people you meet that you have lost someone. It's a social signal that alerts them that you may need support, or just some empathy. *Habouba* means "lovable," and she was. But she was also courageous. Born at the end of the Ottoman occupation of Lebanon, she was raised Maronite Catholic in a mountain village near Deyr el Amar.[12]

The Ottoman rule of Lebanon (at the time, part of Greater Syria) gave autonomy to local chieftains especially in Mount Lebanon. But a new Ottoman governor, the Bosnian Jazzar, "Pasha of Acre," came to power in the late 18th century until the beginning of the 19th century. He was a ruthless and cruel ruler, known as "the butcher."[13] The family story I heard was that he laid siege to towns and villages that refused to swear allegiance or pay taxes. My grandmother's village, Bey'oon, located southeast of Beirut in the Chouf Mountains, was one of these. I vaguely remember hearing that Teta Habouba's village was not spared the many cruelties of World War I, either.

After her parents died (we don't know for sure what happened to them, but it may have been during a time of widespread starvation), Teta Habouba went to live with her brother and sister-in-law, as was the custom for orphans. There was some falling out with her brother over whom she was supposed to marry and, as the story goes, my *teta*, at age eighteen, left her mountain village and headed for Beirut, some sixteen miles away. I try to imagine her walking, scared but determined, stopping at convents and churches along the way. Hospitality is a very ingrained trait in that part of the world. Even so, it was a daring thing to do at the time. When she reached Beirut, the story goes, she found work and boarded with the nuns. Her two other brothers had already left on a ship for Brazil, like hundreds of thousands of Lebanese who headed to North and South America and Australia.

Recently, I came across a rare, early photo of Teta Habouba. I suspect she is nineteen or twenty years old. I'm drawn by the look in her eyes. They are big, wide, and hauntingly dark, with *kohl*, a plant-based eyeliner used throughout the Arab world, highlighting them. Her hair is as frizzy as I remember, but in this photo it is black rather than grey, with the same parting on the left. She is sitting in a chair looking sideways. A cross hangs prominently from a chain around her neck. The chain is not centered on her chest and neither is the cross. Spiral motifs on either side of her dress complete her striking look. Her mouth is set in a paradoxically brave and frightened mien. But it is her fierce eyes that draw me back. I never saw that look growing up. Yet, with my hand, I block out her mouth and nose and see my eyes in hers and hers in mine. I like that. The courage and strength of both my grandmothers had been handed down through the generations. It gave mom the courage to marry the man she loved; it was the courage that allowed me to do the same, and to leave my native country.

8. Young Teta Habouba.

Mami recalls that my father took very good care of Teta Habouba. He would tell her, when she felt she was a burden, "Mama, you are mama." Indeed, he often said he loved her more than he ever loved his mother. And Teta Habouba would refer to my dad as "my son, Kamal."

One night I was woken up by the sound of wings—*takk dee boom!*—beating the walls in panic. I must have been five years old. I dove under the covers screaming. Teta came and quickly dispatched what turned out to be a large locust that had flown through my window. She laughed, soothed my fears, and closed the shutters so there would be no more invasions.

My *teta* was a refuge and a well of wisdom, despite the fact that she was illiterate. I will never forget how she would put her hand on my arm, look me straight in the eye and say, "Lola *habibti*, make sure you study. I used to run away from school so I never learned to improve myself." Life had been her school. Even now I miss her terribly.

Her lap and hugs were especially comforting. When she could no longer live alone she spent half the year with her eldest daughter, Georgette, and the other half with us. I loved watching her pound the meat for *kibbeh* (a Lebanese specialty of lamb, *burghul*—cracked-wheat—and onions) in the *jurun*, the old-fashioned stone basin, adding the spices as she created the tiki-tiki-tak-tak, tiki-tiki-tak-tak sound of the wooden mallet. From the kitchen and throughout the house drifted the melodies from her childhood, old traditional Lebanese folksongs "āala dalō'na āla dal 'ōna...." As Teta Habouba sang, she was accompanied by the rhythmic staccato of the wooden mallet she wielded with gusto. She sang "mountain people" songs in a melodious voice with a touch of yearning. I wonder if she was remembering then her childhood as I am now remembering mine, both of us having left our homes early in life. Little scenes imprinted in the heart bubble up as aromas, sounds and memories nudging each other.

Decades later, when I would visit my mom at the retirement home, she would suddenly start singing these same folksongs from her childhood. They were remnants of memories left in her Alzheimer's brain from another land, another life, another time. It was a bittersweet moment for me to hear her singing these old songs—

some of which I had never heard but which I knew Teta Habouba used to sing to her children.

Mami's singing showed me how far she has regressed with Alzheimer's. Of course, these songs from long ago also reconnected me with my past, and with Teta Habouba. But mostly, their haunting melodies became a new language through which my mom and I could communicate. It brought both of us joy even as this horrible disease stole her away, little by little.

My mother's eldest sister, Tante Georgette, could create a pattern for any style of clothing and used that talent to run a school that taught women to design their own patterns and sew their own clothes. At the end of the school session she would organize a fashion show where her students would model the outfits they had designed and produced on a makeshift catwalk. My cousins and I would also model for her. I remember learning how to walk in a way that enhanced what I was wearing, how to pause, turn and walk back. Looking at photos from those days I see my dad's cousin, Soraya, whom I admired growing up. She was tall and a graceful model. There was nothing strange or unusual about the fact that she was a Muslim woman modeling for my Christian aunt's show.[14]

Tante Georgette was famous for her Yule Log cake, *Bûche de Nöel*, as well as a floor-to-ceiling *crèche* she created in their living room corner. As a little girl, I was fascinated by the brown paper splattered with paint that she would shape into caves and niches. Teta Habouba would have sprouted lentils and wheat ahead of time, which became the grass and trees of this landscape. Then the nativity scene of hewn olive wood from Jerusalem, with Joseph and Mary and the animals, was placed first in a little "cave." On Christmas Eve, after midnight mass, the baby Jesus would be placed in the cradle. My cousin Mona recently reminded me how her mother would "walk" the three kings from place to place around the house each day, symbolizing their long journey, until they arrived at the crèche on January 6, bearing their gifts. I was mesmerized by the artistry of Tante Georgette's creation. I loved to explore that wondrous mountain of paper and watch the lentils and wheat sprout. Papi, Mami, and I celebrated Christmas with her family, but we also decorated our own little Lebanese pine tree.

Standing four feet, eight inches tall, Tante Paulette, Mom's youngest sister, brought joy and the "can do" attitude she shared with Mami. I see her as the Lebanese Mary Poppins. On her visit with us in the United States, I stood in mom's guest room, amazed as my aunt pulled gift after gift from her enormous suitcase: two tall brass umbrella stands which she had very practically stuffed with clothes; a prototype of a sculpture, carved by her late husband and entitled "Ballerina;" special sweets from Tripoli she knew we liked; it went on and on and on. When I asked how she got through customs she sweetly said, "I showed them everything."

That reminded me of my mom's first visit to the United States. Before they left Beirut, my father, the epitome of law-abiding citizenry, kept checking Mami's packing to make sure she didn't slip in *maāmool*, Easter sweets. But she simply hid all the forbidden items with our next-door neighbor Nelly, until the last minute. At U.S. customs, my dad's jaw dropped when he realized she had slipped *maāmool* and other goodies into her luggage after all. "Don't worry Kamal," she whispered. I'll handle this!" With the familial sweetness, she explained herself to the customs official, and even offered to share her special, homemade Lebanese Easter cookies with him. He waved her through.

Tante Paulette was the inspiration behind her well-known sculptor husband, Muhammad. But she was always willing to play silly games with me. One day, when I was four years old, we were pretending to be barking dogs and making a racket by the windows just as a colleague of hers walked by. Each time we visit we laugh at that memory. Even now, in her eighties, the twinkle in her eyes, her lightness of spirit, and positive attitude amaze me. She is always game for anything, very curious, interested in my art therapy work, and the world. Yet she has gone through tough times. During Lebanon's civil war, her husband Āmmo (uncle) Muhammad was dying of cancer of the mouth. In those days, no one really knew about the dangers of toxic art materials, especially the dust from his sculptures. She nursed him through the agonizing pain with no morphine available because of war shortages. She told me he would plead with her, "Please Paulette, shoot me!" Yet there is no bitterness, no self-pity. Now in her eighties, she finds joy taking care of her grandchildren.

When my mom came down with hepatitis shortly after I was

born, I was whisked away to live with Tante Paulette and Teta Habouba for a few months. They told me I cried all the time, having been ripped away from my mom. I understand now why I've always felt that both Teta Habouba and Tante Paulette were second mothers to me.

Tante Paulette can fix anything. She uses indelible markers to fix a tiny discoloration in a shirt, a safety pin in a crunch to hold a sagging hem. She also is a great seamstress, and likes the work (Mom was also a great seamstress, but she never did like it). Before coming to visit us in the United States, Tante Paulette asked me what I'd like from Lebanon. I told her that if she ever found a dark burgundy Damascus tablecloth large enough to fit our fully extended dining room table for Thanksgiving and Christmas, I would pay her for it. "But don't worry if you don't find it," I said. Well she didn't find one. But she made me one, not with the Damascene embroidery, but with her own appliqués of fall color leaves she had admired in the United States during her first visit. It was just the right color and length. Whenever I use it I feel a mixture of sadness and a warm feeling of being much loved. And all the wonderful memories from my childhood with her come flooding back.

Papi's Family

When I was born, my parents lived with Papi's mother, Teta Hajjeh, and Papi's surviving brother, Āmmo Khaled. My paternal grandfather and the oldest son Muhyidin had died years before my parents married. In Lebanon, it was traditional then—and remains so today—to live near your kin or with them.

As a child I remember a few of the older women in Papi's family, like my Muslim grandmother Teta Hajjeh, loosely draped white scarves around their heads when they went out in public. But, so did my Christian grandmother and her friends, especially on their visits to church. It was like anybody's grandmother putting on a hat when she went out. Teta Hajjeh's first name is Khadija; *Hajjeh* is the female title bestowed on someone who has made the pilgrimage—or *hajj*—to Mecca. I'd like to imagine that the white scarf was worn as a badge of honor.

The story goes that Papi suggested to his French superiors in

Beirut that they would be wise to bring in more Muslims into their administration.[15] They, it seems, had been unaware that Papi was Muslim. So he was immediately dispatched to the Northern Lebanese front outside of Tripoli to "oversee security." Teta Hajjeh died after a fatal stroke the year we lived in Tripoli, Lebanon. My parents left me with the Italian nuns there without telling me they were going to Teta Hajjeh's funeral. I was four years old then, so I only have a faint memory of her when she was bedridden: a large, imposing woman, à la Queen Victoria in her older years ordering everyone around from her bed. She was known to be an iron lady who ruled the family, including all her brothers. Stories of her arm-twisting abound. Steve tells me they remind him of stories about his maternal grandmother, who, like many Victorian-era women, hemmed in by social mores, used the intelligence that they could not apply elsewhere to dominate the family.

Teta Hajjeh chose the name Hala for me when I was born. My dad did not agree, so he always called me Lola. Interestingly, there are two versions of the name Hala in Arabic. The one that Teta Hajjeh chose means "welcome" as in the greeting "*ya hala, ya hala!*" That became my official name in Arabic. The other version I chose to use later in my life, written the same way in English but differently in Arabic, is pronounced *Haala*, which I liked better and means the halo around the moon.

Teta Hajjeh's brother and his family lived not too far from us. My father's side of the family was larger than my mother's, and they all welcomed and embraced my mother as their own. Some were practicing Muslims; most were not, especially among the younger generation. None of my younger Muslim female relatives "covered." I feel there was, in my father's family, an unspoken belief that one carries one's faith inside one's heart; this belief was common in the Lebanon of the 1950s and 1960s. I asked my Muslim cousins, recently visiting here in the United States, if they have similar memories of this time. They too didn't recall any peer or religious pressure dictating what women wore, or who prayed, or if the men had to go to the mosque. In the 1960s the hems would rise and fall according to the prevailing European fashion. I remember "mini-skirts" were the rage. Lebanese women of all religions were then, and continue to be, impeccably dressed. The older generations, like my grandmothers', were more traditional.

I remember Āmmo Khaled as a kind man—a second father to me—especially since he never had children of his own. He ran interference between his mother, Teta Hajjeh, and everyone else. He knew that my dad would not tolerate her shenanigans. I remember him putting down his prayer rug in his room for the noon prayer. I cannot remember if he prayed at sunset, but I do know he enjoyed his glass of *arak* (an anise drink, similar to *ouzo*) or beer with his lunch, despite Islam's injunction against alcohol. Late in life he married an Italian woman, Sylvia, who moved in with us. Her husband, Āmmo Khaled, mom, and I were the only ones who could understand her compost of Italian, French, and Arabic. As a result, Italian is a language I can mostly understand and love.

The fact that my dad was not a practicing Muslim was never a bone of contention. His moral values replaced dogma. Besides giving generously to the poor and those less advantaged, my father was the kind of boss who stood up for his staff. I always thought that a man I called "Āmmo Bshara" was related to us. But in fact, he was my dad's subordinate at work, who remained in touch with my father throughout his life. (In the Arab world, one uses the terms Āmmo and auntie, *Tante* or Āmti, for close friends as well.) The day after Papi died, Āmmo Bshara called us in Washington. Using a respectful word for "Mrs.," "*Sitt* Jeanne," he said to my mother, "How is Sayyid Kamal?" When my mom told him that Kamal had just passed away, this seventy-year-old cried over the phone and told her that he had dreamt of my dad the night before, and felt the need to check on him. Eerie perhaps, but Bshara's dream reminded me of the respect, love, and loyalty my dad inspired among colleagues, friends, family, and others.

My father's cousin, Samir, was like a big brother to me. He recalls taking his youngest sister, Fadwa, and me to the only public park in Beirut, the *Sanayīi*. After Papi died, Samir and his wife Sano became more like my second parents. He is so much like my dad that we used to joke about it. Immigrants pay a high price in giving up regular face-to-face connection with beloved relatives. I worry about my family in Lebanon and I pray that they and the country stay safe despite the crazy Syrian civil war, ISIS next door, and foreign interference.

Generally speaking, my Muslim relatives were bilingual, conversing in English and Arabic, with some French; my Christian relatives spoke French and Arabic, with some English. So, we called my aunts on my father's side of the family "auntie" instead of the French "*tante*." In the 1950's and 60's, with some exceptions, most Lebanese Christians were educated in French-speaking schools and most Muslims in English-speaking schools. But Lebanese usually are fluent in both, and of course Arabic. As a result of the Freedom of Education Act, (Article 10 in the Lebanese Constitution), schools became free to create their own curricula. While this ensured excellence in education, it also forced it along confessional lines. Except for the French Lycées, the best schools were founded by missionaries from different countries: French Catholic, American Protestant, British Evangelical or maybe Anglican, German Lutheran, as well as Lebanese Orthodox Christians and Muslims. Historically, Lebanon was the place that everyone passed through—invaders, conquerors, occupiers, merchants, and educators. Naturally, some travelers stayed, even some crusaders, whose lineage can be seen in the blue eyes of some Lebanese and Syrians.

As for the rest of my Dad's family, they were always welcoming and embracing of Mom and me. They always made sure to cook my favorite dishes when I visited, such as the Sultan Ibrahim fish and deep-fried tiny sardines called *bizri*. Growing up, I enjoyed visiting my paternal great uncle's family of five children, including Samir. I remember them as always happy and joking. When they disagreed, it was never disagreeable. The Lebanese in general are very expressive and gesture a lot. The moment I stepped into their apartment, I became part of a large, boisterous family; for an only child, it was great fun. The youngest girl, Farida, was closest to me in age and my close friend. The middle son, Walid, would save me the French comics such as *Spirou, Tintin,* and *Asterix,* and we would talk endlessly about our favorites. I knew that their mother, *Imm* or *Um* (mother of) Abed, prayed five times a day, but that did not interfere with anything. I don't know who else prayed; it was not something anyone spoke about. None of the women covered, nor were they any different from my Christian cousins. Farida would later marry a Greek Orthodox man. In Lebanon, one's family name indicates what religion one belongs to, as well as your social, economic, and even political background; your name is like an open

ID. But for some reason, up to this day, unlike many Lebanese, in some cases I can't tell a Muslim family name from Christian one. Perhaps because my family never emphasized religious differences and I never became interested in making that distinction.

Belly Dance

My birthday parties were always an intergenerational celebration that included the entire extended family, as they are in many communitarian cultures. Everyone from both sides of the family—grandparents, parents, children, aunts, uncles, cousins, and good friends who held the "auntie" or "uncle" honorific—would be there. The table was laden with food and the wonderful cakes and desserts for which my mom and aunt were famous.

My dad was an avid and prolific photographer; his record of our lives is especially precious for so many of us who have left the country. Someone would put music on—the latest favorites from Europe and from the United States, sung in French, English, even Italian, as well as Fairouz—Lebanon's own singing star—and good belly dance music. Young and old, male and female, even toddlers would all get up and dance. The young people would showcase their dance prowess in solo performances.

9. My birthday with all the family.

10. Soraya belly dancing at a family gathering.

11. Other cousins dancing at a family gathering in our house.

For a time, Papi was in charge of screening movies for distribution for the *Sûreté Générale*. We had the luxury of our own little "cinema" at home. He had cut a panel from one of the doors of our sitting room and installed a glass window to block out the racket made by the reel-to-reel 16-millimeter projector. As a result, prior to television, I grew up watching current American movies, especially the musicals. I still remember Cyd Charisse, Fred Astaire, Ginger Rogers, and the routines of many others. American movies depicted this perfect, easy-going, Technicolor place with happy people and happy endings. Maybe that's why I always felt at ease in American culture. It was in some way familiar to me even though it was an idyllic version that Hollywood created to cheer Americans up after World War II.

Thanks to my exposure to such talented dancers, I fell in love with dance and began dreaming of a career as a ballerina. My French ballet teacher in Beirut, Madame LeCourt, dashed my hopes: "*Tu est trop longue et trop mince, ma cherie*" (You are too tall and too skinny, my dear). She came from a strict classical background where female ballerinas could not be taller than their partners. But I did appear with my fellow ballet class on TV, dancing the Spanish Dance in Tchaikovsky's Swan Lake.

Fifty years later in Washington D.C., missing dance, the closeness of family gatherings, and needing core strengthening, I took up belly dance lessons, which had become popular in the United States. It was fun to be taught the names for moves I could do but never officially learned. I discovered my body easily remembered how to respond. It would follow the music without any guidance. I enjoyed learning the essential ingredients of isolating hips and torso in tandem with coordinated arms, shoulder, and hand movements.

As fellow students struggled, somewhat embarrassed, and unable to move their hips the way the teacher was demonstrating, they would ask me, "How come you can do it so easily?" Before I could answer, the teacher, a Jewish-Irish young woman with an adopted Arabic dance name of *Amira* jumped in, "She's nay-tiv you know!" Native? Did I come out of the womb swinging my hips, dressed in leotard and a jingly scarf?

I laughed and explained to my classmates how belly dance was something most people in Lebanon did at every family gathering, and I had grown up moving my body in ways they maybe did not. Most Americans perceive belly dance as exotic, sexually provocative, and even taboo. But Al-Rawi writes that as Western women learn the belly dance and allow themselves "...to experience unfa-

miliar movements," they can learn new "…body wisdom and rituals so that the dancer becomes physically aware of her culturally
acquired conditioning, repression, and blockages."[16] It struck me as
ironic that in Middle Eastern cultures often perceived as backward
and sexually repressed, the women are more grounded in their second chakras (belly area) and more comfortable in their bodies than
most women I encountered in classes in the United States. So much
for the stereotype of the "poor oppressed Arab" or "Muslim wom-
en."

Although I enjoyed learning various movements, after a while
I felt Amira's instructions were too restrictive; my body yearned to
be free to respond to the music. As students and teacher focused
on the steps and moves trying to perfect the technique and choreography, my body rebelled. Where was the soulful dance? Where
was the joy in this adopted form? The belly dance I remembered
and loved required no choreography, prescribed moves or specific steps. You just allowed the rhythm and beat to move you and
let your body improvise in response to the music almost like body
jazz in a heartfelt feminine synergy. Our teacher did an excellent
job conveying technique, but it became obvious to me, as my body
remembered the soulfulness in the dance, that she did not understand the magic and joy of belly dance like a "native." For her, it
was about choreography, technique, and the prowess of balancing
a sword on your head while dancing. Although impressive, it was
not what I was looking for.

So, I found another belly dance teacher, a graceful Kurd-
ish-American young woman who taught us the dance by letting
the beat take over. She also used the kind of music one simply cannot resist dancing to. Instead of stressing precise steps and moves,
she encouraged us to let the music move our body and soul. The
gracefulness and sensuousness of the dance came back to me like a
whiff of basil that drifted up as I brushed past it on Teta Habouba's
balcony

I learned that belly dance actually empowers women because it
strengthens the core, which is extremely important preparation for
childbirth. Some hospitals in the United States are even including
belly dance in their pre-natal programs. I've also learned that belly
dance is an ancient ritual, and that there is no one culture from

which it originates. Between the 8th and 13th centuries CE, it came to the West with the gypsies, and later with the Arabs during their rule of Andalusia. It represented a counterculture to the stylized, formal, and restrained dances in Europe at the time.

Al-Rawi writes that such a dance dates back to the era of Goddesses among them Ishtar in the Middle East, Isis in Egypt, Demeter in Greece, Luna in ancient Rome, Shakti, and Tara in the Far East. She provides another interesting angle to belly dance: " It is intended as a bridge towards greater understanding and respect for women who come from other cultures."[17] I am struck both by the word *bridge* and her desire to bring a respectful perspective to this ancient dance that Al-Rawi writes dates back to those ancient matriarchal horticultural and agricultural societies where dancing was so important. In Lebanon and some other Arab countries, there is the family type of belly dance like the one I grew up with. But with the rise of nightclubs and restaurants where women performed for the rich, another type of belly dance emerged, one focused on entertaining audiences. A particularly exotic and erotic version has been imported to the West.

It reminds me of a talk I attended that described how Orientalist art was a perception formed in Western eyes; that it usually sprang from the imagination of an artist who usually never set foot in the Middle East. It's ironic that paintings of scantily clad Oriental women in suggestive poses provided the West with an acceptable "playboy" release from restrictive and stifling Victorian mores, since "proper" European women had to maintain their virtue.[18]

Whenever I feel down, all I have to do is put some belly dance music on and let it lift me up. But it saddens me to see this uniquely female dance transformed into pure entertainment. Hidden beneath is a feminist ritual in which women intuit and move in response to the beat of the *dirbakeh*, the Lebanese hand drum, and other Arab musical instruments.

First Home

The first apartment we lived in was the top floor of a typical, three-story, traditional Lebanese house with a red tile roof, in a predominantly Sunni Muslim neighborhood, *Burj Abu Haydar.* Sandstone and stucco were the main building materials in the city (limestone was predominant in the mountains). Each apartment in the building had high ceilings, marble wall panels, and marble floors in black and white patterns. All had a center-hall that was the living room, with the rest of the rooms and family sitting rooms branching off from it. Each apartment floor boasted the beautiful, triple Arab arch windows inside the house and out, all decorated with lacy Arabesque woodcarvings.

12. Girl on a balcony. Beirut. Watercolor ©Hala Buck.

Being on the top floor, our balcony offered the best panoramic view. Looking to the right, I could glimpse the Mediterranean, but what most fascinated me was the view of the mountains straight ahead. On summer nights, I would follow the stream of lights from the cars winding their way up to homes, rented and owned, where Beirutis escaped from the summer heat.

Looking left, there was the mosque and its minaret. I remember how furious Papi was when they installed loudspeakers and shifted to recorded calls to prayers. He thought it was too loud and jarring. Also, the record would often get stuck and someone had to go and jiggle the gramophone needle to keep it going.

Two other families lived in the large apartments below us. A family with seventeen children from one wife occupied the ground-floor apartment with a garden. I remember watching the mother pick a flower from their garden and put it in her hair, around the time Abdallah, her husband, came home. It was the most organized and well-run household I ever saw. Abdallah would argue with my dad. "Kamal, how can you have only one child? She will be all alone in her life!"

My dad would answer, "But this way I can afford to give her the best education and anything else she wants." Abdallah would reply, "I have seventeen children and my hope is that one or two of them would take care of me and my wife when we get old. Don't you worry about that?"

Neither managed to convince the other. As in most communitarian cultures—where the family and group are central—Lebanese and Arabs consider being alone to be the worst imaginable fate. Traditionally, children helped out in the farms, or in the family business, and became the social security and employment pool for families. There were no nursing homes. It would be shameful to place an elderly parent or relative in such a place. Families expected to take care of their older parents, uncles, and aunts. In return, elders move to highly respected roles as family storytellers and wise consults. They also help with babysitting and cooking, and so remain a vital part of the family system. Decades later, as I painfully navigated caring for my mom as she descended into Alzheimer's, I wondered if Abdallah had a point. Caregiving all by yourself with no siblings or extended family nearby is very hard.

Across the street from us was another traditional house where the Ghandour and Daābool families lived. I used to love the large magnolia tree in their garden and the flowers these families would always bring us as a neighborly gift. Maybe that's why, a continent away, when I spot a magnolia bloom on the tree we share with our neighbor, I gently pick one flower and bring it inside. For a few days, its delicate, lemony fragrance warms my heart and takes me right back to our balcony.

I enjoyed helping the maid wash our marble floors. I was fascinated with the black and white designs of the large slabs and loved to swoosh around in the soapy water that kept them bright. These traditional houses were built for the hot climate and therefore were oriented so that they always caught the afternoon sea breeze. To avoid the summer heat, in the morning we used the sitting room that faced west; in the afternoon we migrated to the rooms facing east. That way it was always cool; in the winter we reversed the process to stay warm. During the summer, the wooden shutters in the other rooms would be halfway closed to keep out the hot sun but allow the breeze in. The thick walls and the marble floors also helped keep the apartment cool, and insulated. In cold weather, the Persian carpets would be rolled out to warm up the floors, the summer slipcovers removed from the furniture: *voila*, the apartment was now in its winter attire. We had no central heat but a large *mazoot* (heating fuel) stove did a good job heating the common rooms, while electric heaters warmed the bedrooms. Papi always made sure my bedroom was toasty warm before bedtime. In the family sitting room the furniture was a modern, Art Deco style. There was a Morris chair I loved, especially when I was sitting on my dad's lap.

Beirut

Lebanon creates its own version of modernity, appropriating from the West what fits its pluralistic identity. Thus, it has always been uniquely open to the outside world, ready to incorporate thoughts, fashion, and knowledge while maintaining a strong attachment to cherished values and traditions. A strong social life naturally brings Christians and Muslims together on a daily basis, just as musicians from different cultures jam together and artists integrate others' artistic expressions. As with many cultural fusions, it seems that artists often lead the way. I am always amazed at the rich cultural and artistic life in Beirut.

Beirut is and always has been a very noisy city. I loved the different chants of the various street vendors as they plied their merchandise throughout the neighborhoods, calling out, "*Aā sikkeen ya batteekh*" (literally, "watermelon on the knife," but it really implies, "I'll cut it to show you how red and tasty it is.") Others sold my favorite—a fresh bunch of green chickpeas, called *immillaybani*. Once my mom had negotiated the price, it was great fun for me to lower the money in the basket that was tied to our balcony. The vendor would replace the money with fruits, vegetables, or both, and my mom and I would pull the now heavy basket all the way up to the third floor. I would sit on our balcony and squeeze each soft, sweet-tasting chickpea out of its pod. For most Lebanese, "working" on eating food makes it tastier, whether that means cracking pumpkin seed shells and extracting the firm seed in one clean tooth and tongue maneuver or grabbing and munching on a chicken leg. It's quite a contrast to my husband, Steve, who likes his food nice and easy, all shelled, cut up, and ready to eat.

Drivers use their car horns either as a substitute for, or in addition to, traffic lights. The traffic cacophony mixes with the call to prayer from the mosque's minaret and the competing church bells all in close proximity of one another. But no one thinks anything of it. While this cacophony may seem conflict-ridden and disturbing for outsiders, it is commonplace for Lebanese. Like other Mediterranean people, Lebanese talk with their hands as well as their mouths. Gesturing, raising their voices, they may appear as if they're scolding or about to kill each other. But it is usually just a friendly argument that ends over a cup of Turkish coffee or with a pat on the back.

My family preferred the beach to the mountains. I have fond memories of spending every summer day at the chalet at the "Acapulco" beach with a good friend and next-door neighbor, Jeanny. Her Palestinian family, like so many others, had fled their ancestral home in Haifa during heavy fighting and terrorism by the Zionist Irgun militia.[19] They never dreamed that they would ever return home. Palestine at the time was under British colonial rule.

Jeanny now lives in Louisiana and we are still as close as we were then, despite the distance. During the summer in Beirut we spent all our time at the beach, surfing with small boards, sunbathing, and talking. I loved being in the water, feeling it carry me as I swam or surfed. Being in the sun all day, I would turn dark brown by the end of summer, much to the dismay of Auntie Munia, who said it ruins the skin. In the early evening, our parents came to join us, with barbecue chicken or *kafta* (a mixture of ground lamb, parsley, and onions on skewers) and have dinner under the stars. All those happy memories by the sea beckon to me today; I still head for the beach whenever I need to replenish or sort things out. I guess it is natural to seek natural settings from one's childhood that are familiar and happy and where one still finds peace and answers.

Bayonets and Bikinis — 1958

The first conflict I lived through, one that reflected Lebanon's vulnerability and inability to find a national identity greater than clan loyalties, occurred in 1958. It also was the beginning of the turmoil that has plagued the country on and off since.

Lebanon was caught up in regional conflicts and the loss of Palestine, which led to a large influx of Palestinian refugees who settled in camps and formed their own militias. This threatened the president at the time, Camille Chamoun, a Maronite Catholic. He actively opposed the rise of Gamal Abdel Nasser's Arab nationalism, which he felt caused division within Lebanon and ignited violence.[20] After the revolution in Iraq that year, at the request of Chamoun, the United States agreed to send troops to Lebanon. This disrupted the delicate and fragile internal balance that Lebanon had so far maintained.[21] One morning, the U.S. Sixth Fleet appeared on the horizon. The Maronite Catholic militia the Phalangists (also known a *Kata'eb*) were happy, as were some Lebanese Muslims like my father who feared Gamal Abdel Nasser's Pan Arab Nationalist agenda. But most Muslims were appalled at having foreign troops landing on Lebanese soil.

What I remember is rushing to the beach with my family and friends to watch the *Amerkeyn* arrive. I can still see it. U.S. Marines in full battle gear pouring out of their landing crafts onto the beach.

I don't know what they were briefed to expect but I'm sure they did not expect a cheering population, curious onlookers (including women in bathing suits, and perhaps even a few bikinis) and the ever-enterprising vendors greeting them with Coca Cola, Pepsi, Fanta and, ice cream.

I also remember walking along the Corniche and watching the "Americans" patrolling it. My friends and I were more interested in how good-looking the guys were. We even devised a secret code word to refer to them so no one would know what we were talking about. It was a silly word we made up: *kokus*. Whenever my friend Dina and I get together, we laugh at our young selves sounding like crazed birds, catching each other's attention by saying *kokus* to the right or left or whatever.

During the 1958 conflict, or what the Lebanese like to call *les évènements* "the events," roadblocks appeared in all neighborhoods, including ours. Armed youth from other Arab countries manned stations where they checked ID cards, which at the time indicated what religious sect you belonged to. That's when my dad decided we needed to move to another neighborhood.

While we looked for a new apartment, we stayed with my mom's school friend, Rita, and her family. Their five daughters became my close friends, especially the eldest, Dina. They lived in a safer area known as Verdun, where the fighting was minimal. Since our parents enjoyed each other's company and we girls got along, it sounded like a good idea to stay with them while looking for a new apartment, at least until one evening when shooting and shelling began that seemed to be aimed at their (our) building. Our parents yelled for all of us six girls to keep our heads down and move into the hallway. We all rushed in our pajamas, huddling in the corridor—the only place with no windows and therefore no danger of shattering glass. The whole building shook and it sounded as if it was going to collapse on us. I had never seen grown-ups so scared. It was terrifying to be trapped in the midst of the fighting, not knowing what would happen next. Would they storm the building? Each side had several militias fighting; it was mayhem.

By morning, things quieted down; I don't remember what happened next. Some truce must have taken place. It was then that we learned that President Chamoun's son Danny lived on the top floor of the building, which explained why we had suddenly become a target.

With fighting going on around us for months, we were housebound. We found ways to amuse ourselves during lulls in the fighting, such as roller-skating on the large verandahs or balconies. Whenever the fighting died down, we would go to the nearby Bristol Hotel to ice skate. It was the only ice skating rink in town. We became excellent skaters both on ice and on marble floors. Thirty-two years later in Ottawa, Canada, where we were posted, everyone assumed that I, the Lebanese-American would have to take ice-skating lessons in order to enjoy the wonderful Rideau Canal. Instead it was Steve, a good New Yorker, who had to learn to skate along with eight ladies from Bangladesh.

Life in Ras Beirut

The conflict died down after only a few months; this was nothing like the civil war still far in our future.

After the fighting, my parents and I moved to a "modern" apartment in Ras Beirut, close to the American University. It was a mixed Muslim and Christian neighborhood where most of my father's family lived. But like most of the newer apartments, this one was not built with the climate in mind. The walls were made of cinderblock, which absorbed the summer heat. Nor was the apartment oriented to catch the dependable evening breeze like our old apartment in *Burj Abu Haydar*.

I remember helping to hang the wash on the roof, watching it snap back and forth in the breeze. I disliked the stiff towels but laundry dried in the sun did smell clean and fresh. Across the rooftops of Beirut you saw many other people's laundry hanging. I loved to imagine the lives connected to each set of clothes. Some people raised homing pigeons on their roofs, and in the afternoon they set them free to fly around before they were somehow called back. Pots of hibiscus, jasmine, and other plants dotted most roofs and balconies, and hosing them down in the afternoon cooled down the houses. These flat roofs provided additional living space as well. You could hear families chatting or enjoying a mild starlit night. My parents hosted dinner parties on our roof where it always felt more festive. In the late afternoon, there was usually a breeze that blew in off the sea, and during the many hot and humid nights, people would sleep on cots on the balconies or roofs.

Papi kept his 1936 Ford convertible into the early 1960s. He had replaced all the old systems in the car with modern ones. Our Ford was famous throughout Beirut. It was famous because it would only start when my mom or dad used a rock that we kept on the floor of the passenger seat to strike a certain point near the accelerator pedal. Mom would tell the story of how people downtown would wait for her by the car to see her perform this strange operation—and cheer when the motor started. On our outings up the mountains, Dad would speed up. When we got to the top of a hill, for a second or two the car hovered in midair before it landed on the downhill; I had this fun and woozy feeling in my stomach like when on a roller-coaster, and we would all shout, "Wheee!"

Because of the steep and windy mountainous roads, everyone in Lebanon is required to learn to handle the common stick-shift car without stalling. In those days, one took the driving test in a Jeep on the hills of *Telli zaātar*. The day it was my turn to take the test I realized the Jeep they gave me had lost its brakes. I thought it was part of the test. So, as my vigilant father had taught me in many emergency drills, I calmly used the handbrake, pulling and releasing it as I completed all the required maneuvers on the steep road, and parked. "Not bad," the snotty examiner said. "Yeah, especially with no brakes," I replied. It was gratifying to see him blush. He had not checked the car! My dad was furious at the carelessness of the people administering the test and read them the riot act, but he was also proud of me. I was proud of myself as well.

The ability to respond effectively in crisis proved to be a godsend later in my Foreign Service life, especially during evacuations from Aden and Oman in the '70s and the Iran-Iraq war in the '80s. I remember the emergency security drill the U.S. Marines at the Baghdad Embassy organized, and how much I enjoyed rappelling down the Embassy exterior to simulate a forced escape.

Papi often told me, "Girls can do anything they want, be whoever they want to be." He taught me to be strong. But he was still the product of his generation. When I said I wanted to learn to play the guitar, he balked, and suggested that perhaps the piano would be a more suitable instrument. A mixed message, yes, but it was not necessarily culture-specific. Many of my American and foreign clients received mixed messages from their parents as well. I may have been disappointed, but I did not begrudge him that. No parent is perfect. Not even my father, whose name, Kamal, means "perfection" in Arabic.

I changed schools four times in Beirut. I first attended preschool at the Carmelite St. Joseph, run by nuns. My mom pulled me out because a French nun declared, in front of me, that I would never be good in math. It infuriated her that this nun would give up on me when I was five years old. After that I went to the Franciscan school, and later the Lycée Français for five years.

At the *lycée*, the written, classical Arabic was taught as a foreign language. There are three forms of Arabic, the local dialect *darjeh* or āameh; the classical *nahhawi*, which is written but not usually spoken (it is the Arabic of literature and the Qur'an); and a combination of newspaper and TV Arabic called Modern Standard Arabic, which almost all Arabs can understand. Arabic is the official language in Lebanon but most people also speak French, English, and a salad of all three; Armenians in Lebanon (who at the time comprised 4 percent of the population) also speak their own language. After the Armenian genocide of 1915 Armenians found refuge in Lebanon. They were granted Lebanese citizenship and were loyal citizens. One particular neighborhood in Beirut was dubbed Little Armenia. They also have their own university, Hagazian College.

My mom told me how when she was a student at a French nuns' school, during the French mandate, they were forbidden to speak anything but French. If you were caught speaking Arabic you were punished. To make matters worse, even during recess, the nuns would post fellow students as spies to report on classmates speaking their native language. I was stunned to hear that, but my mom seemed unfazed. "How did you feel about that, Mami?" I asked her. "We had to learn good French," she responded. Even more shocking to me was a recent conversation with a younger cousin, who said she'd had the same experience—in the 1960s and '70s at her French school that my mom had had. Is it any wonder that people whose countries were colonized, their native language disparaged, their customs, traditions, and language diminished or discarded, can and do develop a serious national and personal identity crisis? To her dying day, my mother could not properly read or write in her native language, nor was she aware of the loss of her linguistic roots. Some identify completely with the occupiers and adopt their language, customs, and beliefs, and participate in the denigration of their own culture. Others develop a distrust of the West and its true intentions. They rebel and become suspicious of anything involving Western powers. The "plot" mentality that is rampant in the Arab world has many smoking guns at its origins.

Perhaps to compensate for Mami's loss and to help people understand current issues in the Arab world, when I lecture about the Middle East, I make sure I emphasize that to succeed in any country, modernization has to remain congruent with the culture. As Karen Armstrong wrote, unlike for the West, modernization in the Middle East has historically been an experience, "not of empowerment, autonomy, and innovation, as it had been in Europe, but a process of deprivation, (by colonizing powers), dependence, and patchy imperfect imitation."[22] The Arab uprisings we witnessed in 2011 show the long, torturous, and painful—but inevitable—growing pains people experience when they try to take charge of their own destiny in a sustainable way. Democracy is more than just about elections. Given the fraught history of Western involvement in the Middle East, democracy needs to be a homegrown, gradual process of integrating the best of East and West free from foreign interference.

To this day, Lebanon and most of the Arab world struggle with the legacy of colonization and betrayal. Graham Fuller, writing about the impact of western colonialism on Muslim societies, argues, "Imperial rule quickly distorted the natural development of the Muslim world, dismantling traditional structures of leadership and governance, destroying traditional institutions, upsetting cultural patterns, while discouraging organic development of native alternatives."[23] All of which still haunt the region.

My Parents Leave Lebanon

In 1970, after our evacuation from Aden to Asmara (then part of Ethiopia), Steve and I were sent to Beirut to await new orders.

While we were there, Steve went to the U.S. Embassy in Beirut and started the process for my parents to apply for immigrant visas. Even though my parents had no intention of leaving Lebanon, he and Karla, a consular officer friend at the embassy, agreed this was a prudent thing to do. If anything ever happened and my parents decided they had to leave, they could do it quickly. Unfortunately, she also convinced my mom that no one in the United States would pronounce her name "Jeanne" (Jaan) the French way, and changed it to Jan. I never got used to hearing people refer to my mom as "Jan."

In 1975, Bashir Gemayel, of the Maronite Catholic right-wing Kata'eb party (Phalangist), ordered an attack on a bus carrying Palestinians—in retaliation for an attempted assassination of his father, Pierre Gemayel. Twenty-seven Palestinians died. My dad correctly foresaw that the tragic incident was the "opening salvo of the Lebanese civil war" as the statesman Sayyed El-Husseini called it. Papi came home that day and told my mom: "Jeanne, it's time to pack our suitcases and leave for the United States. I have our visas. We need to leave now." He was afraid the airport would close. It did close soon after they left.

Mom was reluctant to leave her family and friends. The whole extended family thought my dad was crazy. "Come on Kamal," they would say. "This will all blow over in six months." That was the usual time frame for Lebanese crises. But Papi was adamant, and he told everyone to change their liras into dollars, because he predicted the Lebanese lira would tumble drastically, which it did. Still in demand with very senior government officials, due to his forensic expertise and analysis, he had an unusually insightful view of the dynamics of Lebanese politics.

Within two days, my parents left Lebanon, their home, and everyone they knew behind. They took off on one of the last flights out of Beirut with their dog, Lucky II, and two suitcases each full of memories. Had they glanced down at Lebanon from the small airplane window? What were they thinking, and feeling? Did it hit them then or later that they had left their life as they knew it and their country, for good?

Leaving family and friends behind must have been hard, but my parents always faced any hardship with fortitude. We were posted back in Washington D.C. at the time, so it was comforting and helpful to have us there to welcome them. They stayed with us for a while, then after we were posted to Kuwait, with Steve's parents until they could move into their new home.

Our apartment in Ras Beirut had a large balcony that was like a hanging garden, thanks to Mami having the greenest thumb around. The first thing mom did when they moved into their new townhouse in the United States was to plant *naānaā* (mint), reminding her of her balcony garden in Beirut. It was as if she was planting new roots in her adoptive land.

English being her third language, mom would say "smashed potatoes" and tell friends to "please come drop on us anytime." She fumbled some words that sounded like direct translations from French, but weren't. One time she was giving a recipe to a British friend, Thelma: "First, you rape the orange." Thelma's eyes opened wide in shock. "Jeanne, what are you saying?" Thinking that Thelma had not heard her. Mom repeated, in a louder tone, "You know, you rape it very well!" They finally resolved this when mom realized that the French word for "grating" — *rapper* — did not translate into a phonetic English equivalent. Thelma never tired of telling that story.

Years later, in mom's retirement community, I would come across people in the hallway or dining area who asked me if I knew how funny my mom was. I cannot even remember all the things she came up with, sitting with her friends at Maplewood at happy hour. Words came out of nowhere, and for a moment people were not sure whether she was joking or not.

At his age, with his specialty, it was harder for my dad to find a job. The neighbors across the street became friends, and asked Papi if he would mind having their three kids come to his house after school until the parents returned from work. My dad eagerly accepted, and refused all compensation. For him helping out a neighbor made him feel he was doing something worthwhile. When the kids would come by after school, Papi would have prepared snacks and a *mézzé* for them. They loved it and he enjoyed being a surrogate grandparent. That was before our daughter Katie Leila was born. The kids loved being spoiled that way.

Mom had been mostly a stay-at-home mom during my childhood. She had later worked as a secretary at a friend's office in Beirut. Eventually, mom got a job at Bache and Co., an investment firm in Washington, D.C. During the interview with the brokers she didn't understand why they were so concerned there might be a problem because they were Jewish. After all, my Mom recounted, "During my childhood in Beirut our building was owned by a Lebanese Jewish family. I played with their kids and our parents were good friends to the point that when my father Rizkallah died, the landlord patriach insisted he would wash my father's body. I remember how supportive they were of my mother and us three girls."

Lebanese Jews were established in society at the time. Mami was not aware that anti-Jewish sentiments existed in the United States, and my dad used to recount how as a young man, he would drive down to Haifa, Palestine to visit both his Palestinian and Jewish friends, who had co-existed peacefully for hundreds of years. But with the creation of Israel in 1948, all of this changed and resentment towards the establishment of Israel in what was Palestine began.

A few years later mom was offered a job at Geico, within walking distance of their townhouse. On some evenings she drove to the University of Maryland to take an actuary course to improve at her job. She was a can-do woman of the first order, a great hostess and cook. One especially funny example of her playful, even mischievous, nature took place at Geico. Having already established a reputation for her delicious cakes there, one April Fool's day, she cut a round piece of sponge and covered it with her special icing. Then she took it to the office and put it next to the coffee machine and waited as one by one her colleagues would at first cry out in joy, "Jan's cake!" then get frustrated trying to cut it until they realized her trick. She would then swear them to secrecy, replenish the icing and wait again. She had a reputation for burning food by forgetting it on the stove so we always asked, smelling the burnt aroma coming from the kitchen, if we were being served *la specialitée de la maison* (the speciality of the house). She would snap her head up and answer in a firm but funny tone, *"Hayda ana"* (This is who I am. Take it or leave it.).

She loved her home and, since she could sew beautifully, she was always creating complicated window treatments such as fancy curtains and new covers for sofas and chairs. I was intrigued to learn recently that the word *sofa* comes from French, but originally comes from the Arabic word, *suffa.*

I have vague memories as a child of my mom and dad reupholstering our sofa, working together, stretching the webbed straps and assembling the Morris chair they had ordered from Orosdi Back, a famous department store in Beirut that imported everything. Mami also loved moving furniture and accessories around the house, an interest my dad certainly didn't share. I believe I inherited her design sense and love of beauty.

Mom's greatest skill was her bargaining. Even by Lebanese standards she was famous. I used to be embarrassed by her tenacious desire to get the lowest price possible, which she always got. Beirut's *Basta* was the antique and flea market area. It consisted of rows of shops with large old wooden shutter-like doors, cavernous interiors piled high with an eclectic mixture of European and Middle Eastern treasures: carved desks, chests, screens inlaid with mother-of–pearl, Hungarian Opaline, even Saracen swords and shields (I still have one Mom bought) probably unearthed from an ancient battlefield.

Shopkeepers sitting outside their stores chatting and drinking coffee, smoking a cigarette or a *narguileh* (a water pipe also known as *shisha*), would see my mom coming and know they were in for a long morning or afternoon and would be lucky to keep their shirts on their backs. But bargaining is something expected and enjoyed in the Middle East, a game of sorts. Like a good tennis match, a negotiating marathon is a great workout, and fun for both parties in such cultures. Mom would come home thrilled with her winnings, like the red Bohemian glass oil lamp that she asked dad to convert to electricity. Even in the United States, she'd say to me, "How come you told me people don't bargain here in the States? I just got this wonderful suit for half the price." "Mom," I said, "how did you do it? This is from Lord and Taylor? Was it on sale?" "No," she replied. "But I told them I could only afford half price." I guess in American practices she would be called a highly skilled negotiator.

Mami was a woman of indomitable spirit. A few years after Papi passed away, she was driving some friends to a dinner party in Virginia. For many Marylanders, crossing the Potomac River to Virginia inevitably results in getting lost. My mom was no exception. This was long before the days of cellphones and Homeland Security. So she looked around and saw this large building and proceeded to drive up to its front gate.

Rolling down her window she inquired, "Excuse me sir, I'm lost and I need to find a telephone to call our friends and get directions and tell them we're late. May I use your phone?" "What's your friend's name ma'am?" "Mr. and Mrs. John Warner." Snapping into a salute as he clicked his heels the uniformed young man ushered mom into the building. "Yes, ma'am please follow me," he even dialed the number for her. (Mom didn't find anything strange in that. People are always respectful and kind to elders in Lebanon.)

Connected, Mami announced, "Hi John, this is Jan, I'm sorry we're late but we got lost and this lovely young man was kind enough to let me call you." "WHO IS THIS? I'm not having any Goddam dinner party?!" Perplexed and slightly offended by his tone mom continued. "This is Jan Lababidi, I'm sure the dinner was tonight, ask Betty." "There's no Betty here and my wife would never plan a dinner without telling me." At this point mom thought something was off. Turning to the young man standing by "Are you sure you dialed John Warner's number?" "Yes ma'am, I know it by heart, he's our Secretary of Defense and our boss."

Mom had pulled into the Pentagon and as fate smiled in amusement, the John Warner Mami knew was not the Secretary of Defense. Finally, the young man looked up the address and the correct phone number of the other John Warner and he got the directions. Mami and her friends made it to the dinner party. What had made this so hilarious is that John Warner at the time was divorcing Liz Taylor, and was not amused by the idea that she would have invited strangers without telling him. I imagine mom, unperturbed, probably hugged the young soldier as she was leaving.

Another time she got lost trying to find a friend's house outside of Baltimore. So she stopped and called 911. "Yes ma'am how can I help you?" "I'm lost, please send a policeman to guide me." "Ma'am, that is not an emergency." "Of course it is, I'm an old woman and I'm lost. In D.C., the police help the elderly." The 911 operator did not relent. So mom finally called the friends and they came to guide her.

Children adored my mom; she in return, became a playful child with them. I have wonderful memories of her goofing around with our daughter Katie. She would scoot around on the floor with Katie, letting her pull her hair, then play câche-câche (hide-and-seek) behind the curtains. Dad would put Katie on his back and crawl around their living room floor or throw her up in the air and catch her as she squealed with delight. When mom volunteered at the Bradley Hills Elementary School, she taught the kids, both girls and boys, how to crochet. They loved it, and so did their parents. They say that people with Alzheimer's regress back into childhood. But Mom always had that impish childlike quality.

My mom loved to sing in the choir of her Presbyterian Church. Singing was a magic balm for her and later for me as well, most probably because the songs carried the haunting melodies of her childhood and mine. I wrote about those songs in a journal I kept during my mom's slow decline and my journey as a witness to it. Almost to the end, she never lost her *joie de vivre*, unless she was being hijacked by her brain.

As mom descended further into dementia, we decided to consolidate our safe deposit boxes. As I opened her box, I saw several manila envelopes inscribed in my dad's elegant, meticulous, upright script. One contained their U.S. citizenship certificates. Another held documents in Arabic translated into English by the Lebanese Embassy, which I guess they had needed to start a new life here. The last envelope had just one word written in Arabic, *Kitab*. As I opened it, two yellowed papers fell out of the envelope, one in Arabic, the other translated into English. There I was, for the first time seeing and holding my parents' marriage contract, a fragment of my own beginning. Standing in the safe deposit's tiny cubicle holding this document in my hands, I felt tears welling up. I murmured to myself, "This is where my bridge began."

As I ran my fingers over Papi's beautiful Arabic calligraphy I imagined him organizing their documents before they left Lebanon at the beginning of the civil war. The *Kitab* emigrated with my parents, halfway around the world to the United States. It remained the only document attesting to their marriage. I sat down as tears rolled down my face. Papi had died eight years before, yet I could sense his commitment to three major steps in his life: marrying my mom, being a devoted dad, emigrating and leaving all that he was in Lebanon to start a new life in his late sixties in the United States, a country he had always admired.

He was always super organized, responsible, and dependable. As they hurriedly packed their suitcases, had he felt any sadness, regret, or anxiety? I will never know. Papi was not one who showed his emotions. His actions bespoke them, and later his clinical depression. Immigrating in your elder years is hard. He found that here, unlike in Lebanon, people did not respect their elders. There is no role to move into. I think he missed the dignity that cultures in the Arab World reserve for their elders. There you transition to a place of heightened respect and honor, in which you still have much to contribute. Here, as our daughter Katie, many years later wrote in her play "I Site,"[24] he was treated like "an old man with an accent." Katie later went by her middle name Leila. So both names will appear in various parts of my story.

Dignity is something that everyone needs regardless of age or how "foreign" they look or sound. As my parents' roles were reversed and Papi was unable to get a job, he slid into depression. Twice he decided to return to Lebanon during the civil war; I guess these were efforts to regain his lost self. He would take the dog with him and tell Mom to follow him in a few weeks, after he organized everything in Beirut. But the Lebanon he left was no more, and after two weeks, he would call my mom from Beirut and tell her to stop packing and stay put. A few days later he would return, with his dog, Lucky II, his large suitcase full of his tools, Lucky's toys, and whatever else he had taken with him, but never with the dignity and identity he left behind.

He descended deeper into depression. When we tried to get some help for him, I was shocked by the cultural insensitivity and disrespect with which the team at the hospital treated my dad. This eventually pushed me to go back to graduate school and become a therapist, focusing on cross-cultural education and training of others. After the hospital mismanaged his depression, he refused any further treatment.

In the end, Papi's depression ended his life. After a car accident and a couple of falls, he stopped eating and passed away in 1995. In the nursing home, where he died, he had waved Steve and I away because, I believe, he hated us seeing him so vulnerable, and he wanted to spare us any pain.

He chose the five minutes my mom stepped out of the room to pass. Having read *Final Gifts*,[25] written by hospice nurses who documented how people choose to die—I learned that some people will wait until everyone they want to see has gathered; others want to die alone. Having that in my mind, I knew that my dad would choose the latter option. It helped assuage my guilt for having left him.

I remember rushing back to his side, having left him only half an hour before. His body was lying there, but his spirit was gone. Before that moment, I had never realized how at death we transition into the mystery of another reality. Since then, I have sensed his continuing presence, supporting and protecting us, especially as my mother slipped further and further into Alzheimer's.

During his lifetime, my dad taught me to be strong and compassionate. Whenever I was afraid, he would look me in the eye and say with a serious half-smile: *"Are you a girl? Or a mouse?"* I interpreted it to mean that girls are strong and should not be afraid.

Watching him struggle with depression and death, however, helped me realize that I also needed to embrace and not fear my own vulnerability. In death, as in life, he was my greatest and most loving teacher.

> *To be born is to be chosen. No one is here by accident; each one of us was sent here for a special destiny.*
> —John O'Donohue.[26]

2

Cruel Encounter and Beyond

What determines a person's affiliation to a given group is essen-
tially the influence of others: the influence of those about him
relatives, fellow-countrymen, co-religionists who try to make
him one of them; together with the influence of those on the other
side, who do their best to exclude him.

—Amin Maalouf[27]

Lebanon—the Nation

Lebanon has always been a mercantile culture with a high lit-
eracy rate. Being the most religiously diverse country in the
Middle East, with its various allegiances Lebanon is like a kalei-
doscope. Its pluralistic culture and geographical location on the
Eastern Mediterranean between Europe, North Africa, the Arabian
Peninsula, and South Asia has always made it the swinging door
of the Middle East and a barometer of geopolitical gamesmanship.
Throughout Lebanon's history and into the present France, Egypt,
Syria, Israel, the United States, Russia, and Iran have supported
different Lebanese factions. Tiny Lebanon, however, has not just
been a battleground but also a refuge for many people—Jews, Armenians, Palestinians, Iraqis and most recently Syrians.

In 1943, when the state of Lebanon was being formed, Maronite
Christians wanted continuous French protection. Sunni Muslims
wanted independence with no strings attached. The compromise
was the National Pact, an unwritten agreement which spelled out a
confessional power sharing in a parliamentary democracy.

The National Pact was Lebanon's charter for independence

overseen by the French who continued to protect the predominance of Maronite Catholics. According to Petran, "The National Pact was intended not only as a *modus vivendi* between the Maronite and Sunni communities, but also as a means to break a popular drive at the time for secularization led by the then young Druze deputy Kamal Jumblatt."[28] It was designed to assuage fears of most religious sects. However, as Petran writes, from the start the French — who had been governing Lebanon since 1920 — weighted the system in favor of their Maronite Catholic protégés, thus ensuring their continued influence in Lebanon. It was the old adage of "divide and conquer" that still plagues the nation. To this day the president has to be Maronite Catholic, the prime minister Sunni Muslim, the head of parliament Shi'a Muslim, and so forth down the chain of command. This was based on a 1932 census, a dubious one and the only one ever taken.

The Pact made it possible for Lebanon to exist as an independent country with a parliamentary democracy. While it carried the seed of a unique, peaceful pluralistic identity, it also brought its biggest threat by ensuring divided loyalties. As a result of the confessionally-based nature of the government (a system that deliberately mixes religion and politics), the primary allegiance remained to the *zaeem* (leader of the religious sect in parliament).

In addition to internal conflicts, Lebanon has regularly been affected by the involvement of Syria, Israel, the United States, Iran and others. In the 1990s Syria took over Lebanon. In 1982, Petran writes, Israel's massive invasion and occupation of Lebanon, with the tacit accord of the United States, left tens of thousands dead, especially Shiites — leading to the rise of Hezbollah. Later, and in 2006, Israel's devastating bombing of Lebanon, cost thousands of lives. It also destroyed buildings, factories, and roads and disabled the airport — in short the entire infrastructure that had been rebuilt after the civil war was destroyed.

Internal jousting for power, exacerbated by foreign meddling and proxy wars, has repeatedly threatened to tear Lebanon apart. Alliances continue to shift with the prevailing political pressures, foreign interference, and the usual reluctance of Lebanese leaders to give up what little power they have. The nation and its people survived a civil war that lasted fifteen years, between 1975 and 1990.

Despite the violence experienced (and perpetrated) on all sides, the Lebanese dusted themselves off and got on with life. Somehow, since the end of the civil war Lebanon has managed to pull back from the brink of hell, despite its lack of a "visibly" dominant national culture.

Polling in the Arab world showed people's identity is contextual. Depending on what is going on in the region and the West— people identify themselves as citizen of a country or Muslim or Christian or Arab or even citizen of the world. But this survey also showed that Lebanon is unique in the Arab World. Paradoxically, when this tiny nation is threatened by foreign intervention in any way, the Lebanese of all sects set aside their differences and instead rally around their common Lebanese identity. According to Shibley Telhami, this fear for the tiny state overrides civil war, sectarianism, and multiple foreign interventions; it keeps this country of four million intact.[29] Until there is peace and stability in the region, the Lebanese people need to continue to put their national identity ahead of sectarianism and foreign meddling. Perhaps that is why people told me the civil war was a helpful vaccination of sorts. Lebanon's national culture, like its cedar, is resilience. It reminds me that the title and refrain of Lebanon's national anthem is *"Kulluna lil watan"* (All of us for the nation).

My Beginnings

I came into the world in defiance to a forced sectarian compromise that discouraged mixed marriages like my parents. I was a historically improbable child—yet I was symbolic of what Lebanon could be. I was very lucky to grow up in a loving and open-minded family. It provided a buffer against any prejudice that may have existed around me, and modeled peaceful, mutually enriching co-existence.

The years of my childhood, up until my early teens, were peaceful and prosperous for Lebanon. A great number of Lebanese from different religions and sects lived in mixed neighborhoods. For centuries, Eastern Christians and Muslims have lived, worked, and socialized together. There were probably tensions here and there, but their basic cultures were the same; only the place of worship and rituals differed. Later, the civil war fractured this peaceful coexistence. During the war, except for *Ras Beirut*, which is still mixed, Muslims retreated to neighborhoods heavily populated with Muslims, and Christians to predominantly Christian neighborhoods.

The civil war created many refugees. Many others, like my parents, left by choice. Droves of people from the south and from bombed-out buildings in Beirut became squatters in abandoned buildings and apartments like my parents' apartment. When my parents left Beirut at the very beginning of the civil war, they took nothing besides what fit into their suitcases. Everything else they left behind, and they continued paying rent on their apartment in Ras Beirut, since it held all their furniture and possessions. Luckily Tante Georgette managed to rescue photos, and other items. My old upright piano was carried across the dangerous "Green Line" to the safety of her house. Eventually a cousin shipped them to my parents in the United States

War destroys more than buildings and lives. It brings out the worst in people and strips them of their humanity. As a result of people losing family members and remembering the war, there was more sectarianism after the civil war. Too many conflicts, foreign interventions and power games, together with a confessional democracy, dims the larger vision embodied in what came to be known as the "Cedar Revolution" of 2005. Those who participated called this revolution the "Independence *Intifada*."[30] *Intifada* in Arabic means shaking off, in this case foreign occupation. Many Lebanese participated in it to oust Syrian troops and reduce their heavy influence in government. They succeeded. Their hopes to stop all foreign interference may be somewhat diminished, but perhaps like the cedar tree itself, the movement will one day re-emerge stronger and well rooted.

Regardless of all the problems the country faces, the majority of Lebanese share a love for the land itself, especially its blue-green mountains rising from the coastline, the two main mountain ranges, Mount Lebanon and the Anti-Lebanon, and the beautiful and fertile *Bekaā* Valley in between them that extends the length of the country. It is famous for its vineyards that have been producing great wine for centuries. In winter and spring the highest peaks of *Qurnat al Sawdah* at 10,131 feet and *Sannine* at 9,000 feet—are clad in

13. View of Beirut peninsula from the mountain village of Beit Mery.
Watercolor ©Hala Buck

snow. Lebanon was named after the color of that white snow. From the Corniche along the Mediterranean Sea you experience a picturesque perspective of the coast winding its way north and south against the backdrop of the mountains, with red tile roofs dotting the hills. From the mountain villages and towns, you look down at the Beirut peninsula and coast, with umbrella pines catching your eye along a meandering tour until you reach the sea. Wherever you look, this tiny country rewards you with beautiful views. Not even the scars of war can obscure its natural beauty.

What counters separation and division is the importance and centrality of family. Like other communitarian cultures in the Arab world and elsewhere, the extended Lebanese family always comes first. The individual exists to contribute to the welfare of the group, and in return the group is always there to support you, from the moment you are born till the day you die, and your family after that. This tradition of reciprocity is ingrained in the value of interdependence that those societies share. Sadly, the high rate of emigration during crises frays family bonds. When most of the young people leave, the traditional support system weakens, but it rarely breaks. Even during the civil war, Lebanese immigrants returned to visit family.

I grew up at a time when serious conflicts between religious sects were not evident. I basked in the embracing love of my extended family, and my life seemed seamless and conflict-free. I felt secure and sheltered. There was nothing strange or noteworthy in the fact that one went to church while others usually prayed at home. All the good Lebanese food—*hummos, baba ghanouj, lubye* stew, *kibbeh, tabbooleh, shakshookeh,* and *wara' īnab* (stuffed vine leaves)—was the same in the homes of my Muslim and Christian relatives. Traditions were the same, although the applications might differ. For example, people of all faiths believed in protecting their children, especially newborns, from the envious eyes of beholders. Muslims would pin a blue bead and sometimes a charm miniature of the Qur'an (the Muslim holy book) somewhere on the baby's clothing. Christians would also use a blue bead but with a charm representing the cross, or a gold cross with a blue bead in its center and pin it in the same way. The religious symbol was different but the common tradition and heritage was the same, the blue bead. The hand of Fatima or *Khamsa* was also used by both to ward off the "evil eye."

Recently I was wearing my hand of Fatima as a pendant in the Washington Metro and a woman kept looking at it. Finally, she approached me; pointing to my *khamsa* pendant she began speaking to me in Hebrew, assuming I must be Israeli. I told her I didn't speak Hebrew, but I understood some of what she had said, because Hebrew and Arabic are both Semitic languages.

"Actually," I told her, "what you call the *khamsa* we call the hand of Fatima. It's an ancient symbol in the Middle East." We have a saying in Arabic: *khamsey bi ouyooon al shaytan* (five against the evil eye).

"R-really" she said. "You mean ze *khamsa* is not originally Israeli?"

"My guess is," I continued, "that it was brought to Israel by Eastern Jews who had lived for millennia in the Arab World and who emigrated to Israel."

We had an interesting conversation about food as well. She was shocked that *khommos,* as Israelis pronounce it, is actually one of the main traditional Lebanese dishes, which we pronounce *hummos.* It felt good to reclaim symbols and food for my country of birth, all in one metro ride. We parted in a friendly exchange. I wish the peace process were as simple.

People are surprised to learn that for at least two generations, all but one of my female cousins on my Muslim father's side are college graduates of the Beirut College for Women (B.C.W.), founded in 1924 as the American Junior College for Women by American missionaries. In 1973 it became co-ed and was renamed Beirut University College, or B.U.C. In 1994 it became the secular Lebanese American University (L.A.U.) My cousin Hana and I graduated from the co-ed American University of Beirut which was founded in 1866 and was now a private, nonsectarian institution of higher learning which functions under a charter from the State of New York.

Among the male Lababidis we have several famous poets and writers, going back two and three generations. One story that typifies the seamless interfaith connection between my two families is of auntie Maliha, my dad's first cousin, who would call up my mother and ask, "Jeanne, what's the name of your saint that finds things for you? I lost my keys and I want to ask him for help." "St. Antoine," my mom would answer. So, St. Anthony of Padua gets requests from Christians and Muslims alike in my family.

Cruel Encounter

At Christmas and Easter I would go to church with my mother's sister and her children. On some Sundays, I went with my Christian cousin, Nado, to help the priest set up for mass. Because I was an only child, it was a fun way to spend time with the other children in the family. The church was called the *yasooi'ya*—it was a Jesuit church—and it was part of St. Joseph University. I remember huge, black, wrought-iron gates and wide steps that led into a typical Catholic church, with alcoves for the different saints, candles burning with prayers of supplication and the smell of incense, which I loved, along with the coolness and silence. I helped my cousin with whatever tasks the priest had for us.

One day, I'm guessing I was around six or seven, I followed my cousin Nado into church. A short, rotund priest in brown robes, a crucifix hanging around his neck, his face round and red-cheeked, wobbled down the aisle. He put his hand up like a traffic cop and stopped me at the door.

"You cannot come back in here anymore," he said.

Stunned, I must have asked, "Why not? I've come here before!"

"Because your father is Muslim!"

I will never forget his answer or the sound of his voice. I imagine myself at that moment, a little girl in her Sunday best, skipping happily up the stairs with Nado to do this important job, and looking forward to the smell of incense. I probably had a matching ribbon in my hair that Mom said I was particular about.

Up to that moment, I was unaware of prejudice, fanaticism, and cruelty. The rest played out like a bad dream. I felt something die inside me. I don't know how long I stood there, frozen in place, uncomprehending. I don't remember what happened next. But to this day my body remembers the icy, sinking sensation that rippled through it with paralyzing coldness. This is what neuroscientists refer to as the "freeze" response to trauma.

I wonder if that little girl asked herself, "Why? What's wrong with my father? Papi is the most loving and kind father in the whole world." Doubt must have seeped in. Did that little girl wonder, "Is there something wrong with me because he's Muslim? And what does that mean anyway?" I don't remember. Up until that day, the innocence of childhood had spared me the prejudice that existed in Lebanon as it does in every other country. Sure, I knew there were mosques and there were churches. But I didn't know that where you worshipped made a difference.

As the doors of the church closed, I must have trudged back down the stairs. Did I look back or did I just move on? I don't remember. But I never told anyone about this. I'm not sure why. On the surface, nothing seemed changed. But what happened deep in my soul is something I'm still uncovering. Could it be that by keeping that incident buried inside me I have since lived exiled from myself? That memory remained buried in my unconscious for decades. O'Donohue writes that, "There is some innocent childlike side to the human heart that is always deeply hurt when we are excluded.... Our hunger to belong is the longing to find a bridge across the distance from isolation to intimacy."[31]

I do remember that even then, I somehow knew that this priest was wrong. I obviously did not have the sophisticated cognitive ability to tell him that he was no representative of God, because Allah—the Arabic word for God in both religions—does not discriminate between his children. That no one had a monopoly on God or any house of worship. I can imagine my six-year-old-self standing there, suddenly a lost child, frozen in place, her body recoiling. My father's words that I had heard must have drifted into the wounded part of my soul, countering the poison and the shock. "Remember Lola," he would say, "religions are all the same in their essence. We all believe in the same God whatever name we choose to call him, and we are asked to be kind and do good deeds especially for those who are less fortunate. All the other stuff people teach, they have used to make war and hurt each other. Don't listen to that." I wonder now if Papi expected that I would come across fanaticism sooner or later.

Even though they cannot fully understand what is going on, children know when something is wrong. They possess a truth gauge that either gets reinforced or discouraged. I realize now that other thoughts may have run through my mind at warp speed. *I'm different from my cousin Nado and different is not acceptable.* Such subconscious, mistaken conclusions created what neuroscientists call new synapses, which set the course my life would take from then on. The literature tells us when children encounter abuse, they tend to leap into erroneous assumptions and blame themselves. I think my innate assumption was akin to: *Because my father is Muslim something about me is different, and therefore I don't belong.* Neuroscientists like Bessel Van der Kolk and Somatic Experiencing therapist Peter Levine taught us that we are less damaged by the traumas of childhood than by the traumatic, embodied way we remember them.[32] That explains how that life-changing event remained deeply buried in my body's unconscious memory bank.

I never went again to help my cousins in church, but I continued to visit and play with them in their garden across the street. At Christmas and sometimes at Easter though, I went to church service with my mom, Teta Habouba, Tante Georgette, and my cousins.

I think the priest's actions and words were not as destructive as they might have been because I had absorbed a culture of love and mutual respect that surrounded me. As a therapist, I have learned that the stories we carry, especially when they stay untold, can become an invisible prison. This incident would sink into my subconscious mind like a submarine submerging into the depths; like a captain it continued to steer my decisions throughout my life.

Many years later, after working on this trauma in therapy, I was recounting the story to one of the Christian cousins I grew up with. She did not seem surprised. "He must have found out!" she said. I could not believe my ears. "Found out what?" I asked. I was not aware as a child that anyone in my family felt they had to hide anything. In fairness, it was probably to spare me the pain. I guess it was another secret that was kept from me just like the one about the paternal side of my mother's family having disowned her—and by extension me—for marrying my father. My mom did not see them again except for the times she ran into Tante Eugenie at her sister Georgette's house.

A few years before my mom passed away, I also decided to tell her the story. "*Allah yi'taā deeno!*" (May God cut off his religion!), she exclaimed angrily, instinctively using the inimitable richness of Arabic curse words that always feel so satisfying and cathartic. It's equivalent to "May he burn in hell."

A Year in the UK

Life moved on. When I was nine years old, Papi was sent to England by the Lebanese government to train with Scotland Yard as a forensic science expert and to create a police canine force back in Lebanon. My mom and I went with him. One year before he knew about the assignment, Papi had started teaching me English. He would wake me up early so we could have our English lesson, which he had prepared, before I caught the bus to the Lycée. In those days there were power cuts from midnight to 6 a.m., and I remember sitting at the dining table, by the light of a kerosene lamp at 5 a.m. "It is the wave of the future," he would remind me when I grumbled or when my eyes got sleepy.

Papi, like many other Sunni Muslims (and Shia), attended "Les

Frères"—The French Christian Brothers school. He later taught himself English. In his elegant handwriting he painstakingly filled two notebooks with English grammar and vocabulary—books I have to this day. It was his very own English instruction course for his daughter. Even though I was not too keen about the early hour of our lessons, one never argued with Papi's logic. In his French-accented English he would patiently and methodically explain, "English *grrammar* consists mostly of exceptions to the *rrules*, which makes it *trricky*, but easy to *learrn* if you have a good *earr* and good visual *memorry*." At 5 a.m., I don't think either of those faculties was awake, but I did learn and I am grateful. As usual, he was right about the future, and our studying helped me when we went to England. But I was not fluent yet, and the Yorkshire accent made English sound like a new language. During the first few months I felt as if the words were flying right over my head and past me. I still remember one song in particular that I learned at school there: *This old man....* had one line, which I mumbled through. Only years later would I understand the words *give a dog a bone,* sung fast.

The first principal at the school in Yorkshire assured us with pride that my teacher had been to our country: "Hala's teacher was in Africa for a visit." My parents had to steer him geographically to the right continent—Asia. Kids at school asked if we lived in a tent, how many camels we owned, and did I like wearing British clothes. There was much to teach them. So, I invited my whole class to our rented home in Wakefield to meet my parents and see how we lived. Mom had to borrow teacups from the neighbors to accommodate all my classmates.

Prior to that we had rented rooms with a family in Osset, Yorkshire, which Scotland Yard's constabulary had arranged. It was a very nice family with three boys. What I remember vividly is the amount of snow we had. There was so much that on many days we had to jump down from our bedroom windows to go to school, since the front door was completely blocked. I also remember there were gangs in the town that sometimes pelted the three boys and me with snowballs with rocks in them. The boys protected me. I couldn't understand why they targeted us. Perhaps it was just stupid teenagers, but could it have been because I was a foreigner? Another time, some teenage boys cornered me in the gym. I vaguely remember kicking my way out just as Papi had taught me. "You can defend yourself by using your snow boots to kick someone on the shin." Perhaps he knew I might find myself in such a situation. The memory of my encounter with the priest was still buried deep. My prejudice detector had not yet activated in Yorkshire.

My mom too had to adapt to a new language, but she did well. One day she came home furious because, when she asked the Yorkshire bus driver if his bus went to Leeds, he answered, "Next bush, luv." Papi had to explain that "bush" was really "bus."

We spent a full year in the UK. We ended up in London before we flew back to Lebanon with our very own police dog, who was very patient with our neurotic poodle. I was homesick and glad to get back. As was customary, the whole family on both sides was at the airport to welcome us back.

14. Family welcoming us back at Beirut Airport.

Changing Schools—Again

Upon our return from England, Papi, who "always knew best," transferred me from the French Lycée to the American School for Girls (A.S.G) in Beirut. Founded in 1835 by an American Presbyterian missionary, it was the first girls' school built when Lebanon was still part of Greater Syria and the Ottoman Empire. By the time I attended, it was inter-denominational. I entered this new environment with a full-blown Yorkshire accent, which I quickly lost. Kids were not mean, but it was hard for them to understand me. I find myself to this day still using the British "our" suffix instead of the American "or" in some words, such as "honour." Ironically, an article I wrote recently for a British journal had to be changed back to the British spelling.

I discovered that the students at A.S.G had studied mostly in Arabic for six years. The classical Arabic I had learned at the Lycée in my early grades was so poor that I had to take private lessons to catch up, and I never really did.[33]

Once more I had to adapt to a new school, new classmates, and American English. I remember having a few close friends, but did not want to be part of the "in-crowd." I suspect now that it was the result of that early rejection in the church. In changing school systems, from the French to the American, not only did I cross the divide of language, but also of a whole philosophy of education. The American system included such activities as sports, *dabkeh* (Lebanese folklore dance), and the yearbook committee. Still, I did not see anything unusual about making that transition. It was a "Lebanese" thing to do, adapting to whatever milieu we found ourselves in.

Yet again my diverse background fostered bewilderment in others. Every Friday morning we went into chapel for assembly. One particular Friday morning a visiting American minister was interested in knowing how many students were Muslim and how many were Christian. He called out "How many of you are Christian?" Students raised their hands. "How many of you are Muslim?" Again hands were raised. He noticed my hand suspended in midair throughout and what must have been a confused expression on my face "What is the matter?" he asked me. "I'm half and half," I replied. "Which half is which?," he responded with a chuckle. I knew he meant no harm, but I struggled with that question, feeling I somehow needed to define myself and choose between my seemingly separate allegiances. I had never consciously done this, and had no interest in starting now. As far as I was concerned I was Hala. Why couldn't people accept me as I am?

I was a serious girl who obeyed rules. On cold mornings, waiting for Miss Jreydini to unlock the main doors of study hall, some of the girls would climb in through the windows. But I did not until one day I was freezing and fed up, so I joined them. I was half-way in when I heard Miss J's well-known, scolding voice. "Hala Lababidi, to the principal's office!" Miss Farr and Miss Jreydini were there, looking stern. "You are the last person we would have expected to do this!" they said in unison. But I was angry and felt this was unfair. It was the only time I had broken a rule, and I didn't think they understood the reason I'd engaged in such "unladylike" behavior. "Do you know why all the girls climb in through the windows?" I asked. "It's too cold outside, and if you had the doors open earlier we wouldn't have to climb through the windows." That was it. After that the doors were unlocked earlier.

American University of Beirut

After graduating from high school, it was time to check out universities in Beirut. There were several to choose from. Unlike the Jesuit's Francophone Université St. Joseph, founded in 1881, the Anglophone American University of Beirut and the Beirut College for Women were more heterogeneous and modeled after the liberal, humanist American traditions. Those were the ones I was considering. I chose A.U.B. I was a reserved and serious young person, and I remember feeling that A.U.B's co-ed environment would be better for me. Having grown up with few male cousins, I thought such an environment was healthy and necessary for my growth. I was young, sixteen at the time. I liked the casual atmosphere at A.U.B where young men and women mingled naturally. Students came from all over the world, including the United States. The campus was beautiful, with lush gardens, trees, a spectacular view of the Mediterranean, and its very own beach that one accessed through a tunnel under the Corniche.

15. Green oasis of A.U.B Campus in Ras Beirut.

I was not sure what to major in, so my father suggested that medicine or business administration would be useful. I loved and excelled in biology, I've always loved figuring out how things work, but I did not want to become a doctor or work in a lab. Sitting on the veranda, having our evening meal of watermelon and cheese, Papi would say, "*Ana illee ellik wa inti hurra*" (My job is to tell you and you are free to choose).

One semester was enough to convince me that I hated business and that numbers were not my forte. The only thing I remember from that awful semester was "accounts payable and accounts receivable." Besides the fact that Lebanon, like most countries, is patriarchal in nature, I usually listened to my father, especially because he always seemed to make sense. But now I was finding my own way as an adult. I told Papi that I was changing majors. He accepted my decision and supported me all the way. I finally decided on a double major, in Fine Arts and Education. I had always loved to draw—even the nuns at the Carmelite St. Joseph had called my mom to look at the drawings I made in kindergarten, which they felt were advanced for my age. My major was a perfect fit.

In addition to my internship at A.C.S (American Community School), I volunteered at Father Robert's School for the Deaf and introduced art to the children. It was such an amazing and rewarding experience. I was very moved by the reaction of the students. Parents would call to thank me because their kids were happier. I realized that they now had a new language of expression and communication. Father Roberts wanted to send me to Europe to study further but I was too young and not ready for that. In a way I was discovering the therapeutic benefit of making art. Funny how life brings you full circle: I ended up as an art therapist and teacher.

One thing still bothered me though. I had not been able to bring the level of my classical Arabic up to where it needed to be. Having never caught up at A.S.G., despite the private lessons, the Arabic literature course I had to take at A.U.B. was discouraging, plus it pulled my average down. So at the end of my junior year I went to my Arabic professor and said, "I need to ask you to help me enjoy and appreciate the richness of Arabic literature and our language. But I keep getting a low grade because my grammar is very weak. I don't think that's going to change any time soon. If I take your summer course, would you be willing to grade me not on proper grammar, but on my comprehension and analysis of the literature?" To his credit he did, and he gave me a B+. My parents were surprised that I would give up a trip to Europe with them that summer to study Arabic, but they understood how important it was for me. It's sad that as an Arab speaker, my written classical Arabic never did come up to the level I would have wished, but after that encouraging summer I could read and enjoy the great literature of my culture. My mother never could!

I enjoyed the extracurricular activities that A.U.B. offered: the International Club, with its joint outings with other schools such as the American Community School (A.C.S.); trips; the bridge club; folkdance; and sports. I was on the volleyball team, won medals in broad jump, and learned some tennis.

I also joined the Newman Club near A.U.B., a Catholic club that was open to young adults of all religions. It was fun, and a great way to socialize. I met my first boyfriend there. He too was of a mixed marriage and we dated for three years. I loved to dance and we had many dance parties. I remember the bunny hop and other line dances as well as the usual French, American, and Lebanese songs. There were ski trips to Laklouk and Faraya. I was elected to be on the Newman Club's board, but was later asked to withdraw by the American Jesuit priest, who was a friend of the family. The Board was concerned that during the Club's fund-raising activities, potential donors would withhold contribution when they recognized my family name as a Muslim name. I was so angry that I decided to leave the club.

New York City

After completing my undergraduate degree at A.U.B., I went to Parsons School of Design in New York to study interior design. The wife of the dean at A.U.B. was a graduate of Parsons, and she encouraged me to study there. I was nineteen and a half years old and it was the first time I had traveled anywhere by myself. I think my parents were very brave to let me go by myself to New York, but they did have good Egyptian friends, the Fahmys, who lived in Queens. The Fahmys were to meet me at the airport and house me until I located and settled into the East End Hotel for Women on East River Drive.

Just getting to New York turned out to be an even bigger adventure than living there. I was booked on a student-fare ticket on Lufthansa with a short layover in Frankfurt—in July! After checking in for my ongoing flight, I went down to the gate to board the plane but was told I had no seat because of my discounted ticket, even though I had my boarding pass. So I went back upstairs, checked in again, got another boarding pass. "This time no problem," I was told. My suitcase had of course already left for New York.

But at the gate, the farce was repeated, with the same ridiculous result: there was no seat for me. The crazy runaround lasted for most of the day and left me tired, hungry, and scared I would never leave Frankfurt. The Lufthansa staff was not helpful and rather dismissive of my complaints; who was I to complain, a mere student from Lebanon? The final blow came when the passport control officer's shift ended. He had been the one who had so far been stamping and re-stamping my passport every time I trudged down to the gate, only to be sent back up to the ticketing desk. The new officer took one look at my passport and confiscated it. In sheer exhaustion and frustration, alone and scared, I put my hand luggage down in front of the check-in desk and broke down crying. People waiting in line came to see what was wrong. I told them my story, loudly. That, of course, created a commotion that forced the manager to come out. "Please miss," he pleaded nervously, "quiet down. We'll get you on the next flight." All flights to New York were gone. "No way," I said between sobs. "You've been giving me the runaround all day long, and now I don't have my passport. I'm tired and hungry!"

"I can put you on the flight to Cologne first thing tomorrow."

"No, I'll just be stranded there. I'm sure even fewer people speak English there. I want a written letter guaranteeing I WILL be on that next flight out of Cologne tomorrow morning."

"I can't do that, Miss."

"Then I'll just stay here and keep making a fuss!"

I don't know where I got the chutzpah to follow through.[34] By then some spouses of Lufthansa crews who had had the same problem took me under their wings, and said they'd take care of me and make sure I was on the next flight out of Cologne. I think it was from sheer terror of being stranded in what felt a very unfriendly place. Lufthansa paid for my hotel and telegrams to my parents and the friends meeting me in New York. True to their word, the Lufthansa ladies shepherded me to Cologne and made sure we were all on the flight to New York the next day.

I finally made it to New York, but of course my suitcase with all my belongings for the year was nowhere to be found, having arrived two days before. As luck would have it, one of the luggage porters found me wandering anxiously around the baggage holding area. It turned out he was Iraqi-American. When I told him my predicament he said in the typical helpful Arab way, *"Wa la yihimich ya sitt"* (Don't worry dear lady, I will find it). And find it he did.

The result of this adventure was that I promised myself I would learn German. It was the first time I encountered a language I could not understand or use to communicate. It was scary and frustrating. So when I returned to Beirut a year later, I went to the Goethe Institute and took six months of German, which came in handy when we were posted in Mauritania and I joined the German Embassy ladies to play canasta. Teta Habouba always said, "Every language is a new person." Being trilingual in French, Arabic, and English, and dabbling in German and Italian, I know that each new language I've learned has awakened a new place in my soul.

The East End Hotel was a perfect fit for me. I shared a corner room on the sixth floor with Anna, a lovely, but somewhat spacey, Polish-American young woman from Syracuse. I often had to lend her money to pay her rent. Other friends included Jean, from Texas, and two Jewish young women from the New York area, Diane and Sisi. Both became good friends. After New York I ended up speaking with a mixed Texan-New York accent.

We stayed in touch after New York, but eventually lost track of each other as we all moved around. Recently, Diana tracked me down, and all three of us are in touch again. It was very comforting to renew friendships, even at long distance.

I enjoyed my courses, but developed a love/hate relationship with the city. The pace, crowds, and noise were overwhelming. I craved silence and time alone. On the way home I would go and sit in a little chapel near the hotel just to get some peace and quiet. (How ironic that a church had become a place of refuge, instead of rejection, for me. This shows how repressed that traumatic memory was.)

I felt at home in the multicultural environment of New York. Here many cultures mingled daily. You heard different languages and saw signs in different languages. It was a city where being of mixed background is common. After all, for over sixty years, Ellis Island in Upper New York Bay was the gateway for millions of immigrants to the United States. New York had its share of prejudice as well, but there was a sense of excitement about the diversity that created this country where everyone, except the Native Americans, was from somewhere else. Besides African-Americans who were brought against their will as slaves, immigrants came seeking refuge from discrimination, famine, or persecution; or they were just seeking a better life or following someone they love. Yes, I could live here, I thought, if I just had my family around, and my college boyfriend.

I was there for the 1966 transport strike and the big blackout. During the strike, I remember hitch-hiking back to the hotel when

I was too tired to walk any more, in order not to miss dinner at the hotel. I waited on a corner and waived down an old couple who lectured me on the dangers of hitch-hiking. "I know, that's why I chose you!" I said sheepishly. The blackout was another adventure. I had a design project due the next day. I pleaded with a friend to give me a candle, but it soon burned out. I was nervous the assignment would not be ready. We had no idea of the magnitude of the power outage as radio announcers kept broadcasting that power would "shortly" be restored. One of my friends in the hotel, Melanie, was a hearing-impaired young woman. I thought she must be terrified and lost as darkness descended. I made my way to the door to go find her. As I opened the door two hands grabbed my neck—we both screamed, then let out a relieved laugh. She had made her way to our room seeking comfort just as I was leaving to find her. We had an impromptu party in our room. I supplied the salami which I had put on the window sill. It acted as our free refrigerator in winter.

After one year in New York, I returned to Lebanon because I was homesick. But I also had planned to find a job in Beirut to save money and continue what was for us an expensive postgraduate education in the United States. I did not feel it was fair for my parents, with our income, to continue paying for it. And as a foreign student, in the U.S. I could not get a work permit.

Before I left, I went to pick up the last roll of film I had left off for processing. The owner of the photo store refused to let me pay. "It's a going-away gift," he told me. He was another Iraqi-American. Hospitality and kindness exist in New York in the midst of its frenzy.

Upon my return to Beirut, life would take an unexpected turn. A new plan would play out that was much different than the one I had in mind.

> It is often the way we look at other people that imprisons them within their own narrowest allegiances. And it is also the way we look at them that may set them free.
> —Amin Maalouf, *In the Name of Identity*[35]

3

The Foreign Service

All the hearts of the people are my identity, so take away
my passport!

—Marcel Khalifeh[36]

The "Alien"

My introduction to the U.S. Foreign Service was wading through
and filling out forms. At the time my future husband Steve proposed, State Department regulations stated that an officer request-
ing permission to marry a foreign-born individual had to submit
his resignation letter. If the State Department approved of the pro-
spective spouse, the resignation was rejected and permission was
granted; if not, the resignation was accepted![37]

Steve, knowing the bureaucracy, was more worried than I was.
Steve had pestered everyone he knew at the State Department to
expedite our run through the red tape. Luckily at the time, I was
working at the U.S. Embassy and had been thoroughly vetted. I
passed "the test." Papi liked to tell the story of Steve arriving at
our apartment beaming, and holding a bottle of champagne to celebrate. Soon after, I was required to file for U.S. citizenship and to
give up my Lebanese passport. That decision was later overturned
in the Supreme Court case of Afroyim vs. Rusk. I remember sitting
in the Horseshoe Café in Hamra, sipping Turkish coffee while nib-
bling petits-fours with Monique, my French friend. "*Comment est-ce
que tu accepte cela?*" (How can you accept that?) She was incensed
that I was being forced to renounce my Lebanese citizenship. "Monique," I said, "a passport is just paper, no one can take away my
identity—my Lebaneseness is in my blood."

Decades later, I would hear the world-famous Lebanese composer and singer, Marcel Khalifeh, at the Kennedy Center in Washington, D.C. He gave a rendition of a song he had just composed after a grueling interrogation session by U.S. officials at the airport. It was humorous but also bespoke indignities suffered by anyone from the Arab World, even an older man and famous musician specifically invited by the Kennedy Center. The quote at the beginning of this chapter is the refrain from that song.

At the top of each page and throughout all the immigration documents I had to fill out, the applicant was referred to as the "alien." I found that insulting; images of extra-terrestial creatures popped up in my mind. I bristle to this day at this inhuman terminology, relegating me and others to members of an outer-space galaxy. I did not perceive myself as "alien" to anything, certainly not to American culture or the language; in fact, I was multilingual and a graduate of the American University of Beirut. "I have lived and studied in New York City for crying out loud!" I yelled at the inanimate papers in front of me. Once more, the way others perceived me and the way I saw myself were not in sync. But I still did not comprehend the Gestalt of it. I had now become an "alien," a wandering emigrant in search of home. But I had no time to be nervous or concerned; everything was happening too fast.

U.S. Embassy—Beirut

Let me rewind my story a bit. Upon my return from New York I took a job at the U.S. Embassy working in the Cultural Affairs Office and designing posters for the embassy's cultural center U.S.I.S. I met Steve at an embassy Christmas party given by the Agency for International Development (A.I.D.) director. It was the traditional stand-up embassy function. Steve came up to me and we had a very interesting talk, but he had a way of standing very close to me that made me uncomfortable. Besides, I had come with a date. I kept backing away and he kept following—not the best first impression. But I remember noticing him later on in the embassy cafeteria with his tie flipped to the back so he would not spill on it. I thought that was cute.

I soon found out that Steve was a persistent man. He walked

into my office at the embassy soon after and invited me out to lunch. "*Yee, āalayna!*"—"Oh no!" I said to my colleague, Amal. "I met him at a Christmas party and he stands so close to you. I felt I was being cornered," I continued in Arabic. "I thought he was a little intense. Anyway I don't feel like going out."

Steve was waiting for my reply. I looked up, saw him grinning like the Cheshire cat and remembered he'd told me he was studying Arabic at the Foreign Service Institute's Arabic Language School located then at the U.S. Embassy in Beirut, and had probably understood most of what I had said. Certainly my tone and body language would have filled in any gaps. Blushing with embarrassment, and being a polite Lebanese, I felt I had to accept his invitation, but I had no intention of getting serious. I had just broken up with my boyfriend and I guess I needed time to grieve that; plus, I wanted to save up money to finish my post-graduate degree in New York.

Our first real date was going skiing in Faraya, one of Lebanon's ski resorts. Steve showed up two hours late—he is not an early morning person I found out. I was a beginner, and not very courageous on the slope. When we arrived at the top I was surprised and annoyed that Steve did not spend much time with me. Instead, he took off straight down the slope with his poles tucked under his arms. I thought he must be an experienced skier, albeit a rude date. Half-an-hour later as I carefully snowplowed to the bottom, there he was grinning. He admitted that, in fact, he had never skiied in his life and thought the only way was to shoot for it straight down. Well, I thought, this is one strange and gutsy guy. First he asks me on a date for something so difficult for him and then takes off like a bullet down the slope. What next?

We have our distinct recollections of what happened over the next few months. As we got to know each other I found Steve to be a very intelligent, kind, and strong person, despite always being late. And although we came from two different worlds, we shared similar values. He was easy to talk to and funny. I remember standing on his balcony in Āin el Mreyssi overlooking the Mediterranean, chatting and looking out at the beautiful coastline and mountains in the background. Although he did not propose outright he kept hinting about our life together. I wanted to have time to think things through. I didn't feel I was ready to make such a momentous decision. My parents, though, immediately liked him.

Steve asserts it was "love at first sight" for him. As for me, although I loved him, I was still transitioning out of a three-year relationship and had reapplied to finish my graduate work in the United States. But events were moving swiftly. He received his next assignment just a few months after we started dating, and was due to leave for his next posting six months after that. He pressed me for an answer. To this day I have a hazy recollection of saying I would marry him, even though I was concerned about leaving my family and not sure I wanted to live the diplomatic life. What was very important for me was that he not only spoke Arabic but liked, respected, and understood my culture, just as I spoke his language and understood American culture. This is crucial for cross-cultural marriages to succeed, because it represents the mutual respect and sense of equality necessary to bridge the differences that inevitably appear. My parents were totally on board, even though they knew that I would be living thousands of miles away from them for the rest of their lives. They treated him like a son, and for him they were always "papa and mama."

The only glitch in marrying a foreigner came from Papi's half-sister, Auntie Munia, who was the elder of the family. With one eyebrow raised, she asked me one day, very politely, "*Ma idna shabab biijbookee?*" (Don't we have any Lebanese young man that you like?) I replied, "No, I love this guy," as politely and firmly as is possible for a member of a culture where elders are highly respected. A few weeks later she invited my parents, Steve, and me to lunch at their mountain house in Sofar. After a long and wonderful Lebanese meal that stretched for hours, she whispered to me, "Maybe you should explain to Steve about our custom of napping after lunch, so he doesn't think we are being rude or that we don't like him." "*Bonne idée* auntie," (good idea) I replied in the usual French-English mix. I went to find my fiancé, only to discover he had already claimed a bed somewhere and was fast asleep. When I reported that to Auntie Munia she laughed, "*Khalass!*" (Finish!) "He's one of us now!" she said. And that was that!

The months zipped by like a blur. What with preparing a wedding, and my father having an emergency appendectomy a week before the date, my life was turned upside down. We had our first cross-cultural moment when Steve's dad and sister flew in for the wedding (his mom had died two years before). We met them at the airplane and to my utter amazement he and his dad just shook hands. I could not stay quiet. "What is this?" I blurted. "You have not seen each other for two years and all you do is shake hands? Please hug each other." They did, and since then his family have become great huggers. Steve's sister remembers how shocked she was to see my dad hug and kiss their dad on both cheeks.

As it happened, the chaplain from Yale, Steve's alma mater, was in Beirut, so he performed the ceremony in the small Protestant church next to my high school, A.S.G. My father had asked Auntie Munia what the family thought, and whether they would show up. "Those who come, *ahlan wa sahlan*—welcome. Don't worry about those who won't" was her reply. As it turned out, all my relatives on both sides were there (excepting, of course, those on my mother's paternal side, as I know now, but didn't know then). It was very moving to have all of my Muslim family present. The only comment I heard was from a good college classmate, a Greek Orthodox Christian, who found the Protestant ceremony too simple and strange compared to what she was familiar with.

For our very short honeymoon, we went back to the ski slopes; this time we took a few lessons. We enjoyed skiing together down a gentle slope. On our way we struck up a conversation with a French diplomat who was also enjoying gliding down on a beautiful sunny day. Not realizing where I was from, he spent some time making fun of the Lebanese, going on and on about how they think they are civilized and sophisticated. I gritted my teeth, and my hands tightened their grip around the polestraps, not because it was cold, but to keep my anger in check until he finished. Then I told him I found his patronizing take on my people hypocritical. "So much for Lebanese Christians believing that 'Mother France' cares for them or sees them as their equal!" It was the first time I encountered blatant prejudice towards my Lebanese culture. Perhaps my strong reaction was the first stirring of my six-year old self, who had suffered prejudice before I knew what it was. It would be many more years before I saw such events as part of a new awareness.

In the course of our Foreign Service life, I experienced many such encounters. Another occurred in Asmara, Ethiopia (now Eritrea), where we had been evacuated to from Aden, South Yemen, our first post. We were dining with some people we had met, including a charming Israeli young woman. Without any prompting she proceeded to tell us about the Arabs' ignorance and uninterest in education. "You see I know them. You don't," she said. I was beyond enraged. I smiled, and gave her more rope before I replied. "Interesting to hear about your expertise," I said. "I have to strongly disagree with you. You see, I am an Arab." It was the first time I referred to myself as such. She was speechless. I was getting used to these reactions, but I was always taken by surprise when people casually and unknowingly spewed such glaring untruths; I couldn't believe how prejudiced and misinformed this woman was. At that time, I didn't know about Israel's human rights violations and the plight of Palestinians in the occupied territories, nor about the propaganda machine used to denigrate Palestinians both in Israel and abroad. I guessed this woman had never met any educated Palestinians, seeing that even now there is little interaction between Palestinian Israelis and other Israelis. Perhaps the only Arabs she knew were the gardener or a poor "fellah"—a peasant or construction worker living in the occupied territories of the West Bank, who crossed daily to Israel through cagelike checkpoints to find work.

A Cross-cultural Marriage

By marrying Steve, I had embarked, not without some ambivalence, on a unique adventure, leaving everything familiar in my life and heading for the unknown with a new life companion. Not only had I married someone from another culture, I also was signing on to the challenging life of a diplomat's spouse. I would be packing and unpacking, moving constantly, adjusting, adapting, and trying to find a place for myself, over and over again. I wasn't conscious back then how precarious my sense of belonging was, nor how continuous uprooting would affect me.

For the next thirty-one years, like most Foreign Service couples, Steve and I made a good team; we enjoyed our commitment to forge new friendships and promote understanding and mutual respect between our host countries and the United States. The pressures of moving, transfer orders, instant relocations, two evacuations with forty-eight hours' notice, and a war governed our lives. We would have fifteen moves, including tours back in Washington D.C. Packing entailed mind-boggling decisions about what should go as air freight, luggage, or sea freight, and what we needed to function if any of these or all were delayed or lost.

Throughout our married life, Steve and I negotiated many things and circumstances. One was Christmas. For years, we had a typical American Christmas, until I realized I had been the one doing most of the adjusting in our cross-cultural relationship. It was so natural for me to adapt, but it was important to negotiate and create our own traditions. And so we did. On Christmas Eve we came to celebrate "à la Libanaise," opening one or two presents, and eating lamb, *hummos*, and rice. On Christmas Day we follow the American tradition with turkey and all the trimmings.

Looking back, the most significant conflict in our marriage was a cultural one. For Steve, career came first. When I complained about his working late, Steve would reply, "My dad would leave the house at 7 a.m. and not get back till 7 p.m." So, his norm became long hours at the embassy, plus a busy social schedule. But I remembered how present my dad was in my life. I was used to coming home, along with Papi, for lunch with the family. Time has a different quality and meaning in the East. The post-industrial West's concept of "clock time" dominates and controls life. In the United States, sayings like "time is money" and "time flies" are taken for granted, notwithstanding the dreaded "dead-line;" whereas in the Middle East, one says *"mara' al waet"* (time has passed), like a visitor or more likely, *"īndna waet"* (we have time)—spoken in a very calm tone that does not conjure stress. Or, as an article in the L.A.U. Alumni Bulletin states, "Physics, psychology, and philosophy...embrace the idea that time is flexible, malleable and relative."[38]

I'm not prone to complaining, so I soldiered through, looking for a middle ground between us and our different cultural expectations, especially regarding the balance between career and family. One can say that every marriage is cross-cultural because each family is a culture of its own, but adding a layer of the larger societal beliefs and values makes it more challenging—and potentially enriching.

One week after our wedding, we flew to Aden, South Yemen, our new "post," which is State Department lingo for the assigned country. There seemed to always be some dire need for us to get immediately to our next post; I eventually found out this urgency to be standard practice in the Foreign Service. The sky was always falling somewhere and crises had to be dealt with. How could I complain about Steve "saving the world?"

When I left Lebanon as a new bride, I left all that had been supportive and comforting. I shed a few tears as I walked with Steve towards our plane, but there was no time to grieve. In a matter of a few hours we landed in Aden. Did I wonder then how I would manage this new life? Maybe, but I had so many challenges ahead of me that I needed to tackle: A husband, a different country, the Foreign Service culture, and a nomadic life. By the end of Steve's career, we had served in seven countries, mostly in the Middle East. But we did not return to Lebanon, except for a few months after we were evacuated from South Yemen, briefly in 1974, and much later in 1990.

In my twenty-three-year-old mind, I never emigrated as such. Forty years later I became aware that I married into my immigrant status by following the man I loved and with whom I had chosen to share my life. Unlike other emigrants, who pull out their roots and immediately replant them in new soil, I spent thirty-one years being uprooted, then planting myself again and again, in places mostly not of my own choosing. As I went through every uprooting, I was not totally conscious how difficult the process was. I dutifully bloomed where I landed.

Upon arriving at a new post, Steve was immediately ensconced in an office, with supportive staff and familiar guidelines. Spouses and families on the other hand had to start from scratch—learn where to shop, learn about a new culture, how to navigate the markets, master protocol and etiquette, and organize new social lives. Luckily, I spoke Lebanese Arabic, known as Levantine Arabic, and quickly learned other Arabic dialects. Here I was, newlywed, with no clue of what a American Foreign Service wife was supposed to do, let alone one who was foreign-born. How was I to officially represent *Ameyrka* in my own part of the world? For spouses of my generation, there were almost no reference points for the culture we were supposed to represent. At the time there was no Overseas Briefing Center yet that trains families going abroad, no courses on what a Foreign Service spouse should expect and what was expected of her. There were no Community Liaison Officers (CLOs) at post, no Family Liaison Office (FLO) at the State Department. These offices and others now provide invaluable support and guidance to officers and their families, something that I wish I had had. One thing the Foreign Service now teaches extensively about the nomadic life is the importance of grieving at each departure, of making sure to say goodbye properly, and taking the time for transition before jumping into a new life.

I charted my own way through the maze of unvoiced expectations, feeling more "alien" by the minute. There was a whole protocol about calling cards, where and when to leave them at the ambassador's house, how to support the ambassador's wife, and many other requirements I had no interest in. I also had to learn the jargon: "R & R," for the short rest and recuperation vacations during "hardship posts," and "home leave"—paid vacation every few years back in the United States, where we were sent like trained homing pigeons so as not to forget what America was like. It was also an important time to reconnect with Steve's family scattered across the United States. But it was not where my own relatives were. "Home" is a tricky word for anyone living an internationally mobile, cross-cultural life.

Aden, South Yemen

Aden, South Yemen, located at the bottom left of the Arabian Peninsula, was surrounded by stark, volcanic mountains, baked by intense heat and almost 100 percent humidity. It was not a honeymoon destination by any stretch of the imagination, especially after a war that had just expelled the British, who had colonized the country for over one hundred years. The economy was in shambles since Aden, one of the world's largest harbors, depended on the sea trade through the Suez Canal, which had just been closed. Tanks and armored cars still roamed the mostly deserted streets.

We had a very early morning disembarkation at an airport consisting of one hangar, a small building, and a windsock, which reminded me of the final scene in *Casablanca*. The whole city was deathly quiet. I experienced disorientation and jet lag when I arrived in this totally new place, with no maps, and no Michelin or Frommer's guidebooks. *Lonely Planet* would have been a more appropriate guidebook, considering how I felt; but I didn't have that, either. I came to expect this surreal feeling at every new posting.

During our first night in Aden, my worst nightmare came true. We were invited to a costume party at our chargé d'affaires' house. Everyone was kind and welcoming, but out of hundreds of guests we were, along with another newlywed couple from the British Embassy, the only ones without a costume, having literally just come off the plane. I was wearing a cocktail dress. I remember standing on the lovely terrace looking in towards the elegant living room cleared of all furniture for the party. Waiters circulated with trays full of drinks and hors-d'oeuvres among a room full of people I had never met, all of them laughing and chatting. I stood frozen in place under the fiery bougainvillea covering the garden walls—the smell of jasmine reminding me of Lebanon and how homesick I was. I brushed the tears away, wishing I had refused that lunch date with Steve. What had I signed up for?

Steve immediately sprang into Foreign Service mode and went to circulate among guests. "Working" dinners and receptions are an imperative for any diplomat. Foreign Service officers spend their whole careers uprooting themselves and their families every few years. At every replanting, they work to understand their country of assignment in order to foster better relationships between the host country and the United States. Much of that happens at receptions and dinners.

It is important for Americans to understand the purpose of the State Department and its diplomats, which is to build relationships not only for U.S. national interest, but to help politicians at home and abroad find common ground and keep the world safe.

Steve is the quintessential extrovert who is energized by nonstop interactions with people. And then there's me, a middle-of-the-line introvert who finds it exhausting after a while to entertain large groups of people. For months afterwards, people would remind us that we had met at that costume party. But how could I remember who was dressed as Marie Antoinette or a pirate? Remembering names was always the hardest thing to learn in this transient life. Eventually I found my groove and realized that the Foreign Service in a way is itself a bridge to many worlds, and therefore fit into my life journey.

It was in Aden that I first learned yoga, which was taught by a British spouse. I clearly remember her living room where we would spread our blankets on the tile floor. Then, when it was time for Shavasana, she would turn off the roaring sound of the A/C for a ten-minute, peaceful "corpse pause" at the end.

Since our car, a Volkswagen Bug, had not arrived, I was holed up in the Aden Rock Hotel, which we jokingly referred to as the Eden Rock Hotel. I didn't know how to navigate in a place where armored cars still patrolled and king-size cockroaches roamed. The "pif-paf" man, as I called him, would come daily to spray our room, oblivious to the toxic danger he was spewing. I had to scramble quickly out of the room before I got pif-paffed as well. Many years later, I would be reminded of this on a British Airways flight with Katie, our daughter, when she was a baby. The British steward, handlebar moustache and all, suddenly appeared and started spraying the cabin, and all the passengers, too. I quickly threw a blanket over Katie to keep her away from the toxic mist. When I angrily complained, I was told, "It was to prevent those pesky Arabian flies from entering the United Kingdom." Colonialism was alive and well!

Steve found us a lovely, modern, cantilevered house perched on the cliffs of Ras Marshaq, with a panoramic view of the Gulf of Aden. In the late afternoons, we would sit and watch pods of dolphins frolicking, and gracefully leaping in and out of the water in a joyful dance as if they knew we were watching. It was our first home together and I enjoyed decorating it with things Steve already had collected from his former posting in Algiers, and things I had brought from Lebanon. Like other nomads we carried with us an eclectic mix of things that made a government-furnished house into a home—the late Norma McCaig (who established "Global Nomads") referred to these as "sacred objects." I loved setting up our home. My interior design skills itched to create a new space. When it came to entertaining, I was a fast learner, and my Lebanese upbringing had taught me great hospitality skills. The only drawback was not being well-versed in cooking, food being central to Arab hospitality and hosting dinners. At first, I felt totally inept in the kitchen. Unlike most Lebanese mothers, my mom, had always shooed me away from the kitchen: *"Laahh'a*—you'll have plenty of time to cook later in your life," she said. Teta Habouba gave me the same message. Now in Aden, I had to call my mom in Beirut to get recipes. *"J'ai ce poisson, shoo bāa'mil fiya?"* (I have this huge fish. What do I do with it?) *"Keef btaēmlee samke harra?"* (How do you cook *samke harra*?)

Unperturbed by new occupants, geckos cruised the walls making clicking noises and taking care of the roaches. It was my first encounter with geckos. They were nothing like the cute one with an Australian accent in American GEICO ads. I considered myself very courageous, except when it came to ugly, armored bugs. I jumped out of my skin one day when I was reaching into the pocket of my windbreaker. My hand touched a dried-up object; it took an instant for my brain to register what my senses were telling it. "Yakh, aaaahhh, a dead cockroach!" I screamed. After that, even though I felt uneasy having geckos that seemed to own the house, I tolerated their protective role. However, they must have sensed my basic distaste for them, and waited until Steve was out of town for one of them to drop on our bed just as I was getting ready to sleep. My screams must have reached the servants' quarters because the next thing I knew Ali, our wonderful cook and "houseboy," knocked on my door. *"Sitt Hala, are you alright?"* I quickly threw a wrap on and let him in, pointing hysterically at the gecko now erratically scrambling around the bedspread. Ali caught it and took it outside. For the rest of the night I slept completely under the covers. Better to suffocate in the heat than have another clumsy gecko land on me. In the morning when I opened our bedroom door, there was Ali curled up right outside it, guarding and ready to rescue *"Sitt Hala."* The geckos never dropped their adhesive grip again. They stuck to their territories (i.e. all the walls, ceilings, and door jams of the house). We seemed to have reached a truce of some kind.

My favorite story relates to food shortages, which resulted from the closed shipping traffic. While visiting with our British friends, they offered us British biscuits they were happy to have found in the market, but they became upset when they turned out to be stale.

The husband wrote an irate letter to the company, complaining. This was in the '60s. A month later he received a very proper reply regretting the unfortunate issue and saying a new tin of biscuits was en route. But in their understated British way, they wanted to point out that the inspection slip from that stale box of biscuits indicated they had been produced in 1929! Such unusual experiences should have clued me in to what, in the next thirty-one years, I would be navigating: danger, evacuations, Scud missiles, and more food shortages, but also exciting experiences and definitely much learning. In the Foreign Service, my husband was the only base I had. Later, our nuclear family of three was the only constant that moved when we did. Fortunately for us, as it is for most Foreign Service families, there is a closeness, a sense of safety with each other, although some Americans may see that as excessive.

You may think that serving in another Arab country would have been easy for me because, after all, the Arab world is uniform. The reality is that the countries closest to Lebanon in terms of language and traditions are Syria, Palestine, and to some degree, Egypt. South Yemen was a different subculture, dialect, landscape, and habits. One day I was driving down to the souk and gave a lift to a neighbor's houseboy. He had a big bulge in his right cheek; naïve as I was I asked him what had happened. "Oh, I have a toothache," he answered. Once I learned about *Qat*—a popular narcotic leaf that most South Yemenis chewed in the afternoon and evenings—I realized he had indeed been chewing *Qat*. I guess he didn't want to tell me because it was understood that if you are working in a expat's home, you could not chew *Qat* during working hours.

The beaches were beautiful in Aden but full of dangerous sand sharks. Not to worry, we were told—there are shark nets to keep them out. We joined the club at "Gold Mohur," once the exclusive beach for British colonial expats where the South Yemenis were not allowed membership. One could understand the resentment that this engendered in South Yemenis and other people who were colonized. How would you feel if you were treated as inferior beings in your own country! On my last swim at that club, I went exploring the shark nets and to my dismay found huge, gaping holes that no one had mended. So much for our assumed safety.

Fostering mutually helpful relations between the United States and other countries is central to diplomacy. A sense of purpose and adventure is the name of the game in the Foreign Service. A year into our posting, South Yemen broke diplomatic relations and the U.S. Embassy personnel were given forty-eight hours to leave.[39] This meant that after forty-eight hours, the South Yemeni government would no longer be responsible for our safety. It was our first wedding anniversary and I had finally learned to cook *samke harra*. While Steve was at the Embassy destroying files, Ali and I packed. When you live in "hardship posts," you learn never to throw any carton away. We were allowed one suitcase each on the evacuating plane and in them went photos, rugs, cherished mementos, and some clothes; we could not be sure if we would ever see our stuff again. I learned quickly to assess what is irreplaceable and what isn't. But with the help of our good friends from the British Embassy, eventually our "household effects" (HHE) caught up with us. What I missed was the dog we'd adopted that we were not allowed to bring, and our house in Ras Marshaq, overlooking the Gulf of Aden. We heard later that friends had adopted our dog.

Mauritania

After evacuation to the U.S. Consulate in Asmara, then part of Ethiopia, and four months in Beirut, we were posted to Mauritania in northwest Africa in 1970. It borders the Atlantic Ocean to the west, the Moroccan-controlled Western Sahara in the north, Algeria in the northeast, Mali in the east and southeast, and Senegal in the southwest. In 1970, it was a relatively poor, basically nomadic country. Its people represented a mixture of Arab, Berber, and African. They spoke a mixture of French, Arabic, Berber, and a variety of African dialects. *Il vient d'une bonne tente* (He comes from a good tent) was a familiar phrase. Your social status was not determined as much by the color of your skin as by the repute of your family.

We lived on the Embassy compound that was laid out around a central little garden and flagpole with the Stars and Stripes—sort of Fort Apache style. The few scenes I painted there were of the desert meeting the Atlantic Ocean; men in long, flowing, blue robes called *boubous* gliding gracefully across the sand dunes leading a caravan of camels; or women wrapped in their colorful *malafas*, a one-piece, wrap-around, long cape with enough material to cover the head. Sandstorms made it necessary to have an instant cover within reach to throw over your head, face, and eyes for protection. It was in Mauritania that I learned to love the desert. I remember driving back from Dakar, Senegal, a vibrant, noisy city, and crossing back at Rousso into Mauritania. Steve would stop the car and we would just sit listening to the silence of the desert, feeling totally at peace. The desert is like the ocean. It has a vast beauty and the power to whip up a blinding storm in an instant.

Mauritania was also where I learned about different Arab traditions. One night, the Foreign Minister invited Steve and I and a few colleagues to dinner at his tent in the desert. Even high officials felt the need to escape to their peaceful tent encampments away from the burdens of governing and the hubbub of Nouakchott. We both wore clothes that would enable us to sit cross-legged on the floor, as is the custom in desert cultures and others. We all sat in a circle on beautiful carpets and delicately decorated leather pillows called *Tassoufras*. The servants came in carrying a huge brass tray

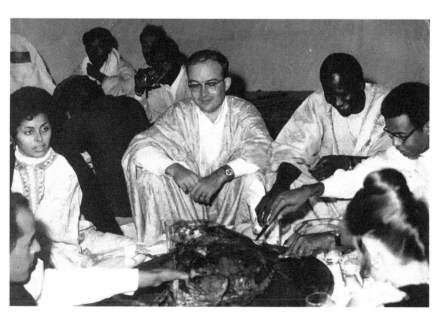

16. "Meshwi" dinner under the tent – Mauritania.

laden with mounds of rice and lamb. They carefully tread between the guests and slowly lowered the tray with obvious relief into the center of our circle.

This was the first time I partook of a traditional Bedouin meal. I watched as our host, Steve, and a few experienced diplomats reached in with their hands for the rice. Its aroma and look I recognized and remembered from my childhood—the mixture of cinnamon, cumin, and a special mixture of *bharat* (a blend of spices)—but their way of eating was something new. Here I was, a Lebanese feeling "alien" in another Arab country just because people ate their food differently. Over the span of many tours in the Arab world, I would learn first-hand how different each Arab country was.

Our host had diplomatically offered cutlery to foreign guests who were obviously not comfortable with the local tradition, but I declined, feeling it would be courteous to follow our host's custom. Also, I didn't want to disappoint our host since he knew I was Lebanese. Steve, as usual, was doing fine and chatting away, completely at ease. I took a deep breath, smiled, and bravely plunged in as well, but rolling the mixture of rice and lamb into a tidy ball, all in one movement, was not as easy as it looked. As I scooped the rice and lamb from the tray I felt some rice and spices getting under my nails and dripping down my arm. When I tried to pop the whole thing in my mouth, some of it ended up on my caftan. But after a few messy attempts I got the hang of it and started to enjoy the flip of the hand that sends the ball of food into your mouth. After that, I was sympathetic with foreigners who are learning to use pita bread (*khibiz*) to neatly scoop up *hummos* or *baba ghanouj*.

The Mauritanians loved dance parties, and we had many, all of them informal, simple, and fun. The men would whirl around in their *boubous*, and the woman in various colorful *malafas*. A few wives came alone and there seemed to be no problem with that. They were open, fun, and interesting.

We loved to venture into the interior or go camping by the ocean. My favorite adventure was setting off in a caravan of Land Rovers into the desert to look for sand roses (crystallized gypsum that looked like roses and take centuries to form in sand). There were only a few very small areas where one could find them. The human "GPS" directions usually included a lone bush or tree (rare in the desert) or an empty Evian bottle filled with sand placed strategically at major crossroads. "When you get to the tree, veer left and one hundred yards beyond you will see an Evian bottle or two, and then you turn right and go two kilometers, until you see another bush, and near it an Evian bottle marking the spot."

On one such outing Steve and Ambassador Murphy were in the front; Anne, his wife, and I were in the back. The rest of the group had sped ahead when our Land Rover suddenly stopped. Steve and the ambassador went out to check under the hood. Anne and I continued our chat. We eventually became aware nothing was happening and heard the following exchange: "Steve, I think it's the carburetor!" "Yes, I think you're right." "Steve, where's the carburetor?" At which point Anne and I looked at each other. "You mean to tell me that Steve doesn't know about cars?" "No. You mean Richard doesn't either?" We got out of the car to take a look. By then the rest of the caravan of cars had disappeared into the distance. Thank God, Papi had always encouraged me to learn about things, and I loved to learn how things worked. That's how I noticed that the distributor cap was off, probably from the rough bumping around on washboard tracks. I put it back and voilà, the car started up. By then the group had come back looking for us. For years, we teased our husbands about that interchange.

One time Steve and I flew with a French pilot, Gallouadec, who was a national legend. He had lived in Mauritania for a long time and married a Mauritanian. I remember him letting me pilot his little plane for a short while. It was the first and last time I did that. It was exhilarating but scary at the same time. From his little plane one could see the vastness of the desert and its beauty. He could spot any little change in the landscape below. He knew all the tribes and every encampment. Looking out his window he would suddenly comment, *"Tien, Mohammed a changé sa place"* — (Oh, see there, Mohammed has moved his camp).

In Mauritania, I developed a love of tea because of my British friend, Jean. She was the widow of a Mauritanian and had decided to bring their son to Nouakchott to get to know his father's country. It was very moving to see the whole family embrace them both. Every afternoon we would take turns visiting and having a "cuppa tea." I thought she was a brave and open soul, and I'm sure she gave their son a grounding in both cultures.

I missed my family very much, especially my parents. West Africa seemed so far away. During our tour there, my beloved Teta Habouba became very sick and passed away. My parents made the common mistake of deciding not to tell me, thinking they were "protecting me." I was still sending Teta letters, oblivious to the fact that she was gone. I found out six months later when my mom came to visit us in Nouakchott. I was devastated. "Why, Mom, didn't you tell me?" "Because you were so far away and we wanted to spare you," she answered. "But I lost the chance to be with Teta and say goodbye. She must have been hurt that I wasn't there." It has taken me many years and grief therapy to come to terms with that. What did she think and feel when I was not there for her? Did she know how much she has meant to me? Death doesn't feel real when you don't say goodbye in some way.

However, there was a little bit of Lebanon even in Nouakchott. Our embassy's "man-Friday" was Sami, a dear man who could do and did everything to help. He had emigrated to Australia, so he spoke English with an Australian twang, and of course mixed Lebanese, Arabic, and French into the pot, usually all in one sentence. One of his favorite phrases was "I *fait c'a bookra*"—English, French, and Arabic for, "I will do that tomorrow."

I was beginning to understand that my origins would be an asset throughout our diplomatic tours in the Arab world. Lebanon held a special place in the hearts of most other Arabs. They knew Lebanon's pluralistic society was able to integrate East and West and still maintain a unique cultural identity. Even though the dialect and social mores were different in each Arab country we were posted to, the underlying values of family, hospitality, good food, mutual respect, and polite discourse created a common bond between us.

At the time, Nouakchott had one paved road, one hotel, one grocery store—manned of course by a Lebanese—a vast desert, and many warm and lovely people. And there were little critters like scorpions and the horrible "monkey spider," as they called them there, which was bigger than a hand. One night, we were saying goodbye to friends who had been dining at our house, as I reached for the doorknob, I saw a huge monkey spider was already attached to it. I think I must have screamed and ended rushing up our stairs.

It hopped around, leaping up four or five feet, before Steve used something to kill it. Our "houseboy" was Guinean whose name was Ba. After hearing stories of other houseboys not well-treated in other embassies, one day he said to me, "*Madame, tu ne m'emmerde pas du tout.*" It's hard to translate *emmerder,* but coarsely this was his way of saying, "You never give me shit!"

Prior to Ambassador Murphy's assignment to Nouakchott and the upgrading of our post to an embassy again, we had a chargé d'affaires as head of mission. His wife, Marguerite (not her real name), was European and nervous about protocol. Early on, she described to me the aptly-named "dragon ladies" — ambassador's wives — with whom she had to work, and the ridiculously strict requirements and protocols they enforced on the other wives. Without thinking, I said, "I don't know how you put up with that, Marguerite. I wouldn't have." She was shocked, but I realized later that she treated me differently after that.

Embassy personnel often meet visiting VIP congressional delegations, or "CODELS," with rolled eyes. Even Nouakchott was not immune to such visits. I read an apt assessment of CODELS recently, which described them as "tax-payer-funded junkets," usually with spouses, on "fact-finding" trips, and usually traveling first-class. The VIPs are wined and dined and catered to by typically short-staffed embassy employees. Shortly after my conversation with Marguerite, we had to prepare for such a delegation. Between the residence and our house, we had four servants to help with the cooking, cleaning, and serving at official dinners, and to help as keep up with the dust storms.

Days before the delegation was due to arrive, Marguerite insisted on us making 400 canapés for the reception. We had one and a half jars of mayonnaise and a variety of tidbits between us. No warnings of mine — about the regular power outages, or the need for the delegation to see the reality of Foreign Service life — could dissuade her. So, for two days she and I and our "houseboys" slapped together whatever mixture of hors d'oeuvres we could muster as she watched the precious mayonnaise with eagle eyes. Finally we put the trays into their freezer. Sure enough, before the VIPs arrived, the power went off for four days, so we had to throw out the whole batch.

As usual, the CODEL had no clue about the "hardship" in hardship posts. Probably they thought we lounged around in splendor, eating bonbons. They arrived with their entourage and proceeded to immediately drop off (literally!) their dirty laundry bags at the Chargé's residence, expecting us to "do the necessary." Being the rebel and knowing Marguerite wouldn't have the courage to do it, I handed the laundry back to them and said we did not have the facility, the manpower, nor, for that matter, electric power for the task.

During the dinner, with tables bedecked with silver candelabra, official china and all, the Gods were watching over us and the power went off again. They, of course, were shocked and amazed when we all just carried on. "This happens all the time," I said. "It's part of the Foreign Service life most people have no idea about." By the way, I asked, what brought you to Mauritania? The answer was not surprising. "We wanted to tell our constituents that we have been to every African country." To add to the delights, our overworked cook, while serving the main dish in relative darkness, tilted the platter a little too much and poured sauce on the minister's wife's dress. To her credit, and my great admiration, she turned to her husband and said, "Dear, you never did like this dress."

Since I was trilingual in English, French, and Arabic, I was asked to interpret for the delegation as they toured Nouakchott and met with the ministers. Thus began my campaign to keep them from offending our host government officials. The official visit to the Minister of Foreign Affairs' office went smoothly, and each congressman was given a beautiful Mauritanian silver gift with its unique design. To my dismay when I took them to the *artisanat*, the official artisan shop, one of the congressmen wanted to trade in the gift he had just received for something else he fancied in the case. I had to restrain myself, but firmly told him he couldn't do that because it would offend the Mauritanians—and surely he could afford to buy his wife something from the gift shop. This was not the best introduction to Congress I could have imagined.

Another time, I was assigned to talk to Mauritanian school children about the "moon rock exhibit" that was touring our embassies around the world. In a secure and hermetically-sealed glass case there was a small black rock' about four inches in diameter. Surrounded by the school kids, I proceeded to explain to them about our Apollo 11 Mission to the moon and how this rock is a piece of what the astronauts brought back with them from the moon. The kids listened very respectfully as they looked intently at the rock. Then one brave soul raised his hand and said "That's very interesting Miss Hala, but we really don't believe this rock came from the moon. You see we have tons of these rocks in our country." So much for promoting American scientific endeavors. I have to say though, I couldn't blame them, the rock did look very ordinary.

We had a Peace Corps program in Mauritania for creating a chicken hatchery. So, Steve and a young Peace Corps volunteer, we'll call him John, would go to the airport regularly to receive a shipment of chicks for the farm, praying that the heat had not killed them on the way. John was very popular with the female Peace Corps volunteers in Senegal, who would show up at our doorstep at all hours looking for him. Steve would then drive them up to the chicken farm.

It was in Nouakchott that we adopted, our beloved mutt Mitzie. During the summer when it was so hot, I would find her immersed up to her head among the papyrus plants in our tiny decorative pool. Two weeks before we left Nouakchott, Ambassador Murphy commissioned me to paint a mural along the drab walls of the changing rooms by the pool. Since we had a lot of pool parties, it seemed like a good idea. So, during our last weeks, in addition to packing, I enjoyed painting a twenty-foot mural I designed with whimsical scenes of rolling green hills and cute animals. Sami had managed to find durable exterior paint. I was amazed many years later to learn from someone who had just visited our embassy there that the mural had held up, even under harsh climate conditions.

Washington, D.C.

After Mauritania, we had a tour in Washington, D.C. I found a job working for the Foreign Buildings Office's (FBO) Interior Design Department. I was the only interior designer there who also was a Foreign Service spouse. During that time, I was assigned to help the famous Shirley Temple Black refurbish the residence in Accra, Ghana, her first ambassadorship. She was, as I expected, charming and smart. A Foreign Service staff member, we'll call him

Joe, accompanied her on her visit to FBO. After looking at all the samples and catalogues, Ambassador Black decided on the usual replacement items such as draperies, bedspreads, and such. But she insisted on ordering all new wall-to-wall rust-colored carpeting for the residence, as well as a special super-firm bed and a new grand piano, although both those items were already there. I knew that State Department budget was—as always—underfunded, and that the cost of ordering all this would mean other embassy families in sweltering Accra would have to go without a sufficient number of air conditioning units.

"Madam Ambassador," I explained, "Accra is a very dusty town. First of all, a rust color would show every footprint. Plus, replacing wall-to-wall every two to three years is too costly and would deny other embassy personnel some basics. I can provide you with new area rugs that are more easily replaced and wear better in Ghana's climate."

She was not happy with my response. Joe took me aside. "Hala, my orders are to give Ambassador Black anything she wants." "I understand your position, Joe. But unlike a political appointee like Ms. Black, I know what it's like in those hardship posts and I need to think of everyone there as well."

Shirley Temple Black took me out to lunch at Tom Sarris's Orleans restaurant, hoping to sway me, I guess. Unluckily for her, I had a long-standing armor that helped me from caving in to authority. I always felt people had to earn my respect, authority or no authority. We had a lovely lunch at the Orleans restaurant in Rosslyn, during which she told me that her dream since she was a little girl was to become ambassador. It was sweet and touching, but I stuck to my guns. I did not grow up in Beirut watching Shirley Temple movies, so I was impervious to that nostalgic tug. I didn't order the rust wall-to-wall. I heard much later from a fellow Foreign Service friend that after we left Washington, the ambassador had in fact finagled the wall-to-wall rust carpeting, which I'm told was indeed a disaster in dusty Accra. That would not have happened with a career ambassador.

Political appointments at the State Department account for roughly a third or more of the ambassadorial pool. Some of them, like Ms. Temple, are good representatives for the United States.

Others can be a great embarrassment. Not having gone up the ranks or lived the Foreign Service life, just about all of them don't have an understanding of what career officers and their families really do and the hardships that can come with that. Many years later, Steve's aunt and uncle happened to meet Ms. Temple and told her they were related to me through marriage. She replied dryly, "Oh yes! I remember Ms. Buck very well!"

As it turned out, while I was working for FBO, Ambassador Murphy, who was now assigned to Damascus, asked for me to refurbish the residence in Syria. I flew to Beirut and was given an embassy car and driver to make the two-hour journey to Damascus. Winding our way up the mountains, Antoun, the driver, was doing what all drivers in Lebanon do: trying to overtake another car at a curve in the road. I was no longer used to this. I asked him to slow down and not do that. He looked at me in his rear-view mirror, smiled and said, "*Shoo sarlik ya sit Hala? Awwee albik!*" (What has happened to you Mrs. Hala? Have courage, strengthen your heart!) "I've been away for a while," I replied, "and this makes me nervous, and hence my heart is not pleased." He laughed and slowed down.

The morning after I arrived in Damascus, Rusty, Ambassador Murphy's golden retriever, managed to escape and darted into downtown Damascus. There we were, the American ambassador, his kids, and I running down the streets of Damascus chasing Rusty. Rusty was having a ball with this crazy game of catch-me-if-you-can.

The ambassador's residence in Damascus was a glorious old Arab house, with a central hall plan, very high ceilings, huge rooms, and lovely gardens. The standard U.S.-manufactured furnishings we were required to procure looked miniaturized by the grand, stately living room. Again, with a limited budget, I proposed using some beautiful velvet with a Middle Eastern design, which had just become available in the United States, to re-cover the furniture and give it some class. Ambassador Murphy hated it, but not Anne, his wife. None of the other swatches I brought looked good there. The irony is that here we were in the city that was famous for inventing brocade, Damask (from Damascus), and other textile marvels, but we had to buy "American," which of course ended up being more expensive, especially with the shipping charges. When I returned to FBO and looked at other options, the velvet was still the most elegant. So, my boss cabled Ambassador Murphy; in reply, we received a short message: "I give in, you can ship the gaudy velvet!"

After the Damascus assignment, I was off to Africa—not the favorite assignment for Interior Designers. I volunteered to travel there—with swatches of fabric, catalogues, and my interior design skills—because I knew that in these extreme hardship posts it was important that staff members as well as the ambassador have a decent house and furnishings; it boosted morale. With little outside recreation, home becomes your whole life. It is where you and your family relax, take recreation, and have representational dinner parties. Since you are always a big fish in a small pond, your home represents and reflects the United States in the local population's eyes.

I started off in Chad (now the Central African Republic), where for the first time in my experience it was impossible to find any local tailor who could reupholster worn out furniture. It also was the first time I encountered the hardships of living in that part of Africa. I stayed with some Italian friends from our Mauritania days. I'll never forget how Vivianne had to put empty tuna cans filled with Kerosene under each leg of her baby's crib to prevent snakes from slithering up. For a special treat, the De Miccos took me out to the only restaurant in town, but warned me of the dangers of all the insects there. It was their mating season, so we had to wear long sleeves in 100-degree weather, spray all our clothes and never, ever, I was told, swat an insect that landed on me, because it created a terrible skin disease. Bugs are things I hate, and that evening was my nightmare come true. Things were crawling around our plates and into them, and dropping from the lovely tree above. I had a hysterical fit and we decided to go back home.

I continued on to Douala in the Cameroon, then Bamako in Mali (where they had just had a flood following which residences needed refurbishing), and finally Abidjan, the capital of Ivory Coast. There, I had to deal with an ambassador's difficult, but very elegant and attractive new spouse, who refused to unpack the lamps she had chosen and ordered from FBO. So, I unpacked the boxes, distributed the lamps around the living room and lo and behold, she thought they looked good. She insisted on having purple everywhere. I remember the scene vividly. Sitting in their family room she turned to her husband who had just walked in. "Darling, Hala won't let me have my purple draperies and rugs and you know how much I love that color." Ignoring her puckered lips, I clarified to the ambassador, "Actually, what I know... is that in two or three years' time, the next ambassador and his wife may not like purple and I cannot afford to replace everything." I made allowance for things that were not costly to give her the purple she needed. Had she been someone who had been a Foreign Service spouse all along, she would have understood my concern. She had already done enough damage by replacing draperies throughout the embassy offices with her favorite chintz, in different colors. She also had the ambassador's settees in his office re-upholstered in turquoise and deep pink satin. The poor administrative officer was beside himself as he showed me the result. "What do you think Hala?" he asked nervously. "It's perfect early bordello," I replied. He burst out laughing. It was the first time I saw him relax.

While in Washington D.C., I also participated in the effort to get some form of compensation for Foreign Service spouses. Our group was in charge of polling other U.S. diplomatic wives for their input. The 1972 directive—as the "Declaration on Spouses" is referred to—declared that Foreign Service wives were private persons and could not be required to carry out any duties for the U.S. government. That meant that the officer's Efficiency Report would no longer rate his wife's "representational" skills and other duties for which, of course, she was never compensated. It also declared that the U.S. government had no right to insist that the wife of an officer carry out such things as representational entertaining, charitable, or other social "duties." It was supposed to solve the problem of "dragon ladies" and liberate spouses.[40] But it had a downside for senior spouses who are still responsible for the official representational duties in support of their husbands—they could no longer demand help from junior spouses. During our tenure, other embassies provided a certain percentage of remuneration for spouses; mostly though, it was added to their husband's salary.

But in fact, to this day, decades after women's liberation, the entrenched expectations continue to be that dinner parties will be organized, that diplomatic functions will be well attended, and that overseeing the expat American community will continue. In addition to the meticulous paperwork, every receipt connected to those representational dinners and receptions must be kept and submitted. Senior wives especially are still expected to be helpmates and hostesses for their husband's career. Some like it, others do not. But I felt that I had to support Steve. I remember though that after we left Jeddah, a female Consul General was appointed and the State Department was planning to hire a paid "house manager" to perform all the duties that senior wives like me performed without pay. I was furious.

Our attempts to find some compensation for spouses who fulfilled those roles failed. Hence the official designation as "dependent spouses," which meant that one's economic security continued to be tied to the officer spouse. Every American at the embassy, spouses included, reflected American foreign policy whether we wanted to or not. Hence the title of a great book: *The Accidental Diplomat.*[41]

On our second tour of duty back in the United States, Steve was sent by the State Department to study Energy Economics at the Fletcher School of Law and Diplomacy and M.I.T in Cambridge, MA. I took advantage of this hiatus to complete my interior design degree at Boston University. I was lucky in that I had a succession of portable careers—interior design, art, and art therapy—and perhaps also because I came from a culture where a career or job was not the defining factor for a person's identity. Many of my generation of Foreign Service spouses enjoyed the vicarious representational role and achievement. I hear that many among the new generation want no part of it.

Kuwait

As we were getting ready to leave for Steve's next assignment in Kuwait, we were overjoyed to find out I was finally pregnant. We flew to Kuwait and for our first eight months there, I fulfilled my contract with FBO to help refurbish embassy residences, including the ambassador's. I found the warehouse full of mismatched furniture that needed to be reupholstered and redistributed to various staff residences. In the ambassador's residence, I also enjoyed designing a room divider-cum-display case that could slide back into the wall for larger embassy functions. Kuwait had many good carpenters and craftsmen, almost all of them foreign workers from the Arab world and the Far East. This, in addition to setting up our house, kept me busy until I had to get on the plane. Even though Kuwait had some modern hospitals, after trying for seven years to have a child, we were not taking any chances.

I flew back to Washington D.C. in my eighth month to be with my parents. Steve couldn't join me right away and was waiting until the due date to join us. As it happened, Katie arrived two weeks early and Steve did not make it back in time. He had planned to spend a couple weeks with us when he did come. The trip from Kuwait in those days took much longer than it does today. We always regretted that he'd missed the opportunity to be there for our daughter's birth. I would have welcomed his advocacy at the hospital. Due to a blizzard, Papi was worried we couldn't get to the hospital in time, so he and mom took me there very early.

I had a long labor and, as it turned out, my wonderful gynecologist, Dr. Becker, was having surgery himself that day. The attending physician who replaced him was not helpful and was actually negligent (the nurses verified this later, even saying I had reason to sue). My mom was my Lamaze coach, but when the time came, she was anxious and worried. I had to calm her down, but when the baby monitor strapped to me started beeping, she rose to the occasion and yelled for the nurses and the doctor to come. I remember them as unfriendly, dismissing my assertion I was ready to give birth. I attributed that to a large number of women in labor that day. But then, after he delivered Katie, the doctor asked me, "Are you crying because it is a girl?" Even through the haze of exhaustion I was taken aback by his question. Only later did I wonder if there had been a prejudiced assumption. Seeing that we were Lebanese-American, mom speaking with an accent, he probably assumed I was sad because I didn't have a boy. "No," I yelled, "I'm crying because I am so happy!" "You idiot!" I should have added. I missed Dr. Becker, who would have been very happy for me since he had seen me through all those years of trying to conceive.

Steve arrived and finally met his daughter. When Katie was six weeks old, I flew back with her in a *Snugli* baby carrier to Kuwait.

The State Department only authorized flights on American carriers because of the Fly America Act, which in fact cost more than other flights and are less convenient. In those days, it was mostly Pan Am and TWA. I remember getting dirty looks from the Pan Am stewardess because I was breastfeeding Katie. I had chosen a seat by the window and had draped a blanket discreetly so as not to offend anyone, yet the crew treated me as if I was some uncouth wretch, my American diplomatic passport notwithstanding. La Lèche League was going strong in those days, and recommended breastfeeding because it had been proven—and has been proven over and over again—to provide great immunity for babies. Especially with all the travels and transits, it was certainly more hygienic than keeping baby bottles sterilized. Overall, my experience over the years with Pan Am and their general treatment of families made me think their demise was well-deserved.

Kuwaitis were the minority in their own country; foreign workers outnumbered them. Besides a few friends we made, Kuwaitis mostly kept to themselves. Old Foreign Service "hands" who were in Kuwait years before us said people used to be much more open and welcoming. I remember one very nice Kuwaiti lady asking how long I would be in the country. Hearing that it would be two to three years, her answer was, "I really like you and would like to get to know you better, but I cannot handle people who keep leaving. So, nothing personal, but I will not invest in developing our friendship." It was the first time I became aware of the effect of our transient lifestyle on the local population and others who stay put. I fully understood how, before the age of email and instant access, that it was painful to constantly put yourself out to form friendships, only to have to say goodbye over and over again. Leaving and being left carry similar pain.

Luckily, Kuwait was a good place to raise a baby. I had household help, an Indian young woman, Postine, who became very attached to Katie. I learned that in the Foreign Service, it is very easy to get sucked into the social whirl and not spend time with your kid. After a loud exchange in which Postine kept saying, "You go to party madam, I take care of Katie," I decided I needed someone different, someone who would babysit when I had to be out, but who had clear boundaries separating her work from primary care of my daughter. I felt sorry for Postine, but I knew it was a slippery slope and I needed to be there for Katie. It's a great temptation to get so totally involved in the duties of social life that kids feel abandoned. The next woman, Erlinda, found the right balance. She had her own children, so she understood I wanted to be there for Katie.

Training staff at every post was part of my job. One day I over-heard Erlinda say on the phone, "I'm sorry, but Mr. Buck is on the toilet." I rushed over and picked up the phone; it was a colleague from another embassy asking for Steve. Later, I explained, "You should not say that. Just say that Mr. Buck cannot come to the phone." "Yes madam, but he was."

From the time she was six weeks old, I would take Katie to the embassy compound every day. We had a large swimming pool that was the center of social life for embassy families. Katie learned to tadpole swim immediately and by the time we left she could jump off the diving board. The embassy staff was congenial and to this day we still have good friends from that time.

Driving through Kuwait was worse than Beirut, since they had highways and Kuwaitis drove at any speed they liked. I honed choice Lebanese curse words driving there. On one day, as a Kuwaiti driver swerved and cut in in front of me, a little voice in the baby seat in the back rang out: *"kiss immak."* It was Katie, with a beatific smile on her face. I won't translate, but after that I bit my tongue driving in Kuwait.

During our Kuwaiti posting, we flew to Iran with good Foreign Service friends from Beirut to visit another friend who was posted at our embassy in Tehran. We arrived just before the Iranian revolution began in earnest. Traveling back and forth with our colleagues from the U.S. embassy, we were surprised that we had to be in armored cars with an armed guard. Even the embassy children went to school in the same manner. In those days our embassies were open, and we moved around in the different Arab countries without fear or security detail. So, it felt strange to us. Steve reminded me how in 1952, Iran had had a democratic election of its leader Mossadegh. But the British were unhappy when he wanted to nationalize the oil fields–basically bringing them into Iranian hands. So, the British and the C.I.A. orchestrated a coup that threw out the Iranian president and reinstated the Shah, who had ruled before the democratic election. Many years later the Shah would crown himself Emperor of Iran. This did not sit well with the Iranians who have not forgotten about our interventionism.

When we arrived in Tehran, the souk had just closed, for a very long time as it turned out. The ambassador at the time was still sending missives to the State Department that declared everything was fine and that the Shah was in control. During this seemingly contradictory situation, we managed to play a couple rounds of tennis as if nothing was going on. The rest is history. Ayatollah Khomeini returned from exile as the revolution gained momentum, the Shah was himself exiled, and Americans were taken as hostages. Americans would only see images of the hostages being dragged around Tehran, but the history leading up to that, as usual, was not reported to the American public.

But even before this scenario played out we decided it was time to leave Tehran and fly to Isfahan, a beautiful, magical city with magnificent mosaics decorating the mosques. Steve and I had an arrangement: when we were in a souk, I would walk ahead of Steve, who was pushing Katie in her stroller. That way I could bargain for a better price before my foreign husband showed up. Suddenly, I noticed that one by one, the shops were closing, the steel doors slamming shut. I ran back to Steve. "Something is happening here. I think we need to get out." "No, remember it's prayer time and you know that they close the souk for that." But my instincts did not agree, and we quickly left the souk. The next day the Iranian revolution started, just as we took off back to the safety of Kuwait.

Being thrust almost overnight into the nomadic, exciting, and demanding life of a diplomat's spouse forced me to develop new skills. At some point during our Foreign Service life I realized that I had stepped out of my initial reserve and into a place of ease in a room full of strangers. The young bride's panic was replaced by an acceptance of my role as a traveling hostess representing the United States. I was still not fond of small talk and tended to plunge into conversations that were meaningful, interesting and, occasionally, controversial. In retrospect I realized the Foreign Service was itself a bridge that fostered connection and goodwill. It was a perfect fit for me. I loved discovering new countries, reaching out, and learning about other people.

17. Matrah Fort and Dhows, Muscat, Oman. *Watercolor © Hala Buck.*

Oman

The Sultanate of Oman is situated at the extreme southeastern corner of the Arabian Peninsula. Its coastline stretches along the Indian Ocean, the Arabian Sea, and the Gulf of Oman. Historically, it was a major link between Africa, Arabia, and India. It is a spectacularly beautiful place with stark mountains, terraced fields and lush oases, fruit orchards in the interior as well as immense and breathtaking deserts—mountains of sand sculpted by the wind. The ruggedly beautiful coastline of the Gulf of Aden framed the entrance to Muscat, where two Portuguese forts, Fort Jalali and Fort Mirani, stood guard. Our embassy was a beautiful, traditional Omani house with stained glass windows, literally backing into the mountains. During Independence Day, we would stand and watch fireworks shooting out of the forts. Graceful sailboats called *dhows* added the last touches to a picturesque and beautiful city.

Omanis are historically renowned seafarers who plowed

through the waters between East and West, sailed to India and China as well as the east coast of Africa, and controlled that part of the spice route. They supplanted the Portuguese in Zanzibar, East Africa, and ruled there for 168 years. Omanis are proud and gentle people with a natural grace about them, a sense of their own worth, shown by the way they move and conduct themselves. Unlike other Arab countries, Omanis had been their own masters for many generations, and despite a strong British influence, they did not suffer from the damaging legacy of colonization—the loss of dignity and a sense that their destiny was in the hands of others. Their body language indicates a secure sense of who they are. They are devout Muslims of the *Ibadi* sect–a tolerant and peace-loving branch of Islam. Omanis are open and accepting of others since they themselves are a mixture of ethnicities. Could it be that their long and rich history as powerful merchants, who came in regular contact with other peoples, made them accepting and open-minded, much like the Phoenicians who sailed from what is now Lebanon? I wondered, if Americans were to travel to meet Arabs on their turf and get to know them person-to-person, might the distorted image of the knee-jerk "terrorist" label change?

A few months after we arrived in Muscat for what would be a four-year tour from 1979-1983, Katie and I were "evacuated" back to the United States with a few other spouses, including the ambassador's wife. We were the only "non-essentials" at the post with accompanying children. The Iran hostage crisis and attack on our embassy in Islamabad had just occurred, and extremists took over the Grand Mosque in Mecca, Saudi Arabia. Since evacuating American families from Saudi Arabia would have been seen as a lack of confidence in the Saudi government, the State Department evacuated "dependents" from smaller Gulf posts such as Oman.

Back in Washington, I found a new way in which the State Department discriminated against family members. There were rules and regulations that made it hard for me to access our winter clothes in storage without Steve's explicit permission. Furious, I pounded on doors and threatened to return to Muscat, with or without the Department's permission. I must have created some panic, because the next day all posts received a directive saying that the return to post of any evacuated member without specific orders would result in the repatriation of the State Department employee himself. So much for my bravado and women's lib. I was definitely not an equal partner in this equation, despite the fact that I had worked hard to carry out all the social duties and entertaining required by Steve's position. Unpaid labor: Great! The rebel in me was not happy. Like most Foreign Service spouses of our era, I was the unrecognized glue that held our family together during each move. To add insult to injury, I went to the training course for "senior spouses" at the Overseas Briefing Center (OBC). Having already "served" as such, I thought it might be helpful to get more guidance. But I revolted when the presenter said, "You need to have two separate kitchens, one for staples you use for your own family, and one for what you use for representational purpose." (That is, for entertaining.) Already fed up with State Department regulations, I shot up from my seat. "How dare you nickel and dime us for flour and sugar when we serve our country without any remuneration? Treating us like petty thieves who might steal flour or sugar or oil, whatever." Then I turned towards the new "senior spouses." "Don't you let them treat you this way. This is demeaning and unacceptable!"

Four months later, Katie and I were allowed to return to Oman thanks to a diplomatic moment. Before the Omani foreign minister's scheduled visit to Washington, Steve and the ambassador asked how the State Department would respond to the minister's questions about why spouses were evacuated, particularly when Washington and Oman were emphasizing Oman's stability. On top of which, if I remember correctly, Congress was planning one of its tax-payer funded "fact finding" trips to Oman, and their wives were coming along. This would appear incomprehensible to Omanis when our own embassy spouses were still not allowed back. We suddenly received our travel orders back to Oman.

Soon after Katie and I returned to Muscat, Steve and I were invited to the British ambassador's residence for dinner. After dessert was served, our hostess stood up and addressed the ladies around the table: "Well ladies, shall we go powder our noses?" I was engaged in some interesting conversation with a male guest and did not hear. "Hala dear, wouldn't you like to powder your nose?"

"No thank you, I don't powder my nose," I replied politely.

"But you must! Dear, we need to leave the gentlemen to enjoy their port, and we will have our sherry in my parlor." I still laugh when I think of that scene, a holdover from the British Raj.

I remember an interesting cross-cultural experience. We were showing visitors around a village above Nizwa in the country's interior. We took pictures in a respectful way, asking people if they minded. As usual, they were gracious about it. But sustained cultural awareness sometimes requires a wake-up call. As we were walking back to our Suburban, a young Omani who had posed for us said, "Please wait one minute." He left and came back with his camera and asked if we minded if he took our picture. Of course, we said yes. But as we walked back to our car we all commented that we had learned something in that interchange. The young Omani helped us to feel what it is like to be on the receiving end of a photo quest, and to be perceived as "quaint enough" to warrant the attention. As "culturally sensitive" as we were, somehow we needed a taste of how it really felt to have someone stop you and ask if they can take your picture. I never forgot that experience and was more mindful aiming my camera and shooting at the "interesting scenery" and its "people."

In each country where we were posted, I had painted only a handful of oil paintings, mostly landscapes and people. It was in Oman, where, in 1980, I picked up my watercolor brushes professionally for the first time. Constantly uprooted, starting over again and again, I discovered that painting was my way of getting to know a place and its people. Perhaps it was my way of putting down a small root and creating my own identity beyond being the "spouse of." It was also a way of capturing and preserving the old world. The country was changing fast, so I felt I needed to record it before the boom of modernity destroyed every vestige of this ancient and special place. Some friends would call to alert me to some old part of the city being demolished and I would rush there with my sketchbook and camera to record it as the bulldozers moved in. I still have a lovely window carving that was about to be carted away. It saddened me to see countries with a rich heritage bulldoze the old in order to modernize and live up to the West's notion of being "civilized." I'm glad that some things were rescued and the country still retains its charm.

Everywhere I turned there was something interesting and

18. Friday Goat Market, Oman Nizwa. *Watercolor ©Hala Buck*

beautiful to paint. The Omani women's dresses, although modest, were colorful, with striking designs and bright hues, a delight to an artist's eye. The men in their bright white *dishdash,* and beautiful *khanjars*—silver daggers attached to ornate belts—inspired interesting compositions.

Later, I realized that the painting exemplified the public vs. private way men and women share power in that part of the world. On the surface, one sees the men strutting around in their impressive outfits and *khanjars* or daggers. Behind the tree the women are taking care of the goats. Now and then, you see one man or another slip behind the tree and consult with the women. The women in fact are the ones who negotiate and set the price, but publicly, the men keep their honor intact.

Most of my paintings there were of the colorful, dignified, and gentle Omani people with the striking backdrop of mountains, oases, the Gulf of Oman, ancient castles, and forts. In Dhofar, in southern Oman, people's features showed their mixed African heritage. In spring, the landscape would erupt in a burst of wild flowers and apricot blossoms, while the gnarled frankincense trees blanketed

19. Painting in Nizwa surrounded by curious helpers, Oman.

20. Dhofari Women, Oman. *Watercolor ©Hala Buck*

21. Sad! *Watercolor ©Hala Buck*

22. Girl in the red dress, Oman. *Watercolor ©Hala Buck*

23. Four kids by a door. Al Hamra, Oman. *Watercolor ©Hala Buck*

24. Women at a Camel Race, Oman. *Watercolor ©Hala Buck*

25. Resting Camel Drivers, Oman. *Watercolor ©Hala Buck*

the mountains. It was an artist's dream. Wherever I sat outdoors to paint, children would gather, adults would come and look, curious, polite, and respectful. No one bothered me, and we would end up talking about their village and why I painted. I explained about paints, they shooed the flies away. I felt accepted and respected. There was so much to paint—from the people, to the mountains and valleys. I painted full time for the four years we were in Oman.

Some of my favorite paintings are the ones I painted in Oman. The ones I kept remind us daily of the country and the wonderful Omanis we met. The artistry in Oman—indeed in all the rest of the Arab World—appears in beautifully crafted silverwork, jewelry, embroidery, window carvings called *mashroobiyah*, weavings and other utilitarian objects. They created intricate door locks called *kadnas*. Copper and brass (lined in tin for safe use) is used in all manner of kitchenware.

I organized three group shows at the Inter-Continental Hotel. I ordered and had shipped not only watercolor paper and paints, but also everything I needed to frame my paintings. It was always a shift for the artist in me to go from the creative mode of paint-

26. On the road. Wadi bani Hani, Oman. *Watercolor ©Hala Buck*

27. Majestic Wadi bani Kharous. Oman. *Watercolor ©Hala Buck*

28. Wash Day. Oman. *Watercolor ©Hala Buck*

ing, to the nitty-gritty of exhibiting and acting as my own business manager. I learned to frame my own work with acid-free material, market it, find exhibition space, and sell it. It is still a wonderful feeling to know that my "babies" are scattered around the world: in a Hong Kong bank, in other Embassies, and safe with dear friends in various countries. Now and then I will meet someone who saw a painting of mine in a friend's house in London or some other place and realized the connection between us. Prior to email and other modern communications, my paintings helped me reconnect with friends all over the world, even years after losing touch. I also learned things I did not know before, such as that camels hate running in a straight line. I was almost killed by one runaway camel at that race had Steve not pulled me away in time.

I often complained to Steve that I had no identity of my own in the Foreign Service. I was always "Steve Buck's wife." He would argue that people knew *me* and liked *me*. But at one Independence Day reception that Steve, as chargé d'affaires, had to host (together with me), he finally realized what it was like to be *me*. Standing in the reception line welcoming our guests, many people would politely shake Steve's hand and then, looking at me, would turn back to Steve. "Oh! You're Hala's husband." They knew me from my exhibits and had purchased my paintings. That night Steve sheepishly came home. Holding me, he said, "I think I now understand what you've been trying to tell me. Now I'm spouse of."

During our Oman tour Katie had her first best friend, Emily from Canada. The girls were inseparable. We still stay in touch with her parents David and Mary Jo; and almost every time we got together, we tease Steve about one special camping trip. We had set up camp in a *wadi*, or riverbed, aware of and watchful for any rainstorm. It could be raining miles away and minutes later we could be swept away by a rushing deluge. Steve and I lay half asleep when we felt some raindrops. Steve is not a morning person, and once slept through a hurricane in his parents' car when he was young, but suddenly he leapt to his feet. Moving at warp speed he roused everyone. "Quick, quick! We have to get to higher ground, it's beginning to rain." In a zombie-like frenzy we threw our camping gear into the back of the Suburban we'd borrowed from the embassy and drove up to a nearby hill. Except for Steve, uncharacteristically alert at 4 a.m., the rest of us were still in a daze. Luckily there was no flash flood. None of us could go back to sleep, so we set up a folding table and sat down to play a couple hands of bridge, as we often did with the Fields. Katie, Emily, and her brother Michael were happily playing. All of a sudden, an Omani shepherd appeared with his flock and stood frozen in place at what must have been the weird sight of these Westerners sitting around a table, in the middle of nowhere, playing a card game at dawn. Because Arabs usually are polite and courteous, we exchanged *sabahh el kheir alaykum,* good morning greetings. I'm sure that our little tableau became a story handed down the generations in his family.

There were many weekends we would go on camping trips with friends. On one memorable New Year's trip, we woke up a little groggy, and had started a fire for our coffee and breakfast when a fishing boat beached near us. Out stepped two Omani men who walked up to greet us. So, Steve and I launched into our series of greetings and to our surprise one of the fisherman switched to perfect American English. "Hi there, happy New Year," he said as we stood dumbstruck. It turned out he had studied or worked in the United States—I cannot recall where—and he was back helping his family.

Everywhere we turned, we found friendly and warm people. At Christmas, a few embassies would get together and have Santa Claus arrive by fishing boat, much to the delight and squeals of the children. It was something that our TCK[42] daughter would later find hard to make her friends back in the United States believe.

We were in Oman from 1979-1983. Sadly, due to our years spent in a transient lifestyle, we lost contact with Omani friends. There was no email, no reliable mail service, and telephone calls were too expensive. Imagine then, when thirty years later, on September 30, 2010, in Washington, D.C., Steve called me. "Love," he said, "you will like what I'm about to tell you." It seems at a reception he introduced himself to the Omani ambassador to the United States, a very elegant and educated woman. "She was very warm and polite when I told her I had been the Deputy Chief of Mission at the U.S. Embassy in Muscat. But when I mentioned that my wife Hala painted extensively while we were in Oman, she suddenly lit up. "You mean you're Hala's husband? I have several of her paintings that my uncle bequeathed to me. I remember her well." It turned out her Cultural Affairs officer also had a painting of mine. It was so heartwarming and affirming to hear that. As a Foreign Service spouse who had to assert her identity, it was gratifying that I had left my own mark in a country that I loved. We extended another year in Oman, not wanting to leave after the assigned three.

Knowing how disenchanted I felt about the State Department towards the end of our career, Steve knew this serendipitous encounter would cheer me up. It did that, but something in me felt lighter as well. I felt that my whole thirty-four years in the Foreign Service was not a waste of my life. Over thirty years may have passed since we were in Muscat, but my paintings remain a testimony to my presence there and my love for the people and the country.

After I hung up the phone with Steve, I called a dear friend of mine, Marilyn, who is an "army wife" herself. I knew she would understand how I felt. We both laughed as we enjoyed this validation of my contribution to my husband's career. We decided to meet and celebrate together. My art once more was a healing salve. Even though they're scattered around the world, living on the walls of friends and strangers, my paintings remain a connecting strand in my wandering emigrant life with Steve. Painting has helped me create my own separate and viable identity in an otherwise blurry revolving door of Foreign Service life.

After Oman, we had a three-year assignment back in Washington. Oman was and remains our favorite posting, especially when the next one was in the midst of a protracted war. But I would soon learn that not all postings are equal, especially "hardship posts." The charm and ease of living in Oman folded into the back pages of our transient life album when we arrived at our next posting, Baghdad, Iraq, in 1986, midway through the Iraq-Iran War.

Iraq

In 1986, just when we received our next assignment, for Baghdad, Iraq, I found out—to our utter surprise and shock—that I was pregnant after many years of trying for a second child. This time however, it caused a lot of agony. I was much older, and we were off to a war zone where I knew that hospitals and doctors would be stretched to the limit caring for the wounded. Even though the State Department and Steve kept reassuring me that the war had "stabilized" and that Baghdad itself was not in danger, my intuition told me otherwise. I decided to stay in Washington, rent out our house, and move in with my parents until either the baby arrived or the war ended. A month later, I had a miscarriage. I found out that most cultures do not help parents mourn their lost child when it's "just a miscarriage." But the grief is just as real. I remember coming home from the hospital, Steve and I sitting on the sofa crying, holding and comforting each other. He had to leave a week later. Katie and I joined him in Baghdad a few months later.

We were in Baghdad during the last two years of the Iran-Iraq War. Iraq is a historically rich and fascinating country, part of the cradle of civilization. Baghdad was also the capital of the great Abbasid Caliphate, the seat of centuries of literary and scientific inventions, and a renaissance that rescued and translated all the Greek philosophers. The ninth-century "House of Wisdom" in Baghdad successfully brought men and women together from far and wide, from all backgrounds and faiths, to work side by side to study and better understand our world.

As Prince Charles remarked, "If there is much misunderstanding in the West about the nature of Islam, there is also much ignorance about the debt our own culture and civilization owe to the Islamic world. . . . The medieval Islamic world . . . was a world where scholars and men of learning flourished. But because we have tended to see Islam as the enemy of the West, as an alien culture, society, and system of belief, we have tended to ignore or erase its great relevance to our own history."[43]

In the mid-1980s however, there was Saddam Hussein, who had U.S. intelligence and other support at the time. When we first arrived I had a comic exchange with a car shop owner. I went to buy new tires for our car and was using the Lebanese word for them, *dawaleeb*. The guy kept talking about *taaeraat*, which for me in Lebanese Arabic meant airplanes. We were going nowhere! Frustrated, I kept saying, "No I don't want airplanes, I want tires for this car!" I gestured like a crazed woman about to take off. "Madame, what language are you using?" he asked. "Lebanese," I replied. We both cracked up, realizing that years of British colonization of Iraq had rendered "tire" in the Iraqi Arabic plural as *taaerat* and a *glaass* for a glass. It was another lesson in the startling differences in local Arabic dialects throughout the Arab world and the influence of history on each. People in the West look at the Arab World and see a monolithic entity, when in fact, there is a huge diversity of geography, history, and dialects. The common denominator is a strong belief in the centrality of family and the classical Arabic language, which later also became the language of the Muslim holy book, the Qur'an.

We slowly adjusted to the ruthless rule of Saddam and life in the midst of a war. The six-year-old Iran-Iraq War had impoverished the country and brought hardships to its people, including food shortages. Priority was always given to Iraqi troops. People lined up to buy a carton of eggs. The only staples we could more or less count on were chicken, yogurt, milk, and pita bread. Occasionally the grocer would save me a couple of edible tomatoes. The war and scarcity of basic food explains why Iraq was considered a "hardship post." Once a year for a few days, the grocers would stack up Romaine lettuce from floor to ceiling, then it was gone till the next growing season. Baghdad was also the only place where the centerpiece at diplomatic cocktail parties was an artistic arrangement of... bananas. They otherwise were never seen in the country due to the war shortages. So, all these diplomats in their fancy dress would be chatting, holding a drink in one hand, and a banana in the other. I spied a few people with bulges in their coat pockets.

It has been estimated that 200,000 to 500,000 Iraqis, Shi'ā, and Sunni, died during that eight-year war with Iran. Sixty percent of Iraqis are Shi'a, and an equivalent percentage served in the army. I remember Steve commenting that, "Iraqis, of both Muslim sects, were the most nationalistic I have encountered in all eight Arab posts I served in. Prior to our invasion, the Iraqi Shi'a were first and foremost Iraqis and part of the secular Bāath regime of Saddam Hussein. What started the sectarian problem was that after G.H.W. Bush liberated Kuwait from Iraq's invasion, we told the Iraqi Shi'ā that if they rise up against Saddam Hussein we would support them. They did, we didn't hold our end of the bargain, and they were massacred."

What remains imprinted in my mind is an image of the plain wooden coffins I saw daily on top of taxi cabs, bringing home the young men fallen during that war. Even now, in the United States, I still shudder when I see ski boxes on top of cars. I immediately flash back to what must have been a terrible shock to a huge number of families. Iraqis have endured so much; as a result, they are stoic and very nationalistic people. That is why our invasion in 2003 was doomed, and why the nine years of occupation were so disastrous for the Iraqi people and us. We could never be "welcomed as liberators," only as occupiers. Iraqis know their history, unlike many in our own government. The U.S. leadership should have listened to its own expert Foreign Service officers like Steve and others who had served in the Middle East. They tried to inform George W. Bush that the British, who had taken over Baghdad decades before, had used the same words as the American general after our invasion: "We come not to occupy but to liberate." And yet both stayed.

Iraq's topography and climate were very different from Lebanon's. I still remember arriving in Baghdad in the middle of the night on a Caravelle aircraft, from which you exited the tail of the plane. As we descended the steps I said to Katie, "Why don't they turn off the engines? It's like a furnace blasting us. Then I realized it wasn't the engines, it was summer in Baghdad, very hot and very dry. Iraq is a virtually landlocked country, the majority of the population is Shi'a and the government leaders were from the secular Sunni Muslim minority. There were also many Christians, mostly Chaldeans, like my hairdresser and the foreign minister. We were surprised to see in our visits to the north how Saddam courted and supported Iraqi Christians.

Baghdad sits on the history-rich Tigris River; I never lost the awe of driving across the bridge or crossing it by boat. I would take other diplomatic spouses and rent a river taxi. We loved the thrill of jumping into a taxi boat and crossing the legendary river to the other bank and the *souks*. These are markets still organized by trade, like guilds. One could drive there, but it was much more exciting to think we were on the ancient Tigris. *Souk al saffafeer*, the copper souk, was my favorite. As we approached it, we could hear the tic-tic-tic of the hammers fashioning copper and brass goods. Further down our senses would be tickled by an overwhelming

29. Souk Treasures. Carpet Souk, Baghdad. *Watercolor ©Hala Buck.*

30. Haydar Khana Mosque. Baghdad. *Watercolor ©Hala Buck.*

31. Cloth Souk. Baghdad. *Watercolor ©Hala Buck.*

array of spices and oils, or the rug souk ablaze in color. Kilims and camel bags hung outside the shops, or stood rolled up and stacked for patrons to sit on as they were served tea. Some of my mom's bargaining skills came in handy there. It was like a dance between vendor and buyer. Today, objects from that souk tie us to memories of our nomadic life and the people we got to know.

At first life in Baghdad-at-war was deceitfully normal except for food shortages and coffins on top of taxis. I marvel now how we carried on and created a relatively pleasant life there. In hardship posts, people create their own form of entertainment, which actually can pass for fun anywhere. Badminton was very popular. We played in our large garden almost every day both as a family, with friends, and also in tournaments. Our Turkish colleague was an avid player, and the expat community joined in too. But one recollection sticks in my mind. The Turkish embassy had brought in about ten Turkish models for a fashion show (another crazy thing, now that I think of it—that's what I mean by a wartime new normal). We were having a big brunch one Friday at our house, and so we invited our Turkish counterparts and told them to bring the models with them. I had scraped together enough food for everyone and was very proud of myself, since there is nothing more shameful for a Lebanese than not having enough food. I thought the table was as heavily laden as possible. In came the Turkish models, all very thin and svelte. I invited them to go into the dining room and help themselves to the buffet. Fifteen minutes later, when I went in to check on the table, there wasn't a scrap of food left on any of my platters. I had never in my life seen anything like it. I'd never, ever run out of food, but these skinny models wiped everything out. And it wasn't like we could run out to the grocer and find more food: that was it! Steve and I were stunned. I think I opened a few cans of tuna we used to order from Denmark and other international food suppliers, and created some concoction with it. Life in Baghdad was always an adventure.

For all Saddam's well-known cruelty, under the secular Bāath regime women were well-educated; they held positions as doctors, dentists, and engineers, as well as in the military. Fast forward to the aftermath of our invasion. Steve laments that what the Ayatollah in Iran could not do, i.e. take over Iraq, we enabled Iran's strong influence through our invasion, destruction, and occupation of the country. It started with our dismantling of Iraq's military and police force. Since our invasion in 2003, the Shi'ā dominates the government, which is no longer secular; and the lack of security has set women back, some say by at least fifty years. In addition to having lost family members and suffered like everyone else, women now feared for their lives, and had lost freedoms they had enjoyed under Saddam. In the 1980s, the women who wore *abayas* (black robes) were the older and poorer women, who told me this saved them money on dresses. Now, they cover to stay safe.

I am not embellishing life under Saddam. I could sense the raw terror that permeated the country, the fear of drawing the attention of Saddam Hussein's goons. But as Steve says, "It was a viable country with a well-educated, highly-functioning, broad middle-class and a professional military able to secure its borders. Its people, of all sects, were first and foremost nationalistic Iraqis."

Because of the food shortages, U.S. Embassy personnel took turns driving twelve hours down to Kuwait to stock up on bananas, potatoes, meat, and other basic necessities at the Safeway there. On one such trip it was our turn and my college classmate, Fatima, and her family accompanied us. The drive down was smooth. It was always a spectacle for Kuwaitis and expats at the supermarket to watch these crazed Americans from Baghdad zooming around, dragging several shopping carts laden with items from embassy personnel wish lists and coolers full of fresh and frozen food. The staff there knew the drill.

All packed up, we left for our trip back to Baghdad. As we were leaving Kuwait, a sandstorm was brewing. We had lived through these *khamseens* when we were assigned to Kuwait, and we thought we could outrun it. No such luck. This one persisted and followed us for what turned into an eighteen-hour drive back to Baghdad, with nothing to shelter us along the way. There was nowhere to stop and take cover. We were out on an open desert road. The sand pitted our windshield opaque, it pelted our car and stripped off the paint. It became impossible to see anything, and night was falling, so Steve and I took turns driving, with one of us hanging out the window checking for other cars, or more dangerously, army trucks with broken rear lights. We learned later that seasoned desert drivers cover their windshields with saran wrap and pull off the road to preserve themselves and their cars. In retrospect, I see we should have waited it out in Kuwait.

The fact that I was born in Lebanon was helpful in meeting Iraqis, but art was my main connection. In Baghdad, I discovered an active, though frustrated, group of talented Iraqi female and male artists. No Iraqi could leave the country without special permission, which was almost impossible to get. Artists were isolated from the global art scene and hungry for news. A lot of artists made a living by painting Stalin-like portraits that Saddam commissioned, which you could find in every corner of the country. But there were also beautiful sculptures scattered around the city, at every square. One I especially liked was called "Ali Baba." It was a beautiful arrangement of huge ceramic jars that created cascading fountains. It was the work of the world-famous Iraqi artist, Muhammad Ghani. On the day we left Baghdad, Muhammad Ghani rushed over with a farewell gift, a prototype frieze depicting a typical musical and poetry jam session *zajal* so typical in the Arab world. He apologized that the only paint he had was silver, and said I could put a different finish on it. It was a touching gesture, and so representative of Arab generosity and hospitality.

Iraq has a legacy of sculpture and pottery that dates back millennia. I was amazed to find art still alive, although somewhat subdued. I had good friends among the many local artists. When I visited them, I would take a taxi, rather than my car with its diplomatic plates, so as not to draw attention and put them at risk.

One of my favorites was the famous ceramist, painter, and sculptor, Nuha Al-Radi, who sadly died of leukemia a few years ago. She had a beautiful house in the midst of an orchard full of fruit trees, flowers, and palm trees. It was an oasis in all meaning of the word during that crazy war. We enjoyed talking about our art, and she would show me around her studio. Nuha Al-Radi went on to write a diary[44] in which she recorded life there during the bombings of the Kuwait liberation in 1991. Her house and orchard became the refuge and lifeline for many of her friends and family. During those years there often was no food, no electricity, and no water. The diary gives an honest portrayal of how people suffer when we drop bombs by the thousands from miles above, shielded from the carnage and destruction we deliver to innocent people on the ground. It's true that George H.W. Bush Sr. did not invade or occupy Baghdad with U.S. troops, but until I read my friend's work, I did not realize the extent of the bombing we did there.

I found it very enjoyable to discuss art and the latest trends in Europe and the United States with Iraqi artists. Like all artists, we had our own lingo and would get enthusiastic about common scenes that non-artists don't notice, such as a line of wash hanging in a courtyard, rusted corrugated metal roofs, or TV antennas creating an interesting pattern against the sky. Art materials were hard to come by. One artist had to to use coffee grinds and some kind of paint on glass to produce his art. It was incredible to me that they were still painting and sculpting, and expressing their feelings under such a regime.

The artists were my guides to the culture and the history of what was known as Mesopotamia. The local museum was closed because of the war, its precious objects stored safely in the basement, but Steve and I were lucky enough to get a personal tour. We saw so many breathtaking, beautiful objects; remembering them made us both want to throw something at the TV when George W. Bush talked about "the civilized [meaning Western] world." I cringe when I hear that arrogant, prejudiced word. Even though State Department experts warned that the museum would be looted, we guarded only the oilfields but not the place that held the heritage of civilization, such as the first writing ever created, known as Cuneiform. What did Bush and Cheney know about this great civilization? Would they have launched a destructive war had they learned about the country and its people, rather than falling back on ideology? Iraq's ancient art tradition and history are irreplaceable, and the postinvasion looting of the museum was tragic.

In Iraq, I painted a variety of landmarks that captured my eye, even though it was trickier to paint outdoors. One is the *Al-Mustan-*

31. Taxi? Typical taxi cab. Kerbala, Iraq. *Watercolor ©Hala Buck.*

siriyya (CE 1232), located on the banks of the Tigris. It is one of the oldest universities in the Arab world, the others being Ez-Zitouna (CE 737) in Tunis, al-Qarawiyyin (CE 859) in Fez, Morocco and Al-Azhar (CE 971) in Cairo. All are still functioning.

Before we left Baghdad, I had a solo exhibition in a downtown gallery. I was told the protocol for all exhibits is that Latif Sayyed-Jassem, the Minister of Information, would officiate at the opening. He usually whisks through, drinks a cup of Turkish coffee, and leaves quickly. I had always tried to downplay my connection to the U.S. Embassy, because this was my way of maintaining a separate identity. But the minister was curious about paintings I had up for sale that were not of Iraq. So, I explained that I had painted them in other countries. "How come?" he asked. "My husband is a diplomat." "Ah, and which country?" "Uh, the U.S." I

32. Cloth Souk. Mosul, Iraq. *Watercolor ©Hala Buck.*

33. Mosul sunset. *Watercolor ©Hala Buck.*

thought his jaw fell slightly, since he was not a big fan of the United States (in fact, he was very vocal about it). But he was polite and really interested. He ended up staying for an hour, talking with me about my paintings.

The Iraqi scenes I painted showed daily life in Baghdad, but also Kerbala, Samarrah's spiral mosque turret, Kurdish villages, souk scenes from Mosul, and the rivers Tigris and Euphrates.

What touched me was how Iraqis from all walks of life came to see the show. Shopkeepers, soldiers on a few days of home leave, waiters with their whole families, artisans, and of course the usual diplomatic corps all came out. I was moved by comments in my guest book: "Thank you for reminding us of the beauty in our country," or, "Your prices are high, but a rose even in the dark is still beautiful."

Those who came to the gallery would engage me for hours about a painting, commenting and asking me questions. I remember one visitor who didn't like the fact I missed a detail from a scene he was familiar with, but he listened respectfully as I explained about my artistic license to paint what resonated for me. One Kurdish soldier burst into tears in front of a painting of a village. "That's my village, no one has painted it before," he said. Homesick, perhaps suffering from post-traumatic-stress, his home and his village were precious anchors, even if only in a watercolor. It was very moving. Weeks later, Steve and I were taking a friend visiting Baghdad around the souks. "*Ahlan ya sitt Hala shlonik?*" "Welcome Miss Hala, how are you?" Steve was intrigued that I knew every shopkeeper, and that waiters would pop out of cafés to greet me. "How do you know all these people?" he asked. "They came to my show and we had good discussions about art and what and why I paint."

Since both Katie and I loved to sing Christmas carols, we joined a choir at the main church near the *al-Alawiy'a* club. Every Christmas, when we harmonize together, it reminds us of the fun we had in Baghdad. Somehow, life seemed normal during the two years we were there; at least, normal in the abnormal setting of an eight-year-old war raging at the border, Scud missiles landing outside the capital and, later, within it. Thinking back, I'm amazed at human beings' ability to adjust, no matter how crazy life gets. Also, how stupid we were to be there with our daughter. Yet, at the time, I always felt safe under the protective umbrella of the U.S. Embassy.

The archeological sites of Nineveh, Babylon, Sur, and Samarrah were extensive and impressive, dating back to the history of what was then known as Mesopotamia. They were part of a magnificent civilization. But getting around the interior of the country usually required special permission. When we traveled in northern Iraq, we needed Foreign Ministry approval and an armed escort with us, since the Kurdish rebels had resorted to kidnapping foreigners and holding them hostage. I remember the day we were going to visit the amazing archeological site of Nineveh, outside of Mosul. It was Steve, Katie, myself, and a colleague from the embassy. As we were getting ready to leave our hotel, we realized our escort was not there. So we went to the local police station to ask for support. The police chief was intrigued by this Lebanese married to an American. We politely conversed over several cups of "police station tea" as Katie from then on referred to any tea that was not Twining's Earl Grey. Ultimately, we were given one policeman. This was fine with us. He sat up front with Steve, his rifle between his feet barrel pointing up. Not the most comforting arrangement, but it was better than no escort at all.

We were walking around Nineveh, where they had just uncovered a very important find, when a truck full of Iraqi soldiers screeched to a halt and about twenty men poured out. To our amazement, the captain headed straight for us; he was very annoyed that we had ventured out unguarded. His soldiers had missed us at the hotel and he had been worried about our safety. He was not impressed with our lone policeman. So, we finished our tour with twenty soldiers tagging along. We thought they were being overly dramatic. But later in the day, somewhere else in the north, a Land Rover stopped by the side of the road and men in Kurdish garb tried to wave us down. We all sensed that it would be best to step on the gas instead. It was scary enough for us, and we were taking no chances.

The "stabilized war" lasted for about another year after we arrived, and then it escalated. At the time, U.S. intelligence—first the C.I.A. then the Defense Intelligence Agency (D.I.A.)—was providing Saddam Hussein with tactical intelligence against Iran, knowing full well about his ruthlessness. While at the same time, the Iran-Contra scandal was going on. Although Saddam's regime was dictatorial and brutal, he also brought good things to his people. He helped coalesce and create a secular nation based on the secular Baath party, which was originally founded by a Christian Syrian (Michel Aflak) and an Iraqi Sunni Muslim (Saleh Bitar). Even though there was still poverty and fear, especially during the war, the regime had pulled people out of an antiquated feudal system where a handful of big families owned most of the land. For example, our cook, Ali, was illiterate, but one of his sons was a doctor and the other an engineer; both his son-in-laws were fighting in the war. When we asked him how life was for him, a Shi'a Muslim, he would tell us how now he had a modest house, his own little plot of land, a TV, and free medical care and education. His job with us was sufficient to support all the rest of his family while his sons were fighting in the war.

Iranian Scud missiles fell at least once a week. At first, they tended to be inaccurate and mostly exploded outside the city; we felt we were not in immediate danger. We had one close encounter while sitting at a garden dinner party bedecked with lanterns. We looked up to see beautiful pulsating colorful lights gliding overhead, then realized with horror it was a Scud missile on its way to some target.

One day, at a time of increased incoming Scud missile attacks from Iran, I was getting into the car with Katie when the wife of an Eastern European embassy officer, who lived next door, rushed over. "Hala, are you getting ready to evacuate?" She asked me anxiously. "No." I answered reassuringly, "I'm just taking my daughter to her piano lesson." It reminded me how when living abroad as a diplomat, one becomes a big fish in a small pond. Each member of the family, whether one wants it or not, represents the United States. You lose your privacy—something that was hard for me. That includes the necessity of having live-in help.

By the end of our tour, however, Scud missiles were coming into the city daily, and one landed and exploded close to our house. Had Steve not lobbied the State Department for funds to install Mylar on all windows of embassy personnel housing and embassy buildings, our daughter would have been seriously hurt. Steve and I were out that night at a typical dinner, having left Katie with our Filipina baby sitter, when we heard the two telling booms of a Scud missile—the first when the missile hits and the other when it explodes. It sounded very close, so instinctively all the guests dove under the dining table. When the noise stopped, we all emerged and rushed to the roof to see where the missile had come down. All we could see was the telltale black plume of smoke rising from our neighborhood, al-Mansour. We tried to call home but, as expected, the lines were dead. Like in a slow-motion movie, I still remember feeling disembodied as we drove home finding our way around the now closed streets, praying it had not fallen on our house. It had not, but many of our windows were shattered, including a huge picture window underneath which Katie had been sitting when the missile hit. Thankfully, the Mylar film that had just been installed a few days earlier had held in place and kept the broken glass from injuring her.

Living with danger in Iraq helped me understand how my Lebanese family and friends could respond whenever I called during the civil war. "*Keefkon?*" How are you? "Everything is fine," they invariably responded, as if they had just returned from the movies. "I don't understand how they can say that," I would tell Steve. We knew they were living under constant shelling, retreating to basement shelters for days on end. But, as anyone who has lived in "abnormal" circumstances knows, human beings adjust to a "new normal." You can't survive if you become conscious of how crazy your life has become. Denial or downplaying dangers are survival mechanisms. It is later, when you are back to safety, that the emotional aftershock hits you—and post-traumatic stress can set in.

There was no official evacuation of dependents, but the near-miss on our Baghdad home was too close for comfort. We decided I would take Katie back to Washington to stay with my parents. Our tour was ending in a few months, so we decided I would get Katie settled, then return to Iraq to pack and for my last art show there that was scheduled at a gallery in downtown Baghdad.

On our way back to the United States, at a stopover in the Frankfurt airport in the early morning hours, Katie and I heard what sounded like an explosion. Both of us instinctively dove under the nearest counter, much to the amusement of other passengers, some of whom did not even turn away from their books. We learned later that the Frankfurt police had exploded an unclaimed suitcase. That's when the impact of living in a war zone fully hit me. Years later I would recall that airport scene and the feeling of panic both Katie and I felt. That was when Katie and her boyfriend Adam, were caught in Israel's 2006 punishing bombing of Lebanon in retaliation for the kidnapping of two Israeli soldiers.[45]

They too would also return traumatized. I prepared Adam's family to be patient with Katie and Adam's emotional fragility and nervousness once they were back home. In Katie's case, I was sure it would retrigger Baghdad.

During our tour in Baghdad, I rediscovered my good friends and A.U.B classmates, Fatima and Rima, who were working for UNESCWA in Baghdad, as well as a high school classmate, Rabab. Having them there mitigated the stress and trauma of war Our rekindled friendship in Baghdad ironically helped me recognize the ongoing "in-betweeness" that had deepened during my Foreign Service experiences. One evening at our house I was passing around some hors-d'oeuvres. Fatima declined, so I continued going around the room. Next I heard Fatima say, in her inimitable teasing way, *"Hey! wayn rayhha?"* (Hey, where are you going?) *"Ilteelee ma biddik."* (I thought you said you didn't want any.) She then lovingly and humorously admonished me for losing my manners. *"Sirtee kteer Amerkaniyye,"* she said. (You've become too American.) "Don't you know a guest is supposed to refuse the first time, and you, the hostess, must insist several times that he or she eat? *Sheddee al azeeme!* (You must strengthen the invitation.) This shows that you care." Food of course is the ultimate proof of hospitality and generosity.

Another time, Rima was supposed to come with us and Fatima's family on a picnic. She was slightly depressed and stressed about studying for her GRE exam. When I went to pick her up, she said she preferred to stay home and study. When we went to meet Fatima, her husband and kids, I reported what happened. Again Fatmeh chided me, *"Yeeh, keef bit khalleeya tib'a la wahhda?"* (How did you leave her all by herself?) There is no worse fate in communitarian cultures than to be left alone, unsupported. "She needs to get out and have her friends around her. You know she's depresssed." So off we went, back to Rima's apartment, and to my utter surprise, a few minutes later, having been adamant about not wanting to come, she emerged with Fatima and we proceeded to have a wonderful picnic at Lake Tharthar.

Maybe it was because I was an only child who relished her time alone that I didn't see anything wrong with Rima choosing to stay home. I took answers like this at face value. So in those aspects, I'm not one hundred percent like most Lebanese. For them integrating a little *Amerkaniye* is fine because Lebanon is pluralistic and willing to embrace parts of other cultures. But I laughed at where the invisible cut-off might have been. At the time of that picnic, Steve and I had been married for twenty years. I felt comfortable being both American and Lebanese, there was no dissonance there for me. What I understand now and appreciate about my birth culture is that this was an example of how people look out for each other, and how everyone feels they have a safety net with family and with friends. It dawned on me how much I also liked the directness of American rugged individualism, while Fatima's friendly chide reminded me of my nurturing roots.

Decades later I would come across two research projects that exemplified how people relate to each other in different cultures. Results showed that schizophrenic people in some countries, like India, not only fared much better than in the United States, some actually were cured. Bewildered by this finding, Western researchers repeated the longitudinal study only to find the same results. What they finally understood was that in communitarian cultures, these "mentally ill" members of the group were not sent out to an institution to be isolated and medicated; rather, they were embraced even more closely by the whole community, and that helped them get better.[46] We are social beings. All the new findings in neuroscience and interpersonal neurobiology have discovered that our brain is a "social brain."[47] We are wired to connect. This is crucial not only for survival, but for mental health. The difference between cultures is how people choose to connect, get involved, and even meddle in other people's lives to show they care.

I lived in both an American and Arab world during our postings in the Middle East. I felt comfortable in both milieus. As the unpaid, unrecognized spouse, I also helped my husband bridge the two worlds, and helped to promote understanding, all while performing the requisite large amount of entertaining. At times I was Hala, the Lebanese wife of the American diplomat; other times I was introduced as the Deputy Chief of Mission's (DCM) wife, thus losing my own identity. Through my art and its connections to others, I resurfaced and nurtured my own separate sense of self. Arabs in all our posts embraced me as one of their own and were kind and hospitable. They included me in activities to which other diplomatic spouses had no access. Lebanese were especially welcomed and liked. So, while each Arab country was very different from Lebanon, there was always a sense of collective heritage that kept me from feeling entirely "alien."

As a Foreign Service family, one of your main goals is to get to know the local people and the culture to create a bridge of understanding, respect, and trust. In Baghdad, however, Iraqis were scared to be seen with foreigners, let alone diplomats, for fear they might be perceived as spies. Most people at the embassy were alienated and hunkered down in our increasingly fortified compound. I remember a cartoon in the *Foreign Service Journal*. Two people on the street are looking at the high walls of a U.S. Embassy compound with no visible entry door. One character asks: "How does one get in?" The answer: "You have to have been born there." Since that time our embassies have become even more like fortresses.

Steve and I worked hard to raise the morale of the embassy community who felt hemmed in by lack of knowledge about the culture and the Iraqis' reluctance to make contact with any diplomat. We knew that those who did meet with us had to report back to Saddam's intelligence service. Steve and I opened our home every Friday (the equivalent of Sunday in most of the Arab world) to all embassy personnel. We wanted to help bring the embassy community together, to interact in a relaxed, non-work setting. They could come by any time on that day, bring games, and preferably something edible to share, since food was scarce. On most Fridays, if you were walking around our large house in Mansoor, you would see someone lounging on some sofa or armchair, reading the paper or a book, another group playing badminton or Frisbee out in the garden, others talking or playing some board game. The regional psychiatrist who visited our embassy was complimentary and very encouraging, saying it was really helping the community, but he was concerned about us, since there was no one to give Steve and me support. But I always had felt very much part of the Foreign Service community. It was our "family on the road," so to speak.

As with all hardship posts, Baghdad required that personnel be emotionally and physically healthy to adapt to the challenges. During one emergency drill organized by the Marine guards, I learned to rappel down our Embassy walls,and found it exciting. But not everyone looked at that type of drill as fun. Some American staff who came with personal problems should not have been assigned there; under the stress of war there was even more backstabbing behavior. Except for Steve and the ambassador, almost no one spoke Arabic at the embassy. Most lacked knowledge of or interest in the Arab world. Many were there just for the "danger pay" and future promotion for having accepted to go to a danger post. The lack of engagement surprised me. The Foreign Service had been my "traveling family" during years in which a sense of home came only in brief spurts. Having little say in where we lived, I assumed people joined the Foreign Service because they liked to explore other cultures and meet people who are different. Years later, Steve and I were even more surprised that, according to the Myers-Briggs test, the majority of Foreign Service employees are considered "introverts."

One person, the embassy nurse, a Seventh Day Adventist, I'll call her Diane, was rude and unkind. She told me I had no business as the DCM's wife trying to maintain morale; I was not an employee. At the time, I did not see her actions as prejudicial towards my Arab roots, I just attributed it to her personal dysfunction and insecurities. But during the writing of this chapter, I mentioned the incident to Steve. To my amazement he said, "Oh yes, I remember, you were in tears about it. She basically was saying you're not a real American like us, you're not one of us, and basically shut you out." I understood much later that that was another moment when I ran straight into unexpected prejudice and rejection—for years afterward, I blocked it out.

The personal venom that Diane emitted was something that Arab-Americans would increasingly experience in the United States after 9/11. At the time, I could understand that Diane felt alienated from the local culture, but her disrespect and disdain was shocking. Living under difficult conditions, isolated in our embassy fortress, with little contact with Iraqis, I can imagine some of the staff coped by walling themselves off into a false sense of superiority. From that vantage point, it was easy to perceive Iraqis, and Arabs in general, as inferior, which justified Diane's scapegoating of me. I was naïve to think people could transcend prejudice, or that they could never be so intentionally cruel, nasty, and insolent.

"You were very deeply hurt and I remember it was lucky we were finishing our tour in Baghdad. You were so happy to leave. You did not want to stay," Steve remembered. Now I realize that the Diane incident added to the disenchantment I was beginning to feel towards Foreign Service life. Perhaps the sense of belonging, as transient as it was, had been a mirage. Realizing that even the American Foreign Service community I thought I belonged to and worked so hard to build rejected me, and saw me as an outsider, was another defining moment. It reinforced the reality of being one who will always live in between. Had I not had the history I had, would that incident in Baghdad have triggered so much hurt? I don't know.

Diane had treated me like some street urchin, despite my status as the wife of the Deputy Chief of Mission. At some level, that incident affected me more than I realized. I believe it was then that

I crossed out the Foreign Service family as a community that could accept me as I am, both American and Lebanese. From that point on, I wanted nothing to do with it. I was fortunate that during our next two postings, in Washington and Canada, I did not have to entertain, and I had little to do with the Foreign Service. The anger and resentment smoldered.

Perhaps that's why our last posting, in Saudi Arabia no less, was so difficult. It did not help when the security officer at our consulate in Jeddah, where Steve was head of mission as Consul General (CG), instituted a rule that all embassy family members could no longer just be buzzed into the inner sanctum by the Marine guard; they had to be "escorted in." It felt so humiliating as the CG's spouse, with decades of experience and service of my own, to now be forced to wait until someone came to escort me in to my husband's office. The local employees, true to Arab standards of courtesy and respect, were as shocked as I was. Steve could not do anything about it; this was a security matter, and it applied worldwide. It was instituted after the tragic killing of a secretary by her son at the State Department in Washington, D.C.

In the years prior to Baghdad, the word "foreign" must have been somewhat confusing for me. The Arab world wasn't totally "foreign" to me, even though the way people dressed, the local dialects, and even the food were different. Yet the friendliness and hospitality felt very familiar. Unconsciously, I must have started building an invisible traveling bridge between my Lebanese-Arab roots and the tender roots of my American self. Living in between was not so bad. I was free to be who I am, not bound to any one group, ideology, or rigid belief. I liked that feeling.

While we were young, the Foreign Service was an adventure that gave us a sense of purpose and meaning. I have always loved exploring every new country we lived in or visited. I would drive around each new city we were posted in, discovering the cubbyholes in the souk, looking at everything, from the simplest fly swatters, hangers, and food to beautiful rugs and other handicrafts. I quickly made new friends, learned my way around, hung paintings, and settled in our new "home." All the while, I knew that in time, our new orders from Washington would arrive. Another uprooting from what was home for one, two, or three years would ensue.

Then would come the packing, and making sure that we carried with us all the important papers—school records for Katie, photo albums, and medical records. Another series of farewell parties would herald yet another plane ride, away from everything that had become familiar.

After Katie was born, it was crucial to have important toys, books, and her blanket to help re-establish "home" for her. One never knew when, or even if, our airfreight or household effects (HHE) would arrive. I can't speak for other Foreign Service families, but even now, in retirement, no one in my family can pack lightly, even for a weekend trip. All three of us are so wired to carry all essentials that even a small trip is stressful. We joke about it, much to the consternation of our patient and bewildered son-in-law, who watches our daughter pack one large suitcase and several small bags for a long weekend trip. In danger posts such as Baghdad, we always had a "bug-out bag" loaded with essential papers and valuables, ready to be grabbed at a moment's notice. In the house we also had a "safe room," reinforced area, to which we could retreat in case the war went bad or came too close. Rappelling down a building might have been fun, but the prospect of retreating to the safe room was a little too much excitement for my taste.

"Packing out" was my nightmare. You had to start packing in a counterintuitive fashion. You started with the carry-on luggage we would take with us on the plane. Then there was the airfreight, which had to conform to certain dimensions and weight. And what couldn't fit in either category was relegated to the Household Effect (HHE) pile. Everything had to be weighed, well-marked, and separated, usually in different rooms so the packers didn't mix things up. Usually, half-a-dozen packers would arrive to quickly wrap and put in boxes everything in sight (including sometimes trash cans that had not been emptied.) Keeping track of it all was a difficult task. Overseas, I had our household staff to help me supervise. In the States, I was by myself, since Steve was usually at the office. We had to keep a list of every carton and its contents, and check it off against the movers' list on the way out—and on the way in at the other end. In the many moves we made we lost some things we cared about, but that's just the way it goes.

Overseas, packers were overzealous and used far too much

packing material, but we had almost no breakage. But movers in Washington D.C. were sometimes careless. Despite leaving meticulous instructions to the contrary, we still received the end irons from our fireplace in D.C. in Oman, where winter was non-existent. At one post, our airfreight crates from Washington were lost. No one in customs could find them. Finally, two months later, Steve, with his stubborn streak and a hunch, personally went to the airport and walked around the tarmac. There, sitting in the hot sun, were our crates. I learned from that experience to never, and I mean NEVER, let the movers pack clothes while they were still on hangers. The heat on the runway had literally melted the multicolored plastic hangers onto the clothes. Red and blue streaks adorned quite a few of my dresses and Steve's shirts.

Canada

After three years in Washington, D.C. we arrived in Ottawa, Canada late in the evening of 1989, having driven from Washington D.C. through snow and then, very carefully, over black ice as we got closer to the Canadian border. Everything was closed except for a small grocer near the Minto hotel. I went there to get a few things for the fridge. The owner was Lebanese. I had learned that opening a grocery store or restaurant was the first thing that many new Lebanese or other immigrants did partly because they usually carry their native food recipes with them. When I came to pay I realized I didn't have Canadian dollars yet, so I told him to keep the groceries and I would send my husband the next day with the money. "*La*, just take them, you'll pay me when you can," said the owner. This honor system I knew from Beirut and other Arab countries, but here I was a stranger to this guy. Just my being Lebanese brought out this tradition and kindness that I had not encountered for a long time. I was very moved.

We loved Ottawa despite the freezing cold for about six months a year. The best advice we received from Canadian friends was to get out: skate, ski, or you'll get cabin fever. We followed their advice. Skating on the Rideau Canal was magic. We would stop at the little huts to get warm and to buy a "beaver tail"—the Canadian equivalent of a funnel cake, but shaped like a beaver tail. I learned an American brought the idea to Canada. It seemed to fit in better here than back in the States.

Canada was the only post where, even now, we never lost track of the friends we made. It's relatively close, and our Canadian friends are either retired there or have always lived in Ottawa. It is rare in the Foreign Service to be able to maintain connections across oceans and continents, and address changes. Even if one revisits a distant post, it is never the same: landscapes have changed and people one knew have left. I prefer to keep my memories as they are. Mobile families definitely can't "go home" again.

We found another wonderful family—the Bowers— whose daughter, Gill, was Leila's best friend there. Our Canadian friends have always been and remain truly precious. I still wish I could drop by for a cup of tea and a chat with Jane; after all, that's how my friendship with Jean Abdellahi in Mauritania started. Luckily, nowadays maintaining friendships in the Foreign Service has become easier through email and the internet. Visiting our Canadian friends, like the Fields and the Bowers is possible. Whenever we get together with them, we pick up our bridge game where we left off. I believe they have even kept our score pad.

34. Autumn colors, Minto Bridges, Ottawa. *Watercolor ©Hala Buck.*

35. Sunday afternoon, Minto Bridges, Ottawa. *Watercolor ©Hala Buck.*

36. "Birds of a Feather." Birds & Balloons, Minto Bridges, Ottawa.
Watercolor ©.Hala Buck.

37. Stormy times. Minto Bridges, Ottawa. *Watercolor ©Hala Buck.*

38. Foggy day. Minto Bridges, Ottawa. *Watercolor ©Hala Buck.*

39. Full moon. Interprovincial Bridge, Ottawa. *Watercolor ©Hala Buck.*

I painted furiously during our assignment. We lived on Stanley Avenue in New Edinburgh and my studio overlooked the Rideau River and the Minto Bridges, which, in the fall, seemed to float above the river as if suspended in the fog.

We chose our house on Stanley Avenue so that during the long, cold winters I could paint indoors from my studio window. I had been used to painting in hot climates where it was a race to put the watercolors down before they dried or some fly plastered itself onto the wet wash. I loved to paint this totally different scenery. But there's always a learning curve, especially when we went from 100 or 120 degrees Fahrenheit in some parts of the Middle East to minus 40 Fahrenheit in Ottawa. I prefer to paint outdoors, so I quickly learned that even the protective back of our station wagon wasn't enough shelter, nor were several layers of gloves and hats, even while working feverishly to finish before freezing. Watercolor is a tricky medium, always surprising you, which is both a challenge and what I love about it. It keeps me on my toes. On one outing in freezing temperatures at *Les Chûtes,* I looked down at my finished painting and saw an unexpected, enchanting pattern all over it. It

40. Lost mitten. Rideau Canal, Ottawa. *Watercolor ©Hala Buck.*

41. Snow magic. Minto Bridges, Ottawa. *Watercolor ©Hala Buck.*

only took a few seconds to realize that the paints had frozen on the surface of the paper. I guessed that as soon as they thawed I would be left with a muddy mess. But luckily, having been carefully laid down, it dried fine on the way home in the warm car. After that, I learned to put glycerin in the water when I painted outdoors, but several layers of gloves notwithstanding, it was my frozen fingers that usually brought me inside.

42. Spring ritual. Blasting open the Rideau River, Ottawa.
Watercolor ©Hala Buck

43. Logs on the Rideau River, Ottawa. *Watercolor ©Hala Buck*

44. Last skate. Rideau Canal, Ottawa. *Watercolor ©Hala Buck*

45. Family time. Rideau Canal, Ottawa. *Watercolor ©Hala Buck*

To my surprise, in Ottawa, I encountered a somewhat overt but polite prejudice. The first time was when I agreed to do a lecture on Adlerian parenting for the P.T.A. Mrs. Smith was warm and friendly over the phone as we worked out details. When I showed up for the meeting early, she walked up to me. "Yes, can I help you?" she asked in a polite, but icy way. "Yes, I'm Mrs. Buck, I'm giving a talk for you today." "Oh!" was all she said, but her body language was more obvious; it had registered a shock. Somehow, Mrs. Buck, the American, was not supposed to look like me.

Another time, I was at a neighborhood coffee shop. The server was very engaging and friendly with the customer before me. But that changed when it was my turn. I had several similar encounters in which people were very polite, but the temperature in the room would suddenly drop. I thought I was imagining things or becoming too sensitive. I couldn't put my finger on it, which made it more maddening.

Finally, at a diplomatic wives' party I put the question out. Addressing specifically those spouses who were "visibly different," as Canadians say, I asked, "Have any of you felt some form of prejudice since you arrived here?" No one spoke. "Please," I added. "I need to know, otherwise I think I'm going crazy." Suddenly several of the spouses opened up. One was the wife of a Far East ambassador who was out shopping with her counterpart from the German embassy. The German spouse purchased something and both were taken aback when the salesperson handed the package to the Far East spouse, assuming she must be the maid. Other stories emerged that validated what I had been experiencing. It goes to show that prejudice is a universal, built-in fault line in human beings. What was hard was that I experienced prejudice both as a "visible minority" *and* as an American, because some Canadians openly say that Americans are racist.

I remembered before we left for Ottawa we were "briefed" about our new posting at the Overseas Briefing Center. A Canadian expert explained the differences between the United States and Canada. Most Americans, even today, see Canadians as just northern Americans who add an "eh" at the end of each sentence. Canadians, of course, bristle at this and see themselves as a separate and sovereign entity. "Canadians," he said, "distinguish themselves from their powerful southern neighbors by how they define themselves as *not* Americans. Instead of seeing their multicultural identity as a melting pot like in the United States, they prefer the metaphor of a mosaic, which honors the diversity of its population. In that spirit, the Canadian government provides support to the different ethnic groups to promote their own culture, to set up their own TV station, for example, or whatever else they choose."

I raised my hand. "I have a problem with that metaphor. As an artist, I grant you that a mosaic is a beautiful object, but if you think about it, every piece of mosaic is glued in place and surrounded by grout, hence it is hard for it to move out of its place. While a country is a living, breathing, dynamic, and evolving reality. Doesn't that keep people in their cultural ghettos so to speak? I grant you I don't like our American "melting pot" reference either, because it requires that one shed one's identity completely and dive into that pot. I myself prefer to see us Americans as a great salad, where the different ingredients maintain their essence but become part of and contribute to the whole." It wasn't the most diplomatic thing to say, but it was a gut reaction.

Throughout our tour in Ottawa, I was surprised how often I had to defend the United States against anti-American sentiments; they were much more common than during any of our postings in the Middle East. Fear of "cultural Americanization" is found in many countries around the world, especially with globalization ascendant. I think the difference was that during our postings in the Arab World, people might have been angry with our foreign policy, especially our one-sided support of Israel, but they could separate that from how they felt about the American people. Often that was not so in Canada. Another difference between the intrinsic characters of the United States and Canada is that the United States was born out of a revolution, while Canada was not. It remains a federal parliamentary democracy and a constitutional monarchy, with Queen Elizabeth II as head of state. Canadian playwright Denison sums it up: "Americans are benevolently ignorant about Canada, whereas Canadians are malevolently informed about the United States." "In its most extreme form, Canadian suspicion of the United States has led to outbreaks of overt anti-Americanism, usually spilling over against American residents in Canada."[48]

I think the countries' geographical proximity plays a role; as Pierre Trudeau, former Canadian prime minister and father of the current prime minister, suggested, being the United States's neighbor was like sleeping next to an elephant. Every time the elephant moved it felt threatening.

Our tour in Canada was coming to an end. All three of us loved being there and loved the friends we made. Besides my having a productive and fulfilling art career in Ottawa, Katie and I took tap dancing lessons. She was more adept at remembering all the steps, but I thoroughly enjoyed it. I guess it reminded me of my childhood.

Since we were returning to Washington, D.C., where I had escaped an attack at knifepoint in 1972, I convinced Katie, now a teenager, to take a women's self-defense class with me. Girls and women of all ages were in the class. By the end of the training, for our "graduation" we had to free ourselves from the staged "attack" by a policeman in protective gear pretending to be an assailant. Each of us had to pass the course's final "test." Each woman had to break a piece of 9"-by-6" wood on which she had written her name. We had to use one hand in one swift karate chop, as we were taught. I was the last one to do that. I didn't think I could do it. I was scared I would damage my "art-making" hand. Finally after everyone else successfully did it, I gathered my courage and broke my piece. It was empowering and fun. Katie and I still have those pieces of wood. It reminds us that we can defend ourselves. I think every girl and woman should take such a class.

We carry very happy memories of Ottawa, and found Canadians generally gentle and reserved—at least in Ontario. Back in the United States, Steve and I cringe when we watch the weather channel, which never includes Canada in its broadcast. Canada is seen only as this large blank mass north of the border, seemingly without weather except when the "cold Canadian front" is affecting us. No wonder the Canadians feel miffed. Steve and I have found that, as usual, people in other countries know a lot more about the United States than we know about their countries.

Life in the Foreign Service

The high cross-cultural mobility of the Foreign Service may not be for everyone, but it suited our family. For those times when life seemed overwhelming or dangerous, art and solitude helped me find my center, drawing on it to create home for us time and time again.

But by the end of Steve's career, I had developed a love/hate relationship with the Foreign Service. On the one hand, I enjoyed traveling, getting to know people in different countries, shedding my reserve, and developing close friendships. But I came to dread the constant uprooting. There were also the difficulties of living abroad. Back on our first tour in Aden, the Indian doctor I went to misdiagnosed a serious infection as food poisoning. Luckily, there was a Yemeni doctor who had trained in the United States, who diagnosed my condition correctly and gave me the right antibiotics. The State Department Medical unit in Washington D.C. was very good, but it was for life-threatening situations only. At most hardship posts we were in there was no equivalent to 911 or a Rescue Squad. As a result, when we were on "home leave" I took CPR training and all the First Aid courses I could find. I had to be my family's "first emergency responder." I read up on field medicine to the extent that even now, when a doctor first meets me or I question a decision, he may well ask me if I am a nurse.

I hated the dangers of scorpions, vipers, and sea snakes in Oman. That's where I learned to plug-up all the drains, to construct barriers that kept small vipers from slithering under the outside doors, and to be constantly alert for scorpions, which were potentially deadly to little kids. When Katie learned to walk and would get up at night, I would immediately be on the alert: I'd switch on the lights, quickly check the floors for any scorpions and then, not wanting to alarm her, nonchalantly kiss her goodnight. I learned to never have bedding that touched the floor so they couldn't climb up onto beds; people we knew had been stung by scorpions that way. I was taking no chances with my family. I read a lot about keeping yourself and your family healthy, even in stressful situations.

We did have a resident nurse at some of the posts, and U.S. regional doctors, but at hardship posts, local medical care was spotty, so I learned to always be on my toes. When we were trying to get pregnant, I was sent from Mauritania to our military base hospital in El Torrejon, Spain. Because I was early I was ushered in before the first patient arrived. I questioned whether the results they gave me ("you'll never have children") could have been switched with that patient. When I raised that possibility the doctor and nurses were irritated and angry—at me! Years later my gynecologist in Beirut, who knew my history, confirmed my suspicion and with another test diagnosed the correct problem. In Muscat, Katie suffered many strepthroat infections, so I became very familiar with the antibiotics she needed. One time, the local British doctor, who was known to like his Scotch, gave me a prescription for another antibiotic, which I knew from my readings was for staph infections. So I went back to his office and told him. He was irate, but as it turned out, had mixed up patients' files and had prescribed the wrong medicine. All this probably reinforced my childhood distrust of those in authority—doctors included—and deepened my resolve to rely on my own wits.

Yet despite all the drawbacks, the Foreign Service, specifically the Near East Affairs community, was our home and family for thirty-one years. People unfamiliar with the Foreign Service usually think it's all caviar and champagne. What they don't realize is that during our time, that the percentage of Foreign Service officers who die in the line of duty is higher than that of military officers.

By one estimate, just above 30 percent of political appointees under Republican presidents, and barely a quarter under Democratic presidents, are rewarded with ambassadorhips in the "cushy posts," primarily in Western Europe and the Caribbean; and most receive these in return for monetary contributions to presidential campaigns. Only 10 percent of political appointees accept hardship posts.[49] This doesn't help the morale of the dedicated career officers. Funding for the State Department is miniscule compared to the Defense Department, which Steve tells me has more musicians than the Foreign Service has personnel. As a nation we undervalue diplomacy, and there is no lobby to support the State Department.

Speaking the language of the country you're assigned to, being interested and learning about its people, and acting as a bridge between the United States and the host country can make the Foreign

Service a very special career. Swashbuckling may appeal to the average person, but when Americans can present their best face, with respect for others' point of view, we have a better chance that they might respect us in return, and want to emulate us.

I remember growing up how all the beloved institutions that Americans and American missionaries founded, such as my high school A.S.G., and the universities A.U.B. and L.A.U. generated and fostered goodwill and respect for the United States. These were successful institutions because they had been founded with the host culture in mind. People respond positively to respectful and genuine interest from others.

If you don't discover the shelter of belonging within your life, you could become a victim and target for your longing, pulled hither and thither without any anchorage anywhere.
—John O'Donohue [50]

4

Bridging Worlds—
Parenting "Third Culture Kids"

Home is not a place or a space or a condition. Home is a way of being, deeply connected to your heart's wisdom and guidance.
—Paula Reeves[51]

Dawning Realization

It was in Mauritania that I received the first inkling that I could translate not only words and meanings, but also the reasons for behavior and customs. I had been hired to interpret for a New York lawyer, Richard, who was negotiating an oil concession in Mauritania. At one of our early meetings we were ushered into the Minister of Economy's office. It was a large, sunny room, with overstuffed armchairs, a portrait of the president on prominent display, a large variety of dates pleasantly arranged on a silver tray (there are more than one hundred different types of dates in the Arab world), a box of Kleenex, a large ashtray, and a black rotary phone to the right of the minister.

I sat between Richard and the minister, simultaneously translating the conversation, while the minister's aide sat to his left. As we sipped the three customary cups of mint tea—each less sweet than the last—I could sense Richard's mounting frustration. I noticed his body tensing, his nostrils flaring, and a hissing sound emerging through his gritted teeth: "*Schtupid, usheless, wayshte of prechious time!*" I could tell from the minister's frown and body language that he was not too happy with Richard's mounting impatience and rudeness. Civility and politeness is a strong value in Arab culture. Even if you do not like a person, it's bad manners to be disrespectful or show rudeness.

So, I excused us, stepped outside and asked, "Richard do you want this concession?" "Well of course I do. But this stupid stuff is driving me crazy. What kind of business meeting is this, sipping tea and chit-chatting?" Without thinking I answered, "This is a nomadic culture Richard; they don't have lawyers. They settle disputes by appealing to their council of elders. This is not a "task-focused" culture; it's people-focused, because the emphasis is on nurturing the relationships that help you do a job. My guess is the tradition of the three cups of tea gives them a chance to get to know you, determine whether they trust you, like you, and therefore could do business with you. This is not New York, Richard. Their "stupid" traditions, as you call them, make perfect sense from their point of view. And I can tell you that right now they are not too pleased with you!"

"Wow," he said, scratching his head, his eyes wide open. After a long, deep breath he said, "I never thought of it that way. What should we do now?" "Remember to be respectful, to enjoy the tea and know these people are not your inferiors."

He did that, and won the concession. And I realized I could instinctively understand both the American and Arab culture, which opened the way to becoming a cross-cultural educator. I heard Richard died of a heart attack a few years later. Maybe poor Richard should have learned to relax and enjoy sipping tea.

Years later I would use "the lawyer story" to illustrate how entrenched we can become in our own world view, believing, *assuming,* that our way of working, living, loving, and relating to others is not only the best, but the *only* way.

"No one culture has all the right answers. Each culture has traditions and values that work for its people," I tell those I'm working with. "When it stops working, the culture changes."

A "Human Bridge"

Twenty years after Mauritania, in Ottawa, a huge fragment of my identity crystallized. In 1991, I was preparing a one-woman art show. As I gathered my watercolors, now framed and ready to go to the gallery, I was surprised by how many bridges—more than half of my inventory—I had painted over that past year. True, Ottawa has many beautiful bridges, my favorite being the Minto Bridges. But did beauty and abundance explain why I painted so many bridges?

As I composed a few words for the local paper, I tried to make sense of the realization that there was something deeper at work. From then on, "bridge" denoted more than just a subject matter for my paintings. Bridge became a metaphor, a foundational image that recurred in my life and consciousness, and always brought inspiration. It was essential to my journey of self-discovery.

I entitled the show "Bridges and Beyond." During an interview with the paper's art critic, I said, "Each captured moment I paint is my way of putting down roots and connecting in the transient lifestyle of a diplomat's spouse."

For a long time I reflected on what I had said in that interview. I began to think of bridges in their essence: as structures that connect land with land, which span over water and chasms, and enable crossings. The bridge became more than just a means of connection; it took shape as a metaphor for myself. I had become a *human* bridge, who straddled religions and cultures and helped others to cross between them as well.

It had taken fifty years, but at last I began to consciously understand what it means to be a human bridge. Human bridges live in *and* in between cultures. We are the immigrants who cross oceans and continents seeking a new life; people in cross-cultural marriages and their children; and children of immigrants, or of intercultural adoption. We span languages and traditions, race and religion. Among us are "military brats," "Third Culture Kids" (TCKs), TCK Adults (ATCKs), "Cross-Cultural Kids" (CCKs), and adults who grow up in an international and/or mobile lifestyle. Our numbers even include children of divorce. We do not just straddle cultures through circumstance. We have the natural potential to be connectors and integrators. This ability to live in between is often born of a painful, challenging necessity. But it is also an enriching responsibility, and our journeys involve many crossings.

Bridges across rivers and waterways don't appear out of thin air, but are built block by block, steel cable by steel cable. So, which experiences shaped my sense as a connector, and provided the foundation of my human bridge? More importantly, how did my child-self interpret and use these experiences? What unconscious and conscious decisions did this little girl make about life, and her place in it? And what lessons might that journey have for my own family, and others struggling to navigate multiple worlds?

When I first began to share this metaphor with friends and colleagues, many asked, "What do you mean by 'human bridge'?" But those of mixed heritages, or who had lived in many different places "got it" immediately, and even responded with, "Oh my God, that's exactly what I am, too!" Now I see and hear the word "bridge" being used metaphorically in so many conversations and settings, and I find myself smiling.

Why do I sometimes refer to myself as Lebanese-Arab-American? And do the hyphens connect, or separate? On the one hand, these three words define who I am, my roots. I was born and raised in Lebanon and feel Lebanese at my core. On the other hand, I am also an Arab by virtue of speaking Arabic and having similar cultural values such as the centrality of family and hospitality. I feel it is important to emphasize that the Arab world is not monolithic as many believe. "Arab" represents deep religious and ethnic diversity, and many different dialects, topography, and climates. What Arabs have in common is a rich, classical written language, distinctive poetry and literature and, in some cases, a shared history. And yet, the word can never encompass the whole of my Lebanese identity, and certainly my American-ness has its own, distinctive essence. All three words are needed to describe the many aspects of my childhood origins, and the adult I became.

I wish I could have read Amin Maalouf's *In the Name of Identity* much earlier in life (it was published in 1998). An award-winning Lebanese writer living in France, Maalouf writes about how he is poised between two countries, several languages, and cultural traditions, and that this is precisely what defines his identity.[52] You cannot compartmentalize identity, nor divide it into halves or thirds, he argues. You just have one identity made up of all these components, which creates the unique individual that you are.[53]

When I first came across Maalouf's words, I felt like I had come home. Here was someone like me, whose complex identity straddles languages, ethnicities, and religions, someone who, thanks to that reality has a special role to play in forging links, eliminating misunderstandings. In short, here is another person who bridges cultures.

While in therapy in my forties and fifties, I began excavating childhood memories. The confrontation with the priest from so long ago surfaced. Suddenly, things started to make sense. I had been carrying the pain caused by my first encounter with prejudice and ignorance for a long time. I now understood how that experience unconsciously triggered confusion and damaged my sense of wholeness and okay-ness, and made me conscious of how people outside my family perceived me. This early memory explained the rage I always felt when I encountered injustice, intolerance, discrimination, cruelty, and religious fanaticism of any kind, anywhere. It is why I continue to feel so compelled to speak out, to write this book, to help people see each other with the eyes of compassion and common humanity. As I slowly sorted through the painful debris from the path I had been following, I could see how I had turned the stumbling blocks of my childhood into building blocks for my bridge. I realized that I was born to make many crossings and teach others to do the same.

The harder feelings, the anger and resentment, had given me audacious courage, which could erupt in many situations. In Baghdad, thirty-four years after the priest confronted me. I was by myself in a pavilion at the Baghdad International Fair. It was held in the lovely public garden and showcased crafts from many countries from around the world. Steve had gone to put some baskets we'd bought in the car when two Mercedes sedans suddenly screeched to a halt in front of the pavilion. Soldiers jumped out and rushed in. Tapping me roughly on the shoulder, one of them barked: "Out!" "What?" I said angrily. Turning to what I guessed was their lieutenant I said, "How dare you come in here and order me or anyone else around like that." I could see that some minister was waiting in the car. "I see you have the minister with you and you may be concerned with security. You could have asked me politely, 'Please madam would you mind stepping outside for a few minutes.'"

The guard was speechless. He couldn't know that I was the wife of an American diplomat; I guess he assumed, from my looks, that I was Iraqi. But no Iraqi would have stood up to him. The poor pavilion manager was pleading, "Please madam, leave!" I realized I was endangering her, but I was still furious.

"You should not let them treat you this way," I said as I stepped outside. Not used to being challenged, the soldiers did not know what to do. I was lucky I wasn't carted off to prison. One did not argue with Saddam's "security" squads.

Being a human bridge provided me with amazing opportunities to create connections and help others do the same. Connecting people with each other was easy, natural, helpful, and kept the submerged pain I carried at bay. But this came at a cost: I became trapped inside my bridge identity, inside what Tara Brach calls our invisible "spacesuit," or "small self."[54] Katie shook me up when one day she said, "I don't want, nor need, to see myself as a bridge because people walk over you." It was interesting that although I always felt I didn't fully fit in anywhere, I had never felt I was being "walked upon." Perhaps my rebellious streak helped in that regard.

As I thought about my readiness to help people cross over to the "other," the idea of a bridge as a static thing, stretched to the limit, spanning chasms, began to change. I made several quick exploratory art therapy images. Then I had an "aha" moment: I realized I was also a bridge "builder," not just a means for people to reach across divides within themselves and with the outside world. I didn't need to be stuck in the middle of anything! The bridge was me and became something distinct from me, something I too could use to move back and forth. Even as I provided connection, the bridge would still be there for me—a viable and inviting link to whatever place or person I chose.

46. "Emerging Essence."
Colored pencils ©Hala Buck

47. "I am the Bridge." *Colored pencils ©Hala Buck*

"I Am the Bridge"

This bridge was built out of every piece of my life;
the painful and sad, the joyful and good.

I never realized it was being built
until one day I stood at its center,
and all the way around, I could see clearly.

The sun and the moon create a sacred glow
through the arches of my bridge.
They reach out, flooding me with their light.

Out of the rock of my whole being
I emerged
after all the debris was chipped off.

That colorful essence hidden in the rock
provided the building blocks
of this living bridge that is my life.

I stand, arms outstretched like a butterfly
another transformation has taken place,
I shout to the world, here I am!

I am finally whole!
And with that
I begin my next journey.

Parenting "Third Culture Kids"

When I left Lebanon as a bride to follow Steve, I did not fully realize that I was saying a permanent farewell to everything that had
been important in my life: parents, family, friends, familiar places,
the sea, weather, food, and a sense of home. Except for a short stay
after we were evacuated from Aden and a visit in the early 1970s,
I was away from Lebanon for twenty-five years. During that time,
there was a civil war, my beloved Teta Habouba died, and cousins
I had known as children started families of their own. During my
thirty-one years in the Foreign Service, I would taste the bitterness
international and mobile families experience when they must say
goodbye, over and over again.

From the minute our daughter Katie was born, I became very
aware that her life journey would be even more complicated than
mine. That was an alarming thought. I didn't want her to feel she
was an outsider or different just because of our lifestyle. My parents
had emigrated to the United States, and Tante Paulette came to visit
us when she could, but otherwise we had no face-to-face contact
with my extended Lebanese family for the first two decades of Katie's life.

People focus on the "perks" and glamour of diplomatic life and
gloss over the challenges. One of the most difficult is raising children in a nomadic, intercultural life. It is part of diplomatic life to
keep crossing back and forth between one's culture and the one
you are learning and reporting about. For a foreign-born spouse,
this constant crossing over happens not only in social settings, but
in one's marriage as well. In a cross-cultural marriage, you both are
very aware of things to negotiate and differences to work through.
I probably had to do more crossing over than Steve. Not only had

I been born in another country, I had to learn how to represent *Ameyrka* and be a credible spokesperson for its values. Negotiating, and openly talking about those values (which are not often part of our conscious awareness), was crucial to our cross-cultural marriage. It became more necessary after our daughter was born. We gave her a name from each: Kathryn Leila, a name that reflected an identity even more complicated than mine. After all, I was a mix of Christian and Muslim culture to begin with; and her dad's white Anglo-Saxon Protestant background added another dimension of complexity. Moreover, we knew our Foreign Service journey, with its many immersions into new countries and cultures, would make Kathryn Leila's identity yet more kaleidoscopic. Ours was a globally transcultural family, full of richness, complexity and, at times, confusion and hardship.

In the 1970s and early 1980s, the State Department did not pay much attention to the effect of such a lifestyle on families. Katie is a "Third Culture Kid," (TCK) a term coined by Drs. John and Ruth Hill Useem, both sociologists and anthropologists. The original description is of children and adults who, due to a parent's job, have spent "a significant part of their developmental years outside the parents' culture." Thus, a "...TCK builds relationships to all of the cultures, while not having full ownership in any."[55] TCKs' sense of belonging is in relationship to "...others of similar background."[56] They lead "...ordinary lives lived in extraordinary circumstances,"[57] and as the late Norma McCaig used to say, not in any one, specific geographic location.[58] Adult TCKs (ATCKs) tend to incorporate elements from each culture into their life experience. They are not rootless, but rather are rooted in relationship with their nuclear family and with other people. Furthermore, Katie was a CCK, because she was the child of a cross-cultural marriage.

More recently, the term "third culture" has come to be a "...generic term to discuss the *lifestyle* created, shared and learned by those who are from one culture and are in the process of relating to another one."[59] TCKs develop the ability to walk in others' shoes. Most are risk-takers, yearn for adventure, and are very loyal to friends.[60] As a foreign-born Foreign Service spouse, I found I had a natural identification with ATCKs and their issues.

Before the Overseas Briefing Center and Family Liaison Office were created, my way of handling anything had always involved a lot of research and talking to other people. I interviewed Foreign Service kids so I could parent Katie in a way that minimized the painful aspects of her reality. I especially remember one Foreign Service teen I interviewed about growing up in this lifestyle. "What was helpful and what do you wish your parents had done differently?" I asked him. "I was very miserable at the French school in Paris. We lived in a different part of the city, so I had no one to play with and the French kids were not friendly," he replied. "So why didn't you tell your parents?" I asked. "I couldn't tell them! They thought this would be a wonderful experience for me. They were so excited." His parents never knew of this young man's unhappy years in Paris.

In Oman, I enrolled Katie in a small nursery group run by a British expat. Because she was an only child, I thought it helpful to mix her in with other children her age. Besides, almost all kids her age were in some form of pre-kindergarten. When Katie was having a tough time adjusting and being separated from me, I used her Fisher-Price school set to enact what happens after I drop her off and to reassure her that I would return to pick her up. She would have the "mommy" figure take the little girl to school and then come back to pick her up at noon. That did the trick. Today we would call that play therapy.

We were in an unusual situation because we served mostly in the Middle East, where the culture is similar, but not the same as the one in which I grew up. It was natural for me to speak and read to Katie in Arabic, French, and English. That's typical in Lebanon. Before Katie started kindergarten at the British Muscat English Speaking School (M.E.S.S) in Muscat, Steve had suggested we send her to a local Omani school. I checked it out. I didn't like the way the kids were disciplined. Remembering the story of the young TCK in Paris, we finally decided to send Katie to M.E.S.S, where her friend Emily was. After she had been there for a week or more, she came home one day, and in response to something I said to her, planted her feet firmly on the ground, hands on her hips and faced me: "Speak to me mommy, don't talk to me!" At first I did not understand what she meant, but eventually I realized she had the same reaction every time I spoke Arabic to her. I deciphered it to mean that she wanted me to speak only English.

In retrospect, I should have sat down with Katie and asked her what happened at school that made her not want to speak Arabic. Did kids make fun of her? Sadly, I didn't. I was confused and did not have the parenting skills to inquire about what had happened to trigger that reaction. I recall vividly what went through my mind: "My poor child, she is so angry and scared. In this mobile life, above all else I want her to feel secure, grounded, and to have a sense of belonging. If that means she will not speak my native language, then so be it." I had no family nearby, nor any counselor to ask for advice. Our "family" was the Near East bureau of Foreign Service officers and their families. Steve tried hard, but he could never fully understand the challenges of Foreign Service life for Katie and me. Nor could he perceive the learning curve I encountered in adapting to American lifestyle, or how difficult it was to do this while trying to maintain my identity. We now know from the literature that parents of TCKs, unless they themselves are also global nomads, can never fully understand the impact on their children.

And so, though I probably hesitated and backtracked at first, I stopped speaking Arabic to Katie. It was a defining decision for her and for me, the impact of which I wouldn't understand for sixteen years. I did cheat a little, kept some baby words that use the hard sounds of Lebanese Arabic that are difficult to discern and learn later, such as *bahh*, meaning "gone," *dahh*, meaning "nice," and *kokh*, meaning "bad" or "dirty." She also watched *Iftah ya Sim Sim* (Open Sesame), the Arabic version of Sesame Street in Arabic. I kept some of the Arabic children books, but they didn't interest her. Back then, they were not as attractive as the ones in English or even French.

In 1999, we flew from Saudi Arabia for Katie's senior performance at Wesleyan University. For her senior project as a theater major, she had written and was performing a one-woman show entitled "I-Site." The word itself is a play on a sense of place and identity. It was a gathering of vignettes from her experiences in the Foreign Service and as a cross-cultural person. Sitting in the darkened auditorium, we had no idea of what would unfold. When she played the scene from so long ago about not wanting me to speak Arabic I suddenly burst into tears. In that instant I realized, for the first time, what both of us had given up. Wanting to minimize the difficulties of a nomadic lifestyle for my daughter, I had sacrificed a connection with her that could not exist without her knowing my native language. I had deprived her of a link to half her heritage. There was a part of me, her *teta* and her *jeddo*, that she could never fully understand. She spoke French, Spanish, and English, but had never learned Arabic. She had lived in three Arab posts with us, but never in Lebanon.

It was validating and comforting to me when, in that same play, she talked fondly of the smells of the souk, the anise, and the *hala-wa*. I never thought she would remember, let alone appreciate those elements of the Middle East that appeal to the senses. Since then, Katie has performed "I-Site" across the United States, in Europe, and in China. It was later published in an anthology, *Four Arab American Plays.*[61] Even now, almost two decades later, I run into people who tell me, "Oh, you're Katie's mom. I remember so well her play. It really resonated for my family and me. We could really identify with her story." That's the gift of sharing our stories.

Before leaving a post, in the days of snail mail and diplomatic pouch, I would prepare stamped envelopes with our U.S. address on them to give to Katie's friends, so they could stay in touch. It must be much easier now with social media and the Internet. We also prepared together a "Goodbye House" book with photos and pressed flowers from the garden to honor the transition and allow some closure. The sudden rupture of friendships, the uprooting from home, school, and all that was familiar usually leaves TCKs angry and sad. As a Foreign Service parent, I felt responsible for each goodbye Katie had to say. Each friendship came with a clock that ticked down to a moment in which everything in her life changed, and this repeated every few years. The unfinished grieving and a loathing of packing and of over-packing built up through each post.

But I also knew that the rewards of our lifestyle were amazing. Katie is compassionate, creative, and adaptable—a true citizen of the world, an adult with a broad base of knowledge and wisdom culled from real experiences. Other benefits for TCKs, as the late Norma McCaig pointed out, are confidence, trust in change, and a sensitivity and empathy that helps them respond to world events in emotionally heightened ways.

I did my best to stay ahead of the obstacles, while juggling the never-ending, unrecognized duties of a Foreign Service spouse while Steve rode up the ladder of his career. Like other Foreign Service families in the era of intercontinental flights, we found ourselves with no transition time to review the life we just left. In one plane ride, we had to get ready to start over again in a new place, when we had not yet finished the process of leaving and grieving the multiple losses of the most recent transfer.

Rereading the book on TCKs, I came across the "Coming Home: Reentry" chapter. I was reminded that most globally mobile families, and especially TCKs, expect to come home and fit right into a place where they and their peers look and think alike. People in the "home culture" and TCKs all expect to be in the "mirror box" where we look and think alike.[62] This is what Pollock and van Reken refer to as the "hidden immigrant" reality. TCKs and their peers at home might look alike, but they think and act differently. One would expect this difference in a "foreigner," but not from one's own countrywoman.

When Katie and I were evacuated from Oman to Washington D.C. in 1979, my mom was working at Geico and took Katie, age three, to her office. When they went to get something to drink from the vending machine, our TCK daughter squealed with delight as the cup dropped and whatever beverage she selected was poured. "Look, look *teta*, someone's pouring the 7Up!" She wanted to see who was hiding behind the machine. Mom was embarrassed. Her co-workers were shocked by Katie's ignorance. How could Katie never have seen a vending machine before? She looked like an American kid: wasn't she one?

When Katie was born, because of my history and my own experience of feeling like an outsider, I knew she would need help to overcome confusion and feelings of rootlessness. Steve and I had signed on to this globally mobile life; but for Katie, it was never a choice. For this child of a mixed marriage it was even more complicated. Since Lebanon was in flames during most of her growing up years, we could not visit and have her know that part of her cultural heritage. Lebanon's civil war was deemed too dangerous for any visit, especially by a U.S. diplomat's family. We were fortunate because my parents, at least, had immigrated to the United States. So on home leave in Washington, Katie was able to hear some Lebanese Arabic mixed in with French and English, and experience the food and mindset. Home leave time with extended family is very important to a child for whom "home" is so fleeting. Katie called my parents *teta* and *jeddo*, and her other grandparents *grandpa* and *grandma*. There was little confusion on that front for her. She navigated both worlds effortlessly.

For TCKs "home" is a complex and tricky word. For the time they are at post they feel that *that* is home, because that is where the nuclear family lives. Katie was four years old when we went on home leave to the United States. Whenever people asked her where she was from she would say, "I'm Omani." "No sweetheart," I would jump in, "you're American." She seemed confused. "But Mummy, we visit *teta* and *jeddo* and grandma and grandpa but then we have to go back to Oman. So I'm Omani!" Another time in Muscat, after a Lebanese friend's visit, Katie asked, "Who was the little girl with Najat?" "Her niece," I answered. A little puzzled frown, a tilt of the head, and then a little voice said, "But mummy, can you live in the same place as your family?" "Why of course sweetheart, did you think we couldn't?" "But mummy, when we go to Washington to visit *teta* and *jeddo* and everyone, then we have to leave!" Despite all my efforts to create continuity with our own family traditions, I realized that a child draws her own conclusions about what she experiences and observes.

At that point Steve and I decided it was time to request a Washington assignment. Katie was too confused to know something that Steve and I took for granted. These temporary "homes" were not where we really belonged. For Katie, it was a more complicated concept. She had made her own assumption using the logic of a child. At every transition point in the lives of TCKs, they find themselves re-negotiating this ensuing closeness.

My sense of belonging may not have been very solid, but for Leila "home" was even more fleeting, based on the "familiarity of constant change and an uncharted future."[63] Unlike TCKs, my original community in Lebanon did not move when I did. It was there for me to dip back into, except during the civil war years. Marrying a foreigner and following him around the world was a choice I made. Katie and I may share the fact that we are of mixed heritage, but she did not have the continuity and security of growing up in one place during her childhood. I had issues around not fully belonging anywhere. I had opted to be okay with my reality, but I couldn't begin to understand Katie's constant search to fit into every group she encountered in her life. It was left up to me, I thought, to be her roots, to provide the safety and stability that our Foreign Service life could not provide. Our "tent" alone had to pick up stakes and move on every couple of years, and we had little control over those conditions. The only constant—and hence security—she knew was the closeness of our small nuclear family. Openly sharing our feelings would later seem weird to her teenage American friends. I struggled to balance being the "American" mom, the "Lebanese" mom, and the "Foreign Service" mom. Both Katie and I have a yearning for full belonging, and we each are still learning how to navigate our reality without this yearning becoming the unconscious "pilot" in our lives.

> The nature of belonging, for those not born to it,
> is that it must be found over and over again.
> —Mary Edwards Wertsch[64]

Reentry—Back in Washington D.C.

In 1983 we were assigned back to Washington, D.C. Once more we unpacked quickly and set up the house. The first or second Sunday after we arrived, Steve had just finished setting up our hi-fi (high fidelity tape recorder and receiver) and put on our favorite classical tape. Suddenly, we heard Katie rushing down the stairs all excited. "Friday morning music," she squealed with delight.

Let me explain. In all Muslim countries, the day of rest is Friday, not Sunday. So our Fridays were days off, and that's when we played one of Bach's Brandenburg concertos. We did not realize that for Katie, hearing that familiar music put the finishing touch on "home." This is one of the quirks one finds in Foreign Service life.

As for schooling, I insisted we look for a private school for Katie that went from Kindergarten all the way to high school. This would avoid disruptive transitions for her when we were back in the United States. With all the upheavals in her education and life, it seemed like a good idea to stick to one school. We chose Sidwell Friends for several reasons. We liked the Quaker values, the weekly queries incorporated into the curriculum, and their openness to the world. It was the best decision we made for her. It provided Katie with familiar faces, a progressive teaching style, and life-long friendships that endured even as we hopped in and out of Washington on assignments. Still, for the first few months, Katie would come home somewhat distraught. She liked Sidwell, the teachers and the kids, but she missed her first best friend Emily. "I can't find another Emily!" she would cry.

Eventually Sidwell became an anchor not only for Katie, but for us as well. I volunteered in the parents' association and became part of the community. For twenty years, a group of parents, our kids, and later grandkids would meet the Saturday after Thanksgiving. The fact that we would periodically leave the United States for another posting and then return a few years later did not preclude those friendships.

Being back in Washington, D.C. for a home tour also meant that Katie had the opportunity to develop close ties with both sets of grandparents. We would also visit the rest of Steve's family scattered around the United States. Unfortunately, our transient life and ongoing travel restrictions meant Katie still could not meet her Lebanese cousins.

Challenges and Opportunities

Despite the hardships, our mobility has enabled Leila to experience different cultures and belief systems. It has enriched her life, it has made her resilient, able to adjust quickly, learn languages easily, and use the treasure trove of stories to pursue her artistic dreams. It has given her, like other TCKs, a leg up in a more global, interdependent, and cross-cultural world. She uses her flexible, open-minded, and open-hearted world view to help people connect through her playwriting, storytelling, performing, and teaching.

During the Gulf War in 1991, Katie came home from Sidwell Friends and reported, "During Quaker Meeting today, the Gulf War came up. I was moved to speak and I said, 'as a Lebanese-American...'" I almost interrupted her to say, "But you're not..." I realized, suddenly, "My God, Katie *is* Lebanese-American." I had worked so hard at helping her feel at home in the United States that even I had forgotten that at her essence she will always be a human bridge. This sudden affirmation of her mixed origins had emerged as if out of the fog of war.

The short Gulf War in 1990 to liberate Kuwait was the first U.S. military incursion into the Arab world. Until then, the United States had never been considered in the same vein as European colonizers. Defending Kuwait was well received in the Arab World; certainly the Kuwaitis were very grateful. George H.W. Bush was smart enough to know that continuing on to Baghdad would have opened up a can of worms. His son George W. Bush never understood that. In the 2003 invasion of Iraq, Americans turned on the TV and watched what looked like a Nintendo game with sound and light. But for us, the bombing of Baghdad's Al-Mansoor district brought up images of a real neighborhood where we had lived, of real people, like the kind family who found and rescued and pampered our dog when she escaped from our garden.

I believe that as the world shrinks in this age of instant communication, we all are struggling to learn how to live with mutual respect and peace with others. As huge distances between nations and cultures are now crossed with the click of a mouse or slide of a finger. Instantly we and they appear in our respective offices, homes, laps, or hand. Not everybody is ready to handle such change, but TCKs, ATCKs, and CCKs are well-suited for this new frontier.

For TCKs, home is defined by relationships, therefore "home" usually is "everywhere and nowhere."[65] They assimilate elements from each culture they have lived in while having the ability to "… view the world whole."[66] As "global nomads," they have a heightened sensitivity to injustice, intolerance, prejudice, the pain of others, and even plain miscommunication. This is what makes ATCKs so passionate, so compassionate, and at times so angry and impatient with others who are unable or unwilling to step into another person's shoes. They wear this "differentness" like a badge, resisting anything that threatens the uniqueness of their life.

Foreign Service life was not only about challenges. The fun and enriching aspects of our nomadic life came from the constant adventure and hands-on learning. On our first Christmas in Mauritania, which is mostly desert, trees were extremely rare. To everyone's delight, the local director of Middle East Airline, a Lebanese company, surprised us by flying in live Christmas trees from Lebanon. I made ornaments with whatever I could find, such as colorful key chains and paper flowers I creatd from crêpe paper. Voila! Christmas in West Africa. In Kuwait, I found beautifully embroidered little Chinese horses that I strung up on our artificial white tree. Thus was born a new tradition for the Bucks. Henceforth, I added a new animal to our tree from every post we lived in and each country we visited. Our Christmas ornaments, like my paintings, are part of our portable history. Each object holds a special memory of people and places. It might just be a horse made of straw we picked up in Thailand, or a miniature carousel horse from Washington that reminded Katie of the fun rides at Glen Echo. Decorating the tree at Christmas in our house is setting up the Buck's ATCK zoo.

Like other Foreign Service families, we were adept at setting up home quickly. The "sacred objects" that brought a sense of normality to our life were unpacked as soon as they arrived, and I immediately hung my paintings on the bare walls. In a few days it looked as if we had lived in the new house for years. It was crucial to create "home" quickly, because time was always limited and unpredictable. The sanctuary of familiar objects were not a luxury but a necessity critical to providing, as best as we could, a secure sense of continuity and belonging for all of us, and Katie especially.

TCKs with transient childhoods tend to mature quickly in some ways because they see and experience so much: different worldviews, poverty, even wars. However, the constant uprooting does create some backlash. Adult TCKs or ATCKs may develop an "uneven maturity,"[67] which can often manifest later as a delayed adolescence in their late 20s and 30s. Many ATCKs and Global Nomads develop a "move-on" itch—an internal alarm clock that shouts: "URGENT, URGENT it's time to go! Pick up your life and move—change is in the air." It's important when that clock goes off to consciously acknowledge it for what it is and examine if and what needs change in their lives. Any kind of childhood mobility seems to leave a legacy of "restlessness" in the adult TCK. A kind of constant urge to be somewhere else, but with no clear definition of where that place might be.[68]

TCKs are accustomed to adults and therefore savvy around them. When we arrived in Baghdad, the Ambassador and Mrs. Newton arranged a welcome party, to which of course Katie was invited. Even though Katie, age nine, was usually comfortable conversing with people five times her age, that evening these new faces were of no interest to her. I noticed her off in a corner, feverishly writing. Later she showed us the poems she wrote during that cocktail party. They were later published in the Parent Encouragement Program's newsletter in 1987 Spring/summer issue:

"People"
People are mothers striving hard to do their best.
People are doctors and nurses saving lives without rest.
People are teachers with patience and advice.
People are veterinarians, helping cats, dogs and mice.
And people are people, bringing meaning to life.

"Friendship"
Friendship is a special thing.
Friendship is a bond.
Although there are some quarrels,
Good friends will hold right on.
'Cause friendship is a special thing,
and friendship is a bond.

"Feelings"
Feelings of madness, feelings of shame,
Feelings of happiness, victory and fame:
These feeling are special, each one a milestone,
an endless marking of life.

By Kathryn Leila Buck (Age nine)

The hellos and goodbyes of Foreign Service life can be wrenching experiences for children with this kind of awareness. Katie and her first close friend, Emily Field, had watched Santa Claus arriving in a small Omani boat at Christmas; they had spent the special formative years between two and seven together, often camping in *wadis* (riverbeds) with our two families. No wonder she despaired of finding "another Emily" at Sidwell Friends. Later, the partings from her friends in Baghdad were made even more painful by the ongoing reality of the Iran-Iraq War. Her grief gave way to a yearning for connection that she continues to live with as an adult.

Steve, like most in our generation of Foreign Service families, was completely absorbed in his career and duties as a Foreign Service Officer. You arrive and the social whirl of dinners and receptions starts immediately, even though you still have no dependable babysitter and your child needs you. This is where our different cultural norms created tension in our marriage. For Steve, a product of the hyper-individualistic U.S. culture, work and career seemed to always come first. But for me, family was always paramount. So we negotiated the number of dinners and receptions I would attend. He would tell our disappointed hosts that, "Hala as a rule does not go to "stand up" affairs. She wants to make sure Katie keeps her bedtime routine." This raised many an ambassador's wife's eyebrow. One evening, one such wife took me aside and lectured me: "You know my dear, you can hurt your husband's career when you don't come to the receptions." To which I replied, "Tell me, in five, ten, twenty years would anybody care if I did not come to this or that reception? But I can assure you our daughter will remember I was not there for her!"

That settled it. I found out that other governments' embassies pay their spouses a percentage of their husband's salaries in return for their duties. Our Foreign Service spent a lot of time trying to negotiate with Congress for some form of remuneration, even a social security credit. In the '70s, I worked on what was called the "Foreign Service Spouse Survey." It was mostly the "senior" wives who carried the burden and supported this, and we almost had a bill pass before the Gramm-Rudman-Hollings Budget Control Act put a stop to it. Remunerated or not, coming from the culture I came from, I knew where my priorities lay.

I became convinced that a secure sense of self for TCKs depends on a stable and supportive family. The glamorous life of endless dinners and cocktail parties can easily supersede the needs of a Foreign Service TCK. Katie did not have a sibling to accompany her to the first day at a new school, or to play a game with her when mom and dad had to go out. There was no brother or sister to act as a sounding board. In these circumstances, it becomes even more critical for parents to be available to listen and give comfort. One child of overseas missionaries wrote she could not tell her parents what horrible experiences, and even abuse, she experienced at boarding school, because after all, her parents were doing "God's work."[69] The Foreign Service does not claim to have that power, but it comes a close second. How could I complain that I was not happy in Aden, or insist on asking for a posting in Paris, London, or Rome? "The work is not interesting in those posts," Steve would say. "Everything that's important takes place at the highest political level. Besides," he added, "I like Arabs and the Arab World."

The Foreign Service is an enriching experience, but as I said before, it is important to remember that children of such parents did not choose this lifestyle—that they have had no say in where they live or how long they remain. The sequence of their lives is dictated by a larger entity, the State Department, which has its own culture and agenda. Although the employee has some choice in where he's posted, the children really don't. Choice then becomes something Adult TCKs (ATCKs) will probably struggle with later in life; they may have difficulty planning for the future.

As Katie grew up, we discussed this TCK identity to the point that I think she didn't want to hear about it. She refused to join a newly formed TCK teen group, saying it didn't apply to her. At the time, I thought she was just fed up with my focus on it, but now I realize she wasn't rejecting the label out of protest. At some level she knew that her journey was more complicated. The Foreign Service Youth Foundation at the time did not address TCKs and ATCKs of mixed marriages.

By their early twenties, all young people are looking to find their adult selves. For those of mixed cultures it is even more crucial to start gathering the fragments of their cultural identity. Katie was well into examining her own. As a result, she was determined to learn Arabic. So she did, first at the Middle East Institute in Washington, D.C. By not forcing her and making her hate my language, I believe I helped free her to make her own choice. She later spent two summers in Beirut at the Lebanese American University (LAU), learning colloquial Lebanese Arabic and practicing with my very patient family, who would rather have spoken English or French with her.

I believe it is essential that a mixed couple model mutual respect and understanding of each other's cultures, and teach their children about both lineages. We were lucky because Steve was an expert in the Middle East who genuinely liked the people and spoke Arabic. Katie had to find ways of belonging in both Steve's American birth culture and my Lebanese one. The advantage of being a TCK meant that Katie felt she belonged everywhere. The flip side for most TCKs, however, is that belonging can feel tenuous. Besides the question of "where do I belong?," there is the question of "do I *want* to belong, and at what cost?" I have learned in the art therapy workshops I have led with ATCKs and Global Nomads that they hang on tightly to this special identity of being different, because in their mind, they fear that belonging may mean "…invalidating the only past they know."[70] They feel they have left a piece of their history, of themselves, in each of the places they have lived.

Trying to recapture those memories by going back to those places doesn't quite work. The people you knew are long gone, the country has changed, and even local friends have moved on. It's like Alan Jay Lerner's Brigadoon, a place lost in the fog of time. The only post where our family was able to revisit and rekindle memories and friendships was Canada, because we were never far away. I loved our three years in Ottawa and all three of us were sad when we were transferred. I remember as we drove away from our house in New Edinburgh, each of us had tears in our eyes. But just a few years later we went back to visit friends; we took time to walk along Stanley Avenue and the Minto Bridges across the Rideau River I had painted so often. We stopped in the stores we used to shop at. We could really say a loving goodbye to this part of our life without the heavy heart and tears. It brought closure in some way, something the majority of global families don't get the chance to have. Without it, a low-grade sadness may linger for a long time. Ungrieved losses accumulate and need to be mourned, or they can create new problems later.

Another phenomenon particular to ATCKs and Global Nomads is called "Quick Release Response." TCKs and Global Nomads normally have not had the opportunity to resolve conflicts because they know they will be leaving and will need all their emotional resilience to deal with multiple losses of home, friends, school—everything that has been familiar, at least for a short time. As a result, they often don't have the opportunity to develop conflict resolution skills: There is less pain in leaving problems behind. Time being always short, one packs up and leaves without addressing unresolved issues. Later in life, they may equate conflict with severance of a relationship, which can affect their intimate relationships. The emotional detachment begins a few months before departure as one begins to prepare to leave and to anticipate the grief that is sure to come. Grief also can occur when someone close to you leaves first.

Most of these issues are not part of their conscious awareness. Vicarious, unresolved grief is multilayered and cumulative in this lifestyle and requires time and permission to process. As the late Norma McCaig used to say, TCKs and Global Nomads are experts at planting and transplanting, but little experience in tending a tender root system.

Katie complains that the only good portrait I made of her was a ballpoint pen sketch of her on a TWA plane at age two. It shows her fast asleep, totally at home on a plane to Oman, curled up with her favorite "blankie." Forced to be on the most economical flight by the State Department, we usually had between eight and twelve hours of transit time in various airports around the world. Airport and transit lounges are as much home for TCKs as any place.

TCKs and ATCKs have a well-honed ability to walk in other people's shoes. In her twenties, after 9/11, Katie decided to go by her Lebanese middle name Leila. When I asked her why, she said, "Mom, when I introduce myself as Katie Buck, no one knows I have two identities, my American White Anglo Saxon and my Lebanese one. Leila Buck defines who I am authentically." Leila continues to write and perform plays that help people understand the Middle East through personal and human stories rather than biased, out of context, soundbites that prevail in news reports. Leila still uses her her creative career to build a lasting bridge between two cultures: my husband's and mine.

A few years later Leila married Adam, who comes from a Jewish family, thus expanding the diversity of our family. His family and ours blend in very well and we feel fortunate to have Adam as our son-in-law. For many years Adam's creative work has been exploring narratives about Palestine to counter biased and distorted ones so prevalent in our media. He employs his art as a tool for action by creating projects to support Palestinian children. Adam's documentary film *Qalqilya* follows the story of a young Palestinian skater who dreams of building a club so he can teach children in his community how "to fly." In the process of making this film, Adam and his Palestinian partner found funding to build the first skate ramp in Palestine. This project inspired them to create SkateQilya, a youth empowerment non-profit program using skateboarding and art to teach leadership and community building to Palestinian girls and boys.[71]

Our time back home was ending. It was time to pack-up again and move. So I squeezed every moment to finish my training as a Licensed Clinical Professional Counselor and integrative Adlerian art therapist. Our next tour after Washington D.C. would be challenging.

We are the stories we tell; our words map the spaces of home,
thus binding us in "an act of remembrance."
                                                —Lisa Majaj[72]

5

Saudi Arabia and Midlife Crisis

*To confront pain and demand a gift transforms an enemy into a
teacher.*

— Sydney Barbara Metrick[73]

Prelude to Saudi Arabia

Our tour in Washington from 1992 to 1995 included difficult
times. In addition to going back to graduate school in my forties, finishing my internships, the role reversal in my parents' marriage in the last few years created problems I could not help them
resolve. It was painful for all of us.

After my parents settled in Washington D.C. in 1977 my mom
was able to find a job but my dad, in his sixties and having had a
very specialized career in Lebanon, had two strikes against him. He
never found regular work, and became instead the stay-at-home
partner. Neither of them was equipped to deal with the stresses of
that reality.

To his credit, Papi learned to cook and was proud of it; he became famous among their friends for the *īsmalliyeh* dessert he made
almost every day but try as he may to adjust, slowly he found the
dignity and respect he enjoyed in Lebanon disappear. Papi, like
many immigrants, had an idealized picture of the United States.
What he knew came from descriptions from his good American
friends in Beirut. Fully aware of the corruption and deficiencies
of his homeland, he believed here everything would be perfect.
Little by little, reality set in and chipped away at this impossible
dream. As in any other country in the world, he found good people

and bad people, honest ones and dishonest ones. Accustomed to respect, he was shocked and hurt to encounter prejudice because he looked Semitic, spoke with a French accent, and his name was Kamal. While walking his beloved and well-trained dog, Lucky II, without a leash, in the ironically named Friendship Heights section of D.C., some neighbor shouted at him. "Hey, you, don't you know we have leash laws in this country? Go back to where you came!" My dad, not easily rattled, replied "Tell me, were you ancestors Indian?" Like that man's immigrant forebears, Papi was learning to navigate his new homeland. But he could not regain the sense of meaning, purpose, and dignity that had always defined his life.

In the following nineteen years, both he and my mom carried on as if nothing was wrong. But he grew more and more depressed. I learned later that he took Valium he had brought from Beirut, but that only made it worse. He had two bad falls, broke his leg, and after a car accident it was downhill from there. Papi died on December 16, 1995, eight days before he would have turned eighty-four, on Christmas Eve.

Soon after Papi's passing, Steve came home with news—and a worried look on his face. "Before you say no, please hear me out," he started. Uh-oh I thought, whatever it is, he knows I won't like it. "I've been asked to go to Jeddah, Saudi Arabia as Consul General. It's really my best option and we will be able to pay for Leila's college education. I promise it will be the last assignment I take." Previously, he had turned down an ambassadorship to another state in the Arabian Gulf because I had immediately said no. Usually we sit down and discuss the offer, but at the time, after our traumatic experience in Baghdad, I could not face another posting. So, this time I felt I needed to listen. But my whole being reacted. My resistance to being uprooted and starting over again rose to a crescendo that paralyzed me. I had no energy left for even one more move. It had been an exhausting couple of years dealing with my studies and my parents. I could not face yet another process of sorting, packing, fixing up and renting our house out, moving, and resettling. In addition, I was struggling with perimenopause—made worse by all the stress. I was still grieving my father and I didn't want to leave my mom alone so soon after his passing. Leila was a freshman at university; it would be the first time that our tightly knit family would be separated for so long.

So, we negotiated. I asked that we wait to leave until Leila was a sophomore. Steve used the time for a refresher course in Arabic, which gave me time to finish my graduate courses, complete two research papers for two different universities, conclude my internships and sit for my licensing exam. Finally I had my Masters in Counseling Psychology and became a Professional Member of the American Art Therapy Association.

In my twenties, thirties, and forties, this uprooting and replanting every two to four years was an adventure with many learning opportunities, but by midlife it had become exhausting. I yearned to permanently put down roots and integrate the separate pieces of my life. I especially did not want to go to Saudi Arabia because it followed a unique, ultra-conservative branch of Islam referred to as Wahhabism. According to Al Munajjed,[74] religion and government are intertwined in Saudi Arabia. Sovereignty is based on an alliance that dates back to the mid-eighteenth century between "Wahhabi" religious men (Ulama) and members of the Al Saud family whereby the "Wahhabi" Ulama are incorporated into the administration. Other Gulf countries like Kuwait and Bahrain adopted a more liberal school of Islam (there are four), and religious leaders there have limited authority.

Saudi Arabia is the only Arab country that enforces a mandatory dress code for men and women, and the only country in the world that did not allow women to drive. Me, the rebel, there? We had already moved fourteen times. We'd lived mostly in "hardship posts." This one might be harder than any of the rest.

At one point I told Steve, "I'm willing to stay back in the United States while you go to Jeddah." But as usual he did not want to go without me. Having already given up an ambassadorship. I felt I was placed in a double bind. I knew that turning down another good assignment would have been detrimental to his career; I finally agreed to go—but on a provisional basis; I had the option to go back to the United States and wait it out. As it turned out I stayed, and we were in Saudi Arabia from 1996-1999. It was our last assignment and our fifteenth move.

Art and Grieving

For many years I had been using a simple art therapy random scribble in my journal. I found it was a way to get in touch with my deepest self and my intuitive guidance. Letting the words flow in response to the image enabled me to see, hear, and understand how I felt in any particular moment. In neuroscience, this leads to "bilateral neural integration."[75]

The first scribble I made in Jeddah revealed to me that I was still grieving and lacking stamina for yet another uprooting and replanting.

48. "Grief of uprooting." *Scribble: Colored pencils ©Hala Buck*

"Grief of Uprooting"

Layers of grief piled up in an endless horizon.
Women bent over by sadness,
trying to find support in others.

But the shapes merge and overlap,
not really supporting,
just echoing the pain.

Lost in each others' shadow,
they appear as specters floating in space.
That's how my soul feels,
that's how my soul weeps—on paper.

Yet I am silent in life, unable to grieve
the life I left behind.
I feel dead inside, unable to revive
a spark I had found within me.

Where has it gone, where is it hiding?
I came here knowing it would be hard,
but what makes it harder
is how Steve's career consumes us both.

The Saudis were friendly, welcoming and open. Contrary to what I expected, most of the people I met were willing to discuss my angry resentment of the restrictions, and to talk about the ultra-conservative mores that applied to everyone, Saudi and foreigner alike. They told me how they were working on reform but very slowly, through the traditions and the Wahhabi version of Islam.

The first night I arrived, Steve told me that I was invited to critique an art exhibit by male Saudi artists. I felt it was presumptuous of me to critique. I basically don't agree with the practice of judging art, preferring instead to give encouraging feedback and share my experience as an exhibiting artist. But a few days later, the Saudi women artists wanted me to do the same. I was pleasantly surprised by the art produced by both sexes. They asked me about art therapy and strongly urged me to stay and set up my art therapy practice. They were enthusiastic and more willing to come to therapy than the expats I met.

Jeddah, the Arabic word for grandmother, was thought to be the place where Eve, the famous mother of us all, was buried. Old-timers remembered exactly where her tomb had been, but the modernization of the city had relocated her to another cemetery. When Leila visited at Christmas we went looking for Eve's tomb. Even with our trusted driver, Ali, we still were not able to find it.

Although Jeddah was not the paradise that Eve knew, it sits on the Red Sea, with some of "the most beautiful coral reefs in the world," foreign expat enthusiasts assured me. We went snorkeling in transparent blue lagoons, watching a Technicolor world of fish, corals and an occasional hammerhead shark. It was magical.

The American Consulate was located not far from the heart of Jeddah, a square bloc compound surrounded by high walls with the Stars and Stripes flying in the center. The offices were near the entry and across were with the drivers' offices and maintenance warehouse. Following the driveway that circled around the compound you came to a few houses, only one or two still inhabited, and a large swimming pool. Finally, you came to the Consul General's house, which would be ours. It had a large garden, many date palm trees already laden with dates hanging in pregnant bunches. In front of the house was the oldest row of trees in Jeddah, teeming with hundreds of noisy and messy crows that enjoyed relieving themselves on anyone who dared walk towards the house. From the front door of the "residence" I could see the neon lights advertising Fuddruckers and Wendy's. It all felt surreal.

Even though I agreed to stay, the option to return to the United States was never off the table. It would be difficult, but separations during postings were not uncommon, and they did not spell out the end of Foreign Service marriages. As it turned out, I stayed. What kept me in Saudi Arabia were the people, and the art therapy work I could offer them.

As the commercial center of Saudi Arabia, Jeddah had many merchant families. I found them educated, interesting, open, and hospitable. The women I met had founded impressive centers for the learning disabled. I taught Adlerian parenting at the Maharat

Center. I was delighted to be able to adapt this positive and democratic parenting approach to life in Jeddah. Not only did parents embrace it, but one school principal said she was telling her teachers about it. I was touched and impressed by the openness of so many Saudi families and their willingness to teach responsibility to their children by giving it to them. One prominent family had traveled around the world culling information about centers for children with severe Down's Syndrome. In addition to learning about how those institutions operated, they asked a very intelligent question: "If you had to do this over again, what would you change or do differently?" They brought all that knowledge back and created, the "Al Aoun," or "Help Center." When the former president, George H.W Bush, came to Jeddah, I encouraged him to visit these centers to see another side of the gilded Saudi life.

Back in the early days, when embassies were not allowed in the ultra-conservative capital Riyadh, the American Embassy compound was located in Jeddah. The city was sprawled along the coast and one could only get to the Embassy by driving along the beach during low tide. Since then, the shore has been filled in and now the compound is surrounded by a thriving modern city, with elegant shopping malls offering everything from traditional *hijabs* and gold jewelry to Gucci and Victoria's Secret. Summers are unbearably hot, and much of the population fled to cooler climes in Lebanon, Europe, or the United States. I also took a break of three months, to recoup.

Saudi Arabia was full of contradictions. There was this restrictive, orthodox Wahhabi interpretation of Islam mixed in with Saudi tribal traditions. Yet one would experience a genuine openness among the educated. At Christmas, we would receive a card or a tray from the former oil minister, with the verse from the Qur'an that told the Christmas story with Mary, or Mariam as she is called in Arabic, at center stage. Muslims regard Abraham and Jesus as great prophets who preceded Muhammad, which is why all three monotheistic religions—Judaism, Christianity, and Islam—are considered the "Abrahamic" faiths.

Women and Islam in Saudi Arabia

Like everyone else I was confronted with the Wahhabi strict, patriarchal interpretation of the Qur'an and Islam. As usual, wom-
en were the recipients of the ensuing repression. I was shocked to
learn that Muslim women in Mecca, the most sacred center of Islam, are assigned a separate area in the mosque to pray, usually a
smaller area. I found out that the same restriction applies to Jewish
women in Jerusalem. Israel designates a separate and smaller part
of the Wailing Wall for Jewish women. I don't believe that God ordained treating women that way. However when Muslims at the
Hajj are circumambulating the Kaaba, men and women are walking
together all clad in a simple white wrap. No one covers their face.
In their homes men and women can pray together. During our stay
in Saudi Arabia Steve and I were invited to Saudi friends' home.
Come prayer time we sat there witnessing the simple and peaceful
tradition whereby the men, women and children each spread their
individual prayer rugs and performed the *salat* (prayer) together. It
was very touching.

Since women are not allowed to drive, in families who could
not afford a driver, the men had to do what American women do:
chauffeur everyone around and run errands. If anything will help
rescind that repressive rule, it will be because the men want to be
liberated! Twenty years later in 2017, the new crown prince Mohammed Bin Salman announced that in 2018 finally Saudi women
will be allowed to drive although restrictions still applied.[76]

Eventually, I realized the frustration and depression I felt
masked my own unresolved anger. I learned that I needed to confront these feelings, along with stereotypes I harbored about Saudi
women and their acceptance of the *abaya* and *hijab* (these are not to
be confused with the *niqab*, the full veiling of the face, with which
I still have a problem). In the West, most people mistakenly use
the word "veil" when they are really referring to the scarf (*hijab*).
Indeed, the "veil" has come to stand for everything that's wrong
about Islam and the Arab World. While the word *burka* is often
used interchangeably in the United States, it pertains only to the
garb that women in Afghanistan (which is *not* an Arab country)
wear.

Dressing modestly is an Islamic value that applies to both men and women, and each person chooses how to interpret it. But in Saudi Arabia it was traditional norms and traditional doctrines that made it mandatory. I refused to have a dress code imposed on me. I usually did not wear the *abaya*, nor the *hijab*, unless I was in the souk during prayer time. Instead I had my own "modesty" uniform — baggy pants, long tunics, and a hat with a cape in the winter. It was my way of showing sufficient respect for the cultural mores without compromising my beliefs. I was not Saudi; I was the American Consul General's wife! My Muslim relatives did not "cover." I did not see why I should!

Yet for most expats, including diplomatic wives, the *abaya* was "no big deal." In fact, they would send the more elaborate and decorated *abayas* home as gifts. For them, it symbolized little more than inconvenience. More often than not, they found it expedient to just throw the *abaya* over their tennis outfit, or whatever they were wearing, when they went out.

My strong reaction surprised Saudi women friends. "Hala, you have such a problem with this piece of fabric," they would say as they fingered the *abaya* draped over a chair nearby. "We don't care about it. In fact, it gives us the freedom to do whatever we want to. We are more concerned and determined to take back the rights that the Prophet and the Qur'an gave women and that have been expropriated by men. But we have to do it our way, working in and around the system in place."

Being the rebel that I am, it took a while for me to accept that explanation. But in time I developed a lot of respect for their journey and the strength it takes to challenge the system from within. As an American, I was used to fighting outright for what I believed in, and for the change I wanted to see. But in these older and more traditional cultures, things evolve more slowly. I came to admire these women's courage to persevere in the face of cultural codes as entrenched as Saudi Arabia's.

Considering my Lebanese background, my negative reaction to the Wahhabi interpretation of Islam was no surprise. As I got to know the Saudi women, I realized that I respect the decision of any women to dress as she wants, as long as it is her choice, It took a lot of time and introspection, but eventually I understood that my unresolved anger, sparked by my cruel encounter with the fanatic and close-minded priest, was affecting my perception of the Muslim garb.

The irony was that I had purchased a whole "modest" wardrobe, with long sleeves and no décolleté. But when I arrived, I found that *abayas* were worn mostly in public. That when women entered a private home many of them usually removed their *abaya* and *guatta* as one would a coat. Underneath it affluent women wore the latest fashion from Paris and London. At the first fashion show I went to in Jeddah, I watched each Saudi woman arrive, off came the *abaya*, to reveal the sexiest, most elegant outfits. They were stunning. I, on the other hand, in my conservative dress, looked like Mother Hubbard. In choosing not to wear the *abaya*, I actually found it *harder* to dress in a way I liked and still be respectful of the rules of the country.

I learned to respect their way of obtaining rights that we take for granted. Unlike the United States, which was created through a revolution, the rest of the world usually works through gradual evolution, and takes much more time to change. In addition, globalization has brought about a reactionary movement in many cultures and religions, and has become equated not with modernization but "Americanization."[77] Even in the United States of 2017, as divisions grow, a new expression has surfaced — "cultural anxiety." In her 2001, book, Armstrong argued that every religion was having a problem with a strict orthodox imposition and literal interpretation of religious texts.[78]

One Saudi woman, a client of mine, grew up without the veil in her own family. She was shocked and crestfallen when her new husband insisted that she cover her face. She was furious, but felt trapped. When they went for the Hajj or pilgrimage in Mecca, while circumambulating the Kaāba with millions of other men and women, all wrapped in the required modest and plain white cloth, she turned to her husband. "Do you see all these people in the most holy ground of Islam? None of the women cover their faces. The Prophet and God did not ask that we do that. From now on you will not see me with a veil." And that was the end of that!

After a while it struck me that my main quarrel was not necessarily with Islamic dress, but with women's rights, both in Saudi

Arabia and worldwide. Listening to the women, and seeing how they deal with the mores in their country, helped me realize that I too was importing a preconceived opinion. I could not understand how strong, educated Saudi women—many of whom studied abroad—could accept the Saudi government dictating such a strict requirement for them to wear the *ābaya* and *hijab*. At least, not until one time when Leila was visiting on Christmas break. We went down to the souk with Saudi friends; in order not to stand out, Leila and I each put on a *ābaya* and clumsily draped a scarf around our heads. Walking around in the crowded souks I felt strangely at peace, as if I was in my own cocoon where I could see everything but no one could really see "me." It felt freeing and protective. Interestingly that the word *"hijab"* comes from the verb *"hajaba,"* which means to conceal or render invisible by use of a shield."[79]

I was surprised by my reaction. I expected to feel restricted, disrespected, and angry. My blanket stereotypic perception that Muslim dress is inherently oppressive fell away. I wrapped my *ābaya* tighter—since it was tricky to keep it from flapping open or the scarf from sliding off. At last, I began to understand why my Saudi friends and clients would tell me it freed them to do whatever they wanted.

I still have a strong negative reaction to the *niqab* because, from what the Qur'an in Surah (verse) 24:30 and 31 says, "believing men..." and "believing women should lower their gaze and guard their modesty." Women should "....draw their veils over their bosoms and not display their ornaments and beauty..."[80] But nothing is clear cut. Bowen writes that in a dissertation on *sharī'a* law at al-Azhar University in Cairo, Shaykh Mustafa Muhammad Raashed concluded that the *hijab* is not an Islamic obligation.

So why, I wondered, has there been such a resurgence of the *hijab* and even the *niqab*? When Muslim women, especially the young, choose to wear modest Islamic dress, it is never a simple decision but rather a complex one. I remember back in the '70s, Kuwaiti mothers who did not wear Islamic dress were mystified and worried about their daughters deciding to "cover." "Hala," they would lament, "why are our daughters choosing to cover when we never did?" Part of it may have been peer pressure, but there was a certain rebellion against their mothers' adoption of Western mores at the cost of tradition and Muslim identity.

The *hijab* may be a symbol of oppression in the West, but in the Arab and Muslim world it can represent several things. First, it is a display of women's piety or devotion to God, giving them a sense of inner peace (much like nuns I expect). As more and more women enter the work place and move around in public spaces, it shields them from inappropriate male attention or harassment. In contrast, Leila, like so many women, has often complained of catcalls from construction workers (and other men) on New York City streets. Second, statistics show that Muslim women outnumber Muslim men in higher education by more than half and at every level of the educational system. As some of my Saudi clients used to tell me: "This way, the men are forced to notice my brain instead of my body."

Over the last twenty to thirty years, many women have adopted traditional Muslim dress in reaction to the West's denigration and vilification of Islam. Muslim women in the West have increasingly adopted to wear the *hijab*, despite the harassment, to define who they are and proudly respond to the demonization of their religion.

As more Muslim women take up the *hijab*, a whole industry around attractive—yet traditional—Muslim dress has mushroomed and inspired eastern and some western fashions all around the world.

In Libya, during a teaching cruise, I found out just how attractive this dress could be. The stunning, shimmering *hijabs*, in bright fuchsia and other beautiful fashions, with tighter fitting, long skirts and tops, really surprised me and the Americans who were on the cruise. We had expected women draped in unattractive, drab, black, loose garments. An older relative who was accompanying some of the young women did wear the old *abbaya* and was not too happy when one of the twenty-year-old Libyan women asked if she could take a photo with our group. (In those days, American tourists were a rarity in Libya.) When we got back on the cruise ship, my companions asked me, "Hala, why did you warn us not to stare or take photos? These women were very at ease approaching us!" I had no answer. I was as surprised as they were. In Tunisia, most women did not wear Muslim dress, although I'm told that has changed in the last decade.

We were in Saudi Arabia from 1996 to 1999. At the time Saudi women and men were segregated in public unless the woman was with a male relative. This was another unique aspect of Saudi restrictions. But even this can create more opportunities for women in which they don't have to compete with men. It is similar to the advantage some women in the United States perceive in all girls' schools or colleges. For example, in Jeddah I was invited to the inauguration of a new women's bank, run and staffed completely by women. It has an area for children to play while mom is doing her banking, and safe deposit boxes with twenty-four-hour accessibility, for those evenings when you want to lock up your jewelry on the way home. In recent years, I'm told, there are even more opportunities for Saudi women.

And interestingly, I found that some Americans enjoyed living in Saudi Arabia. So, was my erupting anger and simmering depression more to do with my history than what I saw in front of me? My art journal helped me understand that it was both. I could perceive the seduction of being taken care of on all levels; it's quite a beguiling lifestyle. Some American expats had been there for thirty years. They traveled all over the world, and went back to the United States every summer, and sometimes twice a year. But they led a comfortable, good life with abundant amenities in Saudi Arabia, lives they could not have afforded in the United States. They also enjoyed the slower pace of life and the lack of violence in the streets. They knew they could not live forever in Jeddah and were apprehensive about the alienation they would feel when they had to retire and return permanently to the United States. They worried that they would not be able to adjust after several decades spent in Saudi Arabia, and that no one in the United States would understand what made living in Jeddah pleasant. Surely, people would not believe that the Saudis, under their "repressive" system, could be welcoming, friendly, and likeable. I shared with them what I had learned about Global Nomads and ATCKs, and the concept of the "hidden immigrant." I could see that those American expats were lost between worlds.

Spending my summers back in the United States, I was struck by how a culture shapes women's body image. In some conservative countries and groups, women's bodies are considered tempting, and require complete coverage. In the West, women's bodies are flaunted in advertisements and on the screen more as objects than embodiment of souls. Messages are hurled at us from all directions, pressuring us to fit the fad of the day. As a result, many women threaten their lives with eating disorders, fight signs of aging with Botox, and worse. Pornography and violent, abusive sex can be seen at the flick of a switch.

Tell me, then, is any culture flawless in the way it treats women? Who is to say which is better: the *hijab,* which treats a woman's body as temptation, or pornography, which desecrates it? Sadly, even in those cultures where women "cover," the Western perception of desirability of underweight bodies is creeping in.

As a therapist who worked in Saudi Arabia and now the United States, who has traveled extensively around the world, I found that in almost all societies, women are the ones usually battered, abused, paid less for the same job as their male counterparts, and afforded fewer opportunities in government and the private sector. What gives any culture the right to look down on another? In Saudi Arabia, public segregation is seen as a flagrant symbol of inequality and female subservience. On the other hand, mothers have power in Arab culture. Steve remembers explaining to a high-level Congressional delegation that in Saudi Arabia, "No, you will not be received by the king or others on Friday. That's the day they all have lunch with their mothers. It's sacrosanct!"

Just as the Bible has been interpreted literally by many groups, so too have the Qur'an and the Prophet's teachings. I heard from other Foreign Service friends who served in Saudi Arabia ten years before us that there was less imposition of the dress code on Saudi or foreign women, at least not in Jeddah. To me, this regression into a more insular, fundamentalist stance spoke more to the social and geopolitical issues, and the void created by a sudden leap into the best and the worst of the 20th century and globalization. The social fabric became frayed as Western values, images, and ways of living intruded and sometimes overwhelmed more traditional cultures such as Saudi Arabia. Religious conservatism became the glue that attempted to keep that fabric together. The women were pawns in this game. When I arrived in Jeddah, I felt and sometimes heard the anger, and the depression that some women suffered from.

I came to a deeper understanding of the cultural struggle in

Saudi society that was catapulted from a traditional Bedouin culture into the twentieth century with the discovery of oil. It had become increasingly closed and controlling, likely in reaction to a genuine fear felt by many people that their cultural identity and values were at risk as the rest of the world moved in. With the oil boom came an invasion of sorts: money and foreign trade brought western TV, attitudes, and values. The country seemed to have battened down its hatches, trying to preserve what was familiar, even though it may not have been anyone's ideal. This may explain why traditionalism was on the rise in many parts of the Muslim world.

Saudi Arabia and many other developing, wealthy countries could acquire, in a very short time, the accouterments of "western civilization," the good and the bad. There had not been enough time for society to absorb all this change and integrate it in a way that made it culturally viable. People felt adrift and looked for their moorings.

Religion is one of those moorings, which is why we see a resurgence of religious extremism in all major faiths. For Christians, Jesus Christ, believed to be the Son of God, is at the center of the religion. In Islam Jesus is regarded as a prophet who came before the Prophet Mohammed. Judaism and Islam demonstrate religious belief in the rituals and the daily guidance of the Torah and Qur'an respectively, which touch on every conceivable subject in daily life. This provides security for people hanging on for sheer cultural and religious survival.

The Qur'an and the Torah are "holy books" because they are literally God's words and the path to redemption. Because of this, as I learned years later during a discussion between a Muslim scholar and rabbi at a synagogue in Washington D.C., in many respects, it is really more correct to refer to the "Judeo-Islamic" tradition, rather than the "Judeo-Christian" one.

The Saudi women I met in Jeddah were searching for the Islam they knew in their hearts existed: an "ethical Islam" as Leila Ahmed calls it, that declared more than a thousand years ago the equality of men and women, and conveyed it through such rights as inheritance, unheard of in the West at the time.[81] I learned that the Qur'an asserts basic equality between men and women by giving women equal (though not necessarily identical) rights to those of men, be they personal, civil, social or political, as well as in the pursuit of knowledge and work."[82] These rights had been usurped by men who cherry-picked the Qur'an and *Hadith* (a collection of traditions and sayings attributed to the prophet Muhammad) to support early tribal laws, traditions, and beliefs of the Arabian Peninsula.

In the midst of my rebellious anger over the suppressed rights of women, I was touched by Saudi women's faith. I probably had the only art therapy group where clients took breaks for prayer. "Hala, it's time for noon prayer," they would remind me and the group would disperse around my office. "Don't be surprised," they explained. "Some of us will be done in ten minutes, while others take longer to finish praying." As I watched them, I could sense the peace and grace they found in stopping daily, five times to be exact, and connecting with the Divine. Even though therapists were advised to avoid religion, I found that I needed to integrate their faith, as they experienced it, into their resource list. For them, it was a source of support and guidance. "So, what helps you when you are feeling down or depressed?" I would ask. And for many the answer would be, "I read *surat al bakra...*" (or some other Qur'anic verse) "...and that makes me feel peaceful."

I was moved by the trust that clients had in me, by their willingness to open their hearts and minds, to grow and change. "Although you're not Saudi," they would tell me, "we know you understand and respect us, and you don't treat us like weird oddities, guinea pigs, or aberrations." "When I saw therapists in London," one said, "I felt that for them I was just this exotic, stupid woman they were fascinated by. They could not get past the ābaya: a piece of cloth!"

Being Lebanese, and bound by a general cultural tie, it was easier to be conscious and not apply my Western-acquired skills in a blind attempt to turn Saudis into American women. Western psychology was developed by mostly white males of a certain era, and a lot of it does not apply to communitarian cultures or to western women's psychology for that matter. Miller wrote how society restricts women from expressing anger except when protecting loved ones. Thus anger becomes a threat to women's core identity. While for men, anger has been the main emotion permissible to them.[83] I was careful not to "liberate" and alienate them from their families and society. In the Middle East, generally the terms "women's rights," "family rights," and "human rights" are for both sexes. They include Christian and Jewish women. They reject the western "feminist" label that they see as more relevant to an individualistic culture because women, in most Arab and Islamic countries, seek to improve the condition of not only women, but the whole family by addressing poverty, legal equality, and human rights generally. They combine elements of East and West to develop feminist ideologies of their own.[84]

I was reminded of an American friend who invited me to a "women's lib" meeting in Washington in the '60s. I found the angry demands for equality impressive, but I felt they were missing an opportunity. I suggested that insisting on being treated "the same" would not serve us well unless we also demanded childcare at the work place, time off after giving birth, and a guaranteed return to our jobs. "Equal does not mean the same," I said. "And until men start having babies we need to demand rights that are in line with women's needs." I was almost booed out of the room. I realize now that I was thinking in a more communitarian social context.

Fernea quotes the former Iraqi deputy secretary of the General Federation of Iraqi Women (prior to our invasion) who perceived American feminism as dividing men from women and separating women from the family. Iraq's approach was to support maternity leave, childcare, and other needs that both men and women share; it's a kind of "family feminism."[85] Interestingly, Europe was more in tune with what I was suggesting at that meeting, and European women now enjoy such support. Meanwhile, in the United States, we still have to ratify the Equal Rights Amendment, originally written in 1923, and we still do not have equal pay for women.[86]

In my art therapy work, I intuitively found a way to adapt what I had learned in the United States to what I was discovering about Saudi culture. I created art therapy directives for creative expression that were congruent with their cultural norms and with women's development in general. In the first sessions, clients would usually talk about pain and other physical symptoms while telling me about their problems. More often it is easier to tell someone about your headache or shoulder pain than your feelings of anger and depression. I did not know it then, but I was developing a model of integrative art therapy that bridged art psychotherapy, body psychotherapy, Adlerian therapy, psycho-dramatic techniques, cross-cultural understanding, sand-tray therapy, and mindfulness meditation. To this day, I use that model and I teach it to other therapists and counselors.

Trigger for Change

Katie came to visit us every Christmas we spent in Jeddah. This coincided with the beginning of her own search for identity. Since my history was also part of hers, the missing piece of the puzzle was her Lebanese Arab heritage. We each embarked on an accelerated exploration of selfhood, navigating the strict, traditional values and extreme conservatism and patriarchal mores of Saudi Arabia and the *muttawāa*, the religious police who wielded increasing power during King Fahd's rule. Saudi Arabia turned out to be baptism by fire for both of us. Even though I was angry most of those three years, I understand now that the resulting images and words were important stepping-stones for my own healing, and that Jeddah was a catalyst for my own growth.

Three years in Jeddah also brought home to me how there had always been a mistress in my marriage—the Foreign Service. The full impact of this realization, my unfinished grief for my dad, restrictive Saudi mores, and not wanting to be uprooted again led to a jumble of emotions. They spilled over into images and words in my art journal." Mostly, they revealed piled-up anger. A full-blown mid-life crisis, or as Brené Brown calls it "midlife unraveling," spurred a spring-cleaning of all the psychic clutter that had accumulated over the years, starting with the encounter with the priest and continuing throughout our highly mobile life over which I had had so little control. These feelings coalesced into a need to find a permanent home and put down roots, my desire for adventure was satiated.

I believe each of us at some time in our lives has worn a veil, although usually an invisible one, to hide our true selves. The veil, or cloak, is a metaphor for the illusions we create and perceptions by which we operate.

Random scribbles that I use in my art journal are just that: random, with no forethought in mind. But they can reveal where one

49. "Waves of grief." *Scribble, pastels ©Hala Buck*

is at that moment: body, mind, and soul. At first, the images that appeared in my scribbles seemed as if they were solely a reaction to the restrictions on Saudi women; but I came to believe they also represented my search for my spiritual, whole self. This naturally tied in with my cultural identity that was struggling against the part of my background I had rejected. I rebelled against religious interpretations, always cherry-picked by men, which veiled the essence of women. I respected the right of women who freely choose to cover themselves because they feel it is part of their faith. My strong reaction, as it continued to unfold, was more about the enforced imposition of a strict dress code on women, both Arab and foreign, who do *not* choose to cover. The *Muṭṭawwā's* enforcement felt abusive, demeaning, and more of a weapon wielded by men to control women, rather than an exercise of religious faith. This power play pushed a big button that evoked the feelings of hurt and rage from that early encounter in my life.[87]

My art journal became my therapy, and the images and words

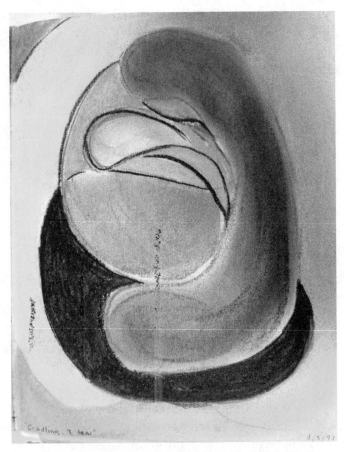

50. "Cradling a tear." *Scribble, pastels ©Hala Buck*

that poured out kept guiding me and showing me the way "home."
I called the unpublished manuscript that emerged *Dialoguing the
Soul©*, because I felt I was doing just that: searching my soul for
who I am and where I belonged.

The restrictions surrounding us all in Saudi Arabia and the
strain of my "senior spouse duties" fueled the explosive anger,
which promptly emerged in my artwork. More incidents from the
past poured into my drawings and words. The incident with the
nurse in Baghdad and also an attack at knifepoint in Washington
D.C., where I luckily managed to escape unharmed, also poured
into the work.

The following are excerpts from that unpublished manuscript:

My own history of unresolved anger led me to react strongly to any injustice, especially against women. I am glad of that, even though it leaves me often shaking with anger.
November 1, 1996.

This next image started off as a contour drawing of an iridescent anemone I had seen while snorkeling in the Red Sea. But images have their own minds. This one morphed and the words poured out as if my pen wouldn't stop, not until the process was spent.

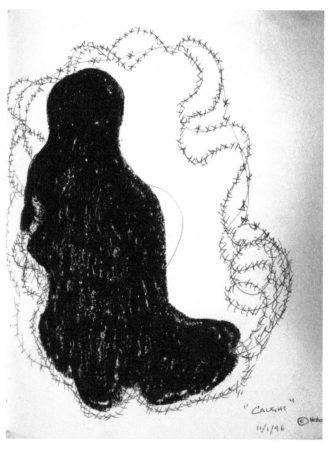

51. "Caught." Scribble: *Pencil and pastels* ©*Hala Buck*

"Caught"

Caught in a barbed wire—unable to move
each movement a jolt of pain.

Caught in the barbed wire, frozen by fear,
alone it seems—in this trap of deceit.

In the name of what, can they inflict this suffering on you?
No God or prophet can speak of love,
and condone such cruelty.

Sitting there surrounded by a windy, tangled wire
that threatens to tear you apart,
you look away—and pretend you're free!

From where I stand I see the truth,
the pointed edges of your prison,
and I yell out in anger.

I cannot free you, I can only tell you
there is a way out, for you and all others.
But only you can say where and how.

You and only you
can break this cage of silence
and cut your way through.

There is pain on your path,
all growth paths do
but there is also life.

A life where barbed wire doesn't threaten
every move you make.
A life where you can speak and be heard,

Where you can follow your dreams.
A life where pain is not a requirement
for being woman.

The images and words kept pouring out, so I let them.

"Tangled in the Web "

Tangled in the web of pain,
A web of power and fear,
of lies and of deceit.

She retreats into her shell,
Yet it offers no real protection—
from the web.

Faced by my own culture's wrongs,
I stand defiant yet helpless,
not because I cannot cut that web
but because the shears should be theirs.

I can only stand in front,
saying, get up
and cut that web!

I feel for my sisters
all over the world,
who are caught in man's web.
I cry for the pain they feel,
and the strength they cannot see.

A strength that comes from deep within one's soul,
a strength that rises up and strikes at injustice all around.
The time will come,
and I will be there![88]

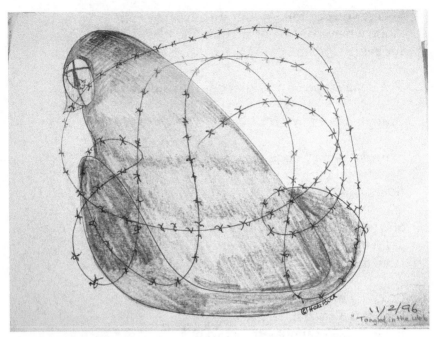

52. "Tangled in the web." *Scribble: Black pencil ©Hala Buck*

These images and words shocked me, and left me shaken. They exploded out of me at a rhythm I could barely manage. Only gradually did I come to understand the many layers they conveyed. Later, what I felt seeping into my soul was perhaps what Estes calls women's "collective rage." "Women who become socially, politically, or culturally conscious often find that they have to deal with a collective rage that seeps upward through them again and again."[89]

The repressive mores of the ultra-conservative literalist interpretation of Islam was not the Islam I knew or grew up with. Which is one of the main reasons I did not want to go to Saudi Arabia in the first place. It sometimes reminded me of the fanaticism of the Jesuit priest: here again were men interpreting a holy book and religion to impose restrictions on women and "other."

My multi-tiered anger also told me I needed to follow my dreams now—even those as simple as living where I wanted to, for however long I wanted to, without a ticking clock determining when I had to leave. The art once more revealed my inner world and allowed a transformation to begin—and with it the healing.

I was constantly exhausted in Jeddah. My professional work, the social obligations, the restrictive culture, and my personal issues exacerbated my health problems. I discovered Reiki, and it became my saving grace. I eventually trained to be a Reiki Master with a friend, Anne, a wonderful American married to a Saudi man. Reiki is a form of healing energy. It was no surprise to my Saudi friends. They said, "Oh yes, we have something similar, called *rokya*." I was intrigued by the similarity between Reiki, *rokya*, and the "laying on of hands" in Christianity. All of them are ancient healing traditions that gestated in the East.

The images that emerged from my Saudi Arabian experience made it painfully clear to me how I had surrendered my own power to the man in my life, my husband. For thirty-one years in the Foreign Service, I had lived where my husband's career dictated.

Suffering, it is said, opens our hearts to compassion. It burns away the "veil" around our hearts. Joan Borynsenko wrote that Americans don't believe in the usefulness of darkness: they need happy perfection. After all "the pursuit of happiness" is enshrined in our constitution. But I found suffering to be a period of initiation. Paraphrasing Thomas Moore, "We need to go through the dark night of the soul in order to be reborn into our new and better selves."[90]

Confronting the lack of choices in the lives of Saudi women, I recognized the lack of choices in my own life, a lack I had not consciously acknowledged and therefore did nothing about. I had contributed to my own disempowerment and sense of helplessness. I have always put my responsibility towards Steve and others ahead of my responsibility towards my own well-being. I was angry with my husband, but even more so with myself. Finally, my body, in response, broke down. On home leave that summer I had to have a hysterectomy.

I needed extra time alone, being in my own quiet space taking care of myself. I did however love helping my clients and teaching; and I focused my energy on that. But I still had to attend to the official duties I was expected to fulfill, after which I would need retreat into a silent sanctuary with my art.

In that solitude it dawned on me: I do not just paint bridges. My writing was creating a bridge between my old self and the one emerging, and eventually between myself and whoever reads this book. It helped me make sense of inner conflicts in my subconscious. This enabled me to understand and accept them, thus allowing the integration that eventually brought me a sense of coherence, or a unity of being. In Saudi Arabia, I came face to face with my own glass wall and gilded cage.

During one home leave trip to the United States, I was on a train bound for New England to attend and teach at the American Art Therapy Conference. As usual I had my art journal with me. I began a sketch of a bridge but it came out in a crescent form. Curious, I allowed that image to develop; I saw an awning shape. I let the process and the art take me where I needed to go. I discovered the healing message awaiting me under that awning/bridge. The first title was "Barbed wire transformed." Until it changed.

53. "Bridgehaven: Barbed wire transformed." *Ballpoint pen ©Hala Buck*

"Bridgehaven: Barbed Wire Transformed"

An awning bridge with solid bases
creates a place of safety.
A grape arbor laden with fruits
provides a place
where change is possible.

Umbrella, parachute,
it spans the distance between two places.
Two places of being and seeing,
two places far apart.

Crescent turned bridge,
barbed wire turned green,
crisis turned into growth.

In that sanctuary they gather,
people of all types and ages,
to marvel at the safe haven
and the commonalities they share.

I am the bridge and the awning,
the vine and the grapes, the people too.
I am part of you — we are all one,

standing in the flow of life
of mother river,
confident that it is safe.
Safe to go with the flow towards our destiny.

Transforming the barbed wire into morning glory was a spontaneous message that originated in my soul. I am the bridge because one side, one foundation, is the Lebanese-Arab culture; the other is the American. I built that bridge over the years to span the divide and endure the separation. The bridge image spontaneously changed into an awning and became a shelter. The vine that I unconsciously added suddenly felt like the barbed wire being transformed from a symbol of pain and confinement into a symbol of beauty, refuge, and growth — for me and for clients.

The train stopped at a station in Connecticut. I looked out to see the name: Bridgeport. I was suddenly aware of the importance of that name for me. Can a bridge also be a sanctuary? Can a bridge be a haven? Maybe "Bridgehaven" should be the title for "Barbed wire transformed." And so it became.

A thought popped into my mind. I remembered how Papi taught me to develop photos in his dark room. First I would immerse the white photographic paper in a pan full of developing fluid. Then, holding it with tongs, I would gently coax the appearance of the picture. It was a process similar to the emergence of the images and words in my art journal. Bit by bit, things became clearer and clearer as their message unfolded. Art revealed what I already felt, but did not necessarily understand.

In Jeddah, I was struck by the necessity of confronting not only the most unacceptable restrictions there, but also the memory of my first encounter with rejection. As a child, I had no resources to fight back and confront the priest. But now I could. The challenge for me was to respond not with anger and hate, but from a deep place of peace and compassion.

So, the crescent turned into bridge, the bridge into an awning, the awning into sanctuary, and barbed wire to vine. It was amazing how everything fit. Transformation and integration! The barbed wire became a symbol of weaving together, of creating healing where there was only pain. The bridge is me, and it stood as testimony to and symbol for my journey of connection, communication, and ongoing transitions.

My experience has taught me that one cannot go back to the past and stay there because it feels safe and familiar. Whether it is an individual or a society at large, each human being needs to study the past, and create a present and a future that feels congruent with values held dear. The backlash and deep divisions we saw in the United States in 2018 results from the same fear that I saw in Saudi Arabia. Whether it is expressed as prejudice against gender, ethnicity, race, or religion. It was fear of the unknown, people seeking comfort in the familiar, no matter how imperfect.

Towards the end of our tour in Jeddah, the images that emerged in my journal showed me how old wounds I had carried were being forced open, cleansed, and hopefully healed. There was more grief to bear. A dear friend back in the United States was dying from breast cancer. Then our beloved dog died. For a dog-lover like me, having had one ever since my childhood, losing a pet was poignant. These new losses seeped into the layers of grief that had piled up before and during the Saudi tour. I was physically and emotionally exhausted after fifteen moves, and found I had to keep lying down to gain the energy I needed for the final pack out. It was time yet again for transitioning and bringing closure through heartwarming farewell parties by friends and colleagues.

In retrospect, the distressing emotions and pain I had explored during those three years did indeed transform an enemy into a teacher. When I look back at all the images and words from this period, I realize this is where the real surgical and healing work of accumulated trauma took place. The restrictions in Saudi Arabia allowed all the anger I had been holding to erupt. Slowly the scribbles changed, as the following images show; art once more was the healing salve.

54. "Spirit trapped"
Scribble: Pastel ©Hala Buck

55. "Weaving a new portrait"
Scribble: Pastel ©*Hala Buck*

56. "What is woman?" *Scribble: Pen and colored pencils* ©*Hala Buck*

A week before we left Jeddah for good, a couple of my clients and their friends organized a public forum for women to talk about domestic violence in Saudi Arabia. This was a first. Admittedly, the attending women and men were segregated, but more than 400 women showed up. The six men representing the *majlis al shoora* (the consultative council) teleconferenced via a giant screen. One of my clients asked if I would agree to speak at the beginning of this "conference." I was touched that they asked me; but I replied, "No, absolutely not; you and your women friends have courageously put this together. I had nothing to do with it. I am so happy for you. But if I go up there, the men will use this as a tool to discredit you and say, 'See, it's the American consulate that put them up to this.' I'll sit quietly in the back cheering you on."

It was the best finale I could have asked for. One by one, women stood up, told their stories and assertively demanded their rights. Meanwhile, one could see from their demeanor that the authorities' representatives didn't know how to respond. They had never been confronted with such anger, or so loudly accused of not supporting women's grievances when they went to court. Nothing like that had ever been publicly revealed. Each woman who braved the great taboo of airing her dirty laundry in public encouraged the next one, and the next. The authorities were stunned to hear the women's heart wrenching stories, almost to speechlessness.

It's easier for us women in the West, who are protected by laws, to defy the establishment. But even here in the in the United States, we have so many cases of sexual and physical abuse that go unreported and unpunished, and far too many shelters for battered women and children; and in them, we only see those who have the courage to run away. There is an increasingly chronic problem around the world of women being harassed, abused, denied their rights, and traumatized. Little did I know that nineteen years later, the #MeToo movement of 2018 would finally erupt in the United States and spread across the world.

Jeddah was an important stepping-stone on my journey towards wholeness. I was able to do a lot of healing, and found clarity about the thirty-one years during which I filled the role of "spouse of." Years of feeling my life was governed by the Foreign Service had come to an end. Steve had a few more years before retirement, but we were returning to the United States for good. My unremu-nerated job was over! With that, my journey continued. I was grate-ful that my professional art therapy work in Saudi Arabia had pro-vided a safe place where my clients could explore their own issues and feelings, and find a way to resolve them. I liked the Saudis, and in my own small way, I felt I was making a difference.

It takes a strong marriage to withstand the pressures of life in Jeddah, and the Foreign Service in general. Ours needed some at-tention. On our way home, we took a houseboat trip through the "Canal du Midi" in France with our good Canadian friends from Oman days. As the Chinese proverb says about older women: "When women wake, mountains move." And so I did.

On our last day, walking towards the *boulangerie* for our daily French baguette, I turned to Steve. "When we get home *habibi* (my love), it's imperative that we go back to couples' therapy." To his credit Steve said, "Okay, if you think we need to." Years later he told me it felt like an ultimatum, which was very appropriate for a diplomat. Yet, he added, it was "the best decision we ever made."

My past was calling for a link to the present. It was in midlife, during a visit to Lebanon, after a twenty-five-year absence, that the puzzle pieces of my identity began to fall into place. Insights emerged slowly and became further catalysts for my art and writ-ing. Being uprooted over and over again with my husband, while raising a daughter—herself an even more complex mixture of iden-tities—forced me to examine my own.

Your pain is the breaking of the shell that encloses your understanding.
— Kahlil Gibran[91]

6

Return to Lebanon

We need to go home again, not to recover it but to sanctify the memory of it.

As a foreign-born Foreign Service spouse who chose the transient life of the Foreign Service, marrying Steve meant giving up my cultural anchor. From then on, my personal story would be radically different from my history.

In the spring of 1999, Steve, Katie (she was still going by Katie then), and I flew from Jeddah to Beirut. It was Katie's first visit ever, and my first since 1974. My mom and Tante Paulette, both of whom had just visited us in Jeddah, had preceded us to Beirut. We flew over the monochromatic, barren Saudi desert, desolate and arid, with one attempt at greening that seemed out of place. After all that parched land that seemed to reject life, I saw through the haze of the airplane window the blue-green mountains of Lebanon with the last remnants of snow on Mt. Sanneen. It was like a magical apparition, a Middle Eastern Brigadoon, something that appears in your dreams, something that suddenly spelled LIFE.

As the plane turned and dipped, there it was. I could see villages with red tile roofs perched on mountainsides, umbrella pines, and green as far as the eye could see. The color was not lush, but it still was green, and hugging the Mediterranean coast—Beirut. I took an involuntary, deep breath. Tears welled up, something caught in my throat. Katie held and patted my hand. I was grateful to have her with us. Now in her early twenties, she was eager to meet my extended family and explore her Lebanese heritage. But would I feel at home? Would I recognize cousins, who were children when I left but now were adults? Had the war created an unbreachable wall of unshared experiences? What would I find? How would my family find me? During the years we lived apart, war and hatred ravaged not only the land, but its people as well: would this have widened the chasm time created between us? Would we meet each other as strangers?

We emerged from customs to find a large number of family members waiting behind the ropes, craning their necks, searching eagerly for us. Perhaps they, too, were wondering if we would recognize each other after all those years? We finally spotted each other: "Lola! Steve! Katie!" "Tante Paulette, Samir, Sano, Tante Georgette, Rita!" We shouted each other's names over the noisy commotion of the arrival hall. Tears of relief broke the tension and it seemed we were all hugging at once. As I expected, they were all fashionably dressed, but the teens were attired like American teens. I was home.

"Home" — such a tricky word in our lifestyle. But family was my home, as were a few buildings I could recognize on the drive from the airport. And the solid mountains still watching over Beirut. But so much had changed, outside and inside. I recognized neighborhoods, but couldn't remember their names. There were ugly grey concrete apartment buildings everywhere, a large number of them with large gaping holes from the war, and laundry defiantly hanging on dilapitated balconies.

Being away from my birthcountry for twenty-five years – during which there was a fifteen-year war – was disorienting to say the least. I wondered if and how did those years change my family and friends? I was too much in shock to register everything I was seeing. Instead, I answered questions about the flight, about how, *ma shallah*, beautiful and grown-up Katie was. Except for Tante Paulette, who had just visited us in Saudi Arabia, it was the first time the rest of the family had ever met Katie, they had only seen photos of her through the years.

Everything had been planned for us. Both my Christian and Muslim families had organized the *ziyarats*—visits. We were to stay with Papi's cousin Samir and his wife Saniyya, or Sano, as we call her. All of us were hanging on to each other, afraid the others would disappear in a magic poof. The offering of food started almost the moment we stepped inside: *Fatayer bi sbanikh, hummos,* a full *mézzé,* followed by sweets.

Food and *Ziyarats* — Visits

The *sobhiyyeh* — morning visits — were my favorite. We'd sit on Samir and Sano's balcony sipping Turkish coffee catching up on twenty-five years. *"Shta'nehlkom."* (We've missed you.) I don't recall the details of the conversations, only the embracing and the homecoming feeling in the midst of my family. They came in waves to welcome us and meet our daughter. People in Lebanon always find the time to drop in and connect. As we sat around savoring yummy chocolates and petits fours, I noticed that we all looked older, some more than others, yet it was as if time had stood still. This was the family I have lived away from for such a long time — yet a family it was. I knew if I needed something, most of them would be there for me.

Sano brought out an album from years past. Most of the photos were taken by Papi. A photograph, as Thomas Moore says, "forces a meeting between the self you are now and the one you have forgotten."[93] As we leafed through the album, each person commented on something they remembered.

When lunchtime, the main meal of the day, approached, someone would eagerly ask, *"Shoo jaābelkum tekloo?"* (What do you want to eat that you crave for?) What amazed me was how the *kibbeh, sultan Ibrahim* (red snapper), and fifteen other mézzé dishes appeared. The warmth, love, and help people gave so freely at once was enveloping, reassuring, and binding. Since it is a communitarian culture, the circle of care is wider than it is in the United States. The bonds of family and friendship make people help each other and ensure reciprocity. This interdependence can feel too binding in some cases, especially if the people you are bound to help are unpleasant or don't reciprocate in kind. But this wide net is what I had missed in my own nuclear, small, and nomadic family. I basked in the warmth of familiar faces who knew my history as no one else does. I did not need to explain who I was: I was Lola, Kamal and Jeanne's daughter. I was part of their history, and they were part of mine. More broadly I was part of a communitarian culture placing high value on others' needs.

I was reminded of an experience in Washington, D.C. Before the voice cues at crossings were installed, Steve and I were stopped at a red light. At the opposite intersection a blind man was waiting to cross. The light changed for him but he did not know it: there were no other pedestrians around, and no one from the cars waiting there jumped out to help. I was beside myself, unable to navigate the crossroads to help him. Steve heard my distress so he dropped me off at our appointment and went back to help. "If it had been in Lebanon, any number of people would have jumped out of their cars and helped that person cross," I told Steve. He nodded in agreement. I'm glad we now have the talking crossing signals in the United States.

Sightseeing

Cousins from both sides of the family took time away from their lives to drive us around the city. New roads, or "autostrades" had taken over whole neighborhoods. The beaches where I had spent many happy summers were now chic beach clubs. I preferred the simple beach huts of "Acapulco" and "St. Michel" I had enjoyed during my childhood. Acapulco, I'm told, had become home to squatters since the civil war. The Mediterranean looked more polluted than I remembered. I missed the open beaches of my childhood. Everywhere I saw tall buildings with balconies, the occasional lonely traditional house with the red tile roof still standing, saved from greed and war. Some buildings were modern and elegant, others were just concrete highrise jungles, hurriedly built. But the beautiful mountains overlooking the city were still there, providing a protective barrier and enchanting vistas, as they have for millenia. The lighthouse in Ras Beirut that I loved had been repaired, and once more shone its light towards the sea, which is slowly retreating as more debris and landfill from the reconstruction projects is dumped into the Mediterranean. Lighthouses have always been a favorite of mine; there is something comforting about them standing watch, guiding, shedding light where there is darkness.

But there was a silver lining to all the destruction. After the war, when rebuilding began in the center of Beirut, layer after layer of ancient civilizations were excavated. "Vestiges of Canaanite, Phoenician, Persian, Hellenistic, Roman, Arab, Crusader, Mameluke and Ottoman remains" came forth.[94] The excavations revealed the ravages of not only conquerors, but also the 7.5 magnitude earthquake of 551A.D. and resulting tsunami that destroyed Beirut. The layers that were excavated were rich with the cultural history of modern Beirut, or *Biruta* as it was called due to abundant sweet water wells flowing beneath the city. ("*Bir*" was the Canaanite-Phoenician, and later the Arabic word, for well.) Historians describe the ancient city as the "intellectual and commercial center of the Roman world… most handsome Berytus, (another name for the city) the jewel of Phoenicia." In the 3rd century A.D. one of the greatest law schools of the Roman-Byzantine world, Beirut School of Law, flourished in Beirut.[95]

Thanks to archeologists from several museums in Beirut, some important ruins were excavated and saved from being buried again with the reconstruction—no small feat since the whole city sits on numerous layers of its rich history. A little park in front of the "Serail," or parliament, was created for concerts and quiet moments in the midst of the city's hubbub. A small stone ampitheatre now watches over some of those priceless witnesses of the city's heritage.

The new, the old, and the damaged buildings all intermingled. Proudly, Samir and Sano pointed out the new *sahet al saāh*—Clock Tower Plaza. "*Shoufti keef āmalo el restoration?*" See the beautiful renovation by Solidère of that area? We walked around the rebuilt Place des Canons and other familiar landmarks. The Lebanese were hungry for something to be proud of and rejoice in; many of the French names I remembered had been replaced by Lebanese ones. We had lunch on the rooftop restaurant of the Virgin Atlantic highrise bookstore, where one could find books and music in several languages, from all over the world. Each floor was assigned a different language.

We had a beautiful view of the Mediterranean. Yes, the water was still blue. I had forgotten that fact, having become accustomed to the greyness of the Atlantic Ocean.

Everything was at once strange and familiar. The smell of the Mediterranean mingled with the aromas my senses remembered, but could not place. The warm, gentle breeze on my skin, the constant noise of cars honking, people talking, gesturing, laughing, and arguing—the continuous hustle and bustle: the sounds of life in Beirut. Memories flooded back. I laughed and cried; it was bittersweet to be so warmly embraced by family and friends while realizing how much shared history we had lost, and how disoriented I felt. I had missed having my whole family around me. I thought of how my 89-year old mother in the United States would have enjoyed all the visits and care an extended family provide. I know I would have welcomed the support and respites.

It was my cousin Raja's turn to be our designated tour guide. He took us to visit *Jbeil*, or Byblos, a town framed in the East by layers of mountains and still visibly green, having been spared, so far, the concrete jungle virus. Some claim Byblos is the oldest continuously inhabited city in the world. The modern alphabet is known to have been developed in Byblos by the Phoenicians in 1000 BC. It was later adopted by the Greeks to create the basis for the Latin alphabet. The word "alphabet" came from the first two letters of the Phoenician alphabet, "alpha" and "beth. The Bible was named after Byblos. It sits perched on the Mediterranean. On a promontory stood a tattered Lebanese flag, a cedar at its center—just like the country it represents, it was at once proud, somewhat battered, fluttering in the winds of time. It was a sad reminder of what this country had gone through, and yet through the loss and pain of war, it remained an emblem of resilience.

I was away during the violence and craziness of the civil war, the 1982 Israeli occupation and bombings, and the Syrian occupation. People who have gone through multiple occupations, invasions, wars, and betrayal seem to develop a lack of trust in their government. They tend to rely on their own judgment and their ability to chart and affect their destiny. The result is a mentality of cynicism, discouragement, and a tendency to see plots everywhere. I had escaped all that. From afar I had worried about them and felt angry that the Lebanese were fighting each other instead of uniting to create a strong government and military.

In Byblos, however, there was a gentle peacefulness that emanated from the ancient stones, as if they were saying, "See, we're still here." We watched school children, boys and girls in crisp uniforms, white sleeves rolled up, playing an energetic game of "balloon chasseur." Red-cheeked, they shouted happily as they hurled the ball at each other in the courtyard of an ancient church. One could still visit the small workshops where beautiful colored blown glass has been made for centuries. As we meandered around quaint little alleys, the first blossoms of spring were poking through new green. The surrounding hills were bursting with red anemones, or poppies—*coquelicots*—cyclamen and yellow flowers called *hummayda*. Beautiful old stone houses with red tile roofs dotted the way back up the hill.

People passed us, nodding in a friendly way, conscious of the fact that we were visitors. Fishermen sat mending their nets that shimmered in the baskets. Some invited us to board their converted fishing vessels with plastic white chairs. Would we want a quick trip out to sea? The waves had gotten rougher; we kindly declined. There was no push for sale except for the little boy who insisted we buy his Chiclets gum. Instead of climbing over to visit the ruins, we opted for one of the charming cafés overlooking the nestled little port. I gorged myself on *Sultan Ibrahim* fish and pommes frites. We ate in silence taking in the beauty and serenity. The sun played hide and seek with the clouds. We watched and marveled at this little oasis, a refuge caught in a time warp, almost free of wartime reminders except for the soldier guarding the entry road into the port. A charming hotel in the same old Lebanese style as our first apartment building overlooked the beautiful setting. I turned to Steve. "Maybe next time we can stay here," I said.

People moved more slowly in this little town than in Beirut. There are at least two or three different kinds of churches and one mosque, all in an area of one square mile. A small souk meanders through its cooler alleys. Katie and I climbed on a parapet at the entrance to the harbor, which had survived earthquakes and invasions, and even a tsunami or two. We just sat there, each lost in her thoughts and feelings. I wanted to go back in time and reconnect with my roots and this sea I missed so much. Sitting on these ancient stones I felt a deep connection to them, and especially to the Mediterranean lapping at my feet. A sense of peace enveloped me as it always does whenever I am by the water. I feel as if I recover something of myself each time. In this land, my ancestors lived and died. I will always belong in some way here. Maybe that's why I want my ashes scattered in the ocean. It touches so many shores, including this one.

We left Byblos and continued our tour. Raja, despite a bad cold, insisted on taking us to *Deyr al Nurriyeh*—the monastery of the gypsy, perched high on the flat plateau overlooking Chekka on the northern coast. "You have to experience this beautiful monastery," this Sunni Muslim cousin said. We passed several Syrian-manned checkpoints. I was a little nervous, having heard stories of people held up by Syrian soldiers. But they waved us through, Steve's white beard having bestowed on him the honorable title of elder, or one who has made the *hajj*—the pilgrimage to Mecca. I was amazed his western features did not raise an eyebrow, until I remembered that Syrians, even more than Lebanese, have a lot of blonde hair and blue eyed people among them, courtesy of the Crusaders, Circassians, and other invaders of non-Arab descent. This beautiful sliver of a country, long poised between East and West, is a bridge of many dimensions—cultural, economic, religious, ethnic and political—a diverse collection of people in that tiny country. You can find blue eyes and brown, olive skin and white, brown and blonde hair—its people a reflection of the continuous wave of conquerors, occupiers, and merchants.

We arrived to find a simple building surrounded by cypresses and a breathtaking view of the bay below. We encountered the typical Lebanese priest clad in black with a long beard who nodded at us with a slightly surprised look. This is not a typical tourist haunt, thank God. As soon as we entered the courtyard we were met with absolute stillness, as if the world had been suspended somewhere outside its gate. I had never experienced such utter, total peace and quiet. I felt I did not want to breathe, for fear that the sound of my breath would break the spell. A small chapel was offering mass to the few devout parishioners who continued to stream in with their scarves and shawls as we stood, somewhat awkwardly in the courtyard. I wanted to stay for a while and meditate. It felt like such a sacred space.

Feeling we were intruding, we went out to walk along the terrace. Straight ahead was the Mediterranean; to the right we could see the old road to Tripoli that I remembered, and in the distance Tripoli itself. To our left we could see a Syrian battalion station.

We carefully aimed our camera in the other direction, luckily that's where the view was. We tried to ignore their voices as they drilled. Life in Lebanon goes on despite their presence. Reluctantly, we left this beautiful refuge and as we did, so did the sun, which set behind a dense row of trees. I have always found some sense of peace by the sea and now, ironically, I found it in this churchyard. Was that a healing gift for the six-year old in me?

It was heartwarming on this first trip to Lebanon for Katie, to acquaint her with the important things from my past and my culture. Memories filled in where places I knew had been destroyed or replaced. Now when I talk about my childhood, she will be able to see, taste, and hear it. I loved watching and listening to her use her newly learned Arabic to understand and communicate with her new instant and welcoming family. *"Ana bhhibkun kteer*—I love you very much," I would hear her repeat daily to my family. In most instances I was much less interesting to them than this American daughter of mine. My heart warmed to see her fall in love with Lebanon. I felt at home with my family, appreciated their loving welcome and embracing of Katie, and Steve as well.

Farida, a dear cousin on Papi's side of the family who married a Greek Orthodox man, insisted on driving us up the mountain, even though we could take the funicular to the famous statue of the *Hareessa* (the protectress), the "Lady of Lebanon" that stands guard over the bay of Jounieh. Farida said she often went there to leave a prayer in its chapel. This Muslim cousin, like the rest of my family, saw no contradiction in that.

Every night, some family member invited us out to dinner or lunch. Samir took us to a beautifully restored Lebanese house turned into a restaurant. It was a tasteful and creative blend of the old and the new. Food as usual was sumptuously displayed, and delicious. Restaurants, like most amenities, are expensive in Beirut. Most everyone whines about the cost of everything, yet every night the restaurants were full. The Lebanese *joie de vivre* was back, making up for fifteen years lost to violence and destruction. Having tasted death for too long, they now needed to live first, and pay later.

Another day we went with Tante Paulette and her family up into the mountains above Tripoli to *Ehden*. We stopped for lunch at one of the plain but quaint restaurants with a gorgeous view of the valley below. Food in Lebanon, like in many Mediterranean countries, is something that brings people together. They linger, savor, and talk. It is a social ritual that cannot be rushed. First comes the *mézzé*—a dozen little dishes with a variety of appetizers like *hummos, tabbouleh, labneh*, olives, and more. A Lebanese beer, *Laziza,* or a little *arak*—an anise drink—go with that. Then the main courses stream in: chicken and *kafta*, the famous Ehden *kibbeh puffs, mishwi,* and whatever else was ordered. For dessert there is always fresh fruit, mostly in season. I had missed the taste of Lebanese fruits. "How small the world has become," I remarked. "Unlike a few years ago, now I can buy *tabbouleh* and *hummos* in grocery stores in the U.S." In the typical Lebanese salad of languages my cousins exclaimed, "*Sahheeh? Vraiment?* Really?"

After lunch, we continued up the mountain to see the legendary cedars. Despite its small size, Lebanon is a land of Biblical reputation. The Lebanon cedar, immortalized in the Bible and history books, the emblem on the nation's flag, is a majestic symbol of endurance and strength. Lebanon continues to need both. These cedars, the most treasured of trees, were used to build temples and palaces for thousands of years. During colonial days, they provided wood for railroad ties for the British Railways. With no replanting, this finally depleted them. These days there are a few reserves that protect the remaining groves of these majestic giants. Luckily, a serious reforestation program has plucked them from extinction, but it will take hundreds and perhaps thousands of years to bring the cedar groves back to their original size. Nowadays people are not allowed to touch any cedar tree, they just admire them. Twenty years ago, UNESCO added the most famous Cedar patch in Lebanon known as the "Cedars of God" to its list of world heritage sites. In a *New York Times* article July 18, 2018, the authors wrote that the "Cedars of God" grove is believed to be where the resurrected Jesus revealed himself to his followers. Unfortunately after thousands of years climate change now is the biggest threat to these ancient giants. I'm glad I have an old photo of me on Papi's shoulders in front of one of those majestic cedars. I was again struck by how their branches stretch out gracefully in a welcoming stance, typical of the hospitality the Lebanese and Arabs in general.

57. On Papi's shoulders at the Cedars, Lebanon.

58. At the Cedars with mom and auntie Rahiba, Papi's niece.

"What do you mean when you say hospitality?" my writers' group asked.

"I don't know how to explain it," I replied. "The warmth, genuine caring, polite, generous welcome one feels in Lebanon. Regardless of how inconvenient it is, or how poor or rich you are, people welcome you with open arms and a hug. Sharing what you have with family and guests is a way of life and a strong cultural value."

"Everywhere you go," I continued, "even in shops you hear the enthusiastic welcome, '*Ahlan wa sahlan!*, *Taffadalo*' (welcome, please come in). Tourists and friends who have lived or traveled in Lebanon comment on this. There are tons of various greetings one learns for every conceivable occasion. It may seem silly to an outsider, but I realized it created a common ground of good will and security."

Mom's niece, Rita, drove us north to Tripoli to visit Tante Paulette. Her apartment was full of her late husband Mohammad's sculptures, furniture that he designed and built, as a three-dimensional collage of Arab and western styles.

Stories from the war started to surface. In the midst of the fighting, Ammo Mohammad died of a painful cancer of the mouth. Back then, artists did not know the dangers of toxic art materials. At the height of the war, his supply of morphine ran out; he had to bear the pain of his cancer without it. I could sense my aunt's agony as she recalled watching him, powerless to relieve his pain. In a calm and even voice of someone who has endured a lot she said, "All medications were hard to get even if they were available. 'Please shoot me,' he would plead with me." Yet despite all that, she maintained a cheerful attitude towards life, never complained, and actively helped her youngest daughter and her family, who all lived with her. "Teta Paula," as her grandchildren call her, is another strong woman in my family. I loved reconnecting with my cousins Maha and May, and meeting their husbands and children for the first time. We sat around Tante Paulette's dining room table for a late evening snack. I said *Khabroona*—fill us in.

Parents I've met everywhere don't seem to tell family stories as they used to. I watched as Katie, my cousins and their children, wide-eyed, took in all the family stories. I felt the comfort of being surrounded by family, and at the same time felt sad. It was clear that I had been on a different path. Simple little things reminded me daily that I was no longer part of life here. In 1999 no one in Lebanon puts their seat belts on. When I reprimanded them I was assured that they put it on when they are on the highway. No statistic I could conjure up changed their minds. At such times I felt like the emigrant aunt from a famous satirical theater group in Beirut, *Le Theatre de Dix Heures*, which we regularly attended while I was growing up. This political satire play had a character, a Lebanese-American "auntie," who was always bragging in a superior tone and in broken Lebanese about *"nihna bil States"* (we in the States). Remembering how ridiculously funny it was to have this emigrant aunt pontificate, I stopped pushing my family to wear seat belts.

Beirut, the capital—which had been known as the Paris of the Middle East—had not lost its charm, despite all the ugly concrete highrises, a lot of them inhabited by squatters who had lost their own homes somewhere else. But gone were most of the green spaces I remembered, except for the American University of Beirut (A.U.B) campus. Even from the mountains, one could see its large expanse of lush green overlooking the Mediterranean Sea. Visiting the campus with Katie was special. She asked "How did you manage to study mom? It's so beautiful, I just want to sit and look out at the Mediterranean!"

As we walked around the campus, memories flooded back. Here I spent four happy years. I remembered being lovingly teased by my classmates. "You're too American," they would laugh because I chose to wear practical raingear—raincoat, boots and all— when the streets were like little torrents. They insisted on wearing stylish stiletto heels and maintaining elegant hairdos—the high chignon was in fashion at the time. My motto was comfort, practicality, and *then* elegance. I would walk into the ladies' room and smile as I watched my classmates standing in front of the electric hand dryers holding their soaked shoes.

American University of Beirut (A.U.B)—Down Memory Lane

A.U.B had always been a microcosm of the whole region. It was founded in 1866 by American missionaries who later turned it into a private, secular insitution officially registered with the New York

Board of Regents. It continues to attract students from every religious, ethnic group from the Middle East and around the world. Despite student political protests and activism among many of those groups, it had escaped serious damage during the civil war. Only College Hall had been hit. It was rebuilt with the same stones from the mountains.

I went to buy some A.U.B sweatshirts from the college store. The same Nivea promotion ball still hung from the ceiling, just with more layers of dust. It was not the only thing that seemed left over from my past. Sami Nassief, whose father used to run the store in my days, recognized my face, though not my name. "Long time since we have seen you here *ya sitt*," he exclaimed with a twinge of reproach. Amazing, I thought. I left A.U.B thirty-four years ago, yet this kind man not only recognized me, but took the time to get to know me again.

It reminded me how back in the States I find it so strange when people get into an elevator and everyone pretends there is no one else there. I guess my Lebanese blood nudges me to first say hello, comment on the weather, or about something attractive they are wearing. It might take a second for people to get over the shock of someone speaking to them, but then they warm up, smile, respond, and we all get off our respective floors as fellow human beings, wishing each other a good day. The warmth and hospitality and awareness of others is central to my birth culture. I guess it's part of my DNA.

As soon as we arrived in Beirut, we were engulfed by the familiar sounds and *fawda*—chaos, the noise, and the aliveness of the place—all unchanged. I re-learned the art of crossing the street Kamikaze-style, or diving in and out of *servees*, the shared car services that comprise the main public transportation in Lebanon (the name is pronounced, affectionately, *serv-ees*, in the French way). In my day, most of the fleet was made up of Mercedes-Benz sedans. They were dependable, rugged, and roomy, taking up to four passengers. They seemed indestructible. The *servees* still runs the same way, but other, less gas-guzzling cars have replaced the sturdy Mercedes. The estimate—as stated in the Fall 2013 issue of the Lebanese University Alumni Bulletin—is that today there are 30,000 service cars circulating around Beirut and up into the mountains.

I still could not figure out the money. I felt like a tourist. When I lived there the servees cost twenty-five piasters, or a quarter of one lira; now it cost 1,500 liras. (A U.S. dollar then was the equivalent of three Lebanese liras, now it was 1,500 liras.) I remembered Papi urging friends and family to exchange their liras into dollars at the very beginning of the war. Few heeded his call, thinking he was too pessimistic. But devaluation of the currency and inflation indeed became another cost of a fifteen-year civil war that had left holes not only in buildings, but in people's souls. It all felt somehow surreal.

Despite, or perhaps because of, feeling powerless to affect change, the Lebanese love to talk politics. They argue loudly, and gesture to accentuate their point. Although they are openly critical of their democratic government and the corruption they see, at the end of the day nothing happens, and they go back to their *mézzé*. Besides the entrenched confessional parliamentary system, young people also feel disenfranchised by the old guard still in power. They don't know how to bring their energy and vision to the seat of power. Outsiders usually only see the apathy, which is real, but sometimes they see something else. Martin Giesen, a German artist who made Lebanon his home in 1973–1985, through the civil war, said that most foreign residents viewed Lebanon's civil war with bemusement rather than heartfelt concern, until the Israeli invasion of the capital in 1982. After that, he notes, in an effort to survive, the Lebanese people bore these convulsive shifts of fortune with "...stoical fortitude, displaying their traditional resiliency and willingness to adapt...."[96] And adapt they did! I believe this is their strongest *and* weakest national trait. Lebanese people bounce back and start over again. He adds: "The house may crumble, but its stone will be used again. Just like the Cedar of Lebanon continues to grow even in bloodstained soil."[97]

But what saddened and infuriated me was the fact that no lessons seem to have been learned. Different Lebanese factions still allow themselves to be pawns in global politics, instead of taking charge of their destiny and their country. Corruption and allegiance to the clan leader supersedes the welfare of the nation. Their tumultous history has given the Lebanese resiliency and *joie de vivre*. They are unsurpassed at knowing how to enjoy life. The lessons of that long, divisive war have only served to exaggerate that zest for life and take it to an unprecedented level. They seemed to embrace every pleasure with frenzy, living more totally in and for the moment than ever before. The restaurants were full, the shops busy, and everywhere one saw the women superbly dressed in the latest French fashion or casual chic, and always impeccably made-up. God forbid you'd run out to the store in your sweatpants, something I quickly learned to give up when I was there.

When I was growing up, everyone had clothes made by seamstresses and tailors. It was very rare and expensive to buy ready-made clothes. I always designed mine, went shopping with mom to find the right fabric, and she would then sew it for me, sometimes with the help of her more accomplished sister, Georgette. I also used to have shoes made to order because I preferred pretty but very low heels and comfort to the the the *talon aiguille*—stilleto heels popular in those days.

We drove by other important landmarks in my life. Our second apartment in Ras Beirut was now a school. It was a Sunday, so we were given permission to visit it. We climbed the stairs, still the same as I remembered and entered. As we moved through what used to be our living room and dining room, now converted into classrooms, it felt almost surreal. It was like walking into a space where only ghosts of the past now reside. It was eerie to know I was in what used to be my old room. At once it felt familiar under my feet, but it was unrecognizable otherwise. I could picture my mom on her lush veranda lovingly watering her plants, while dad smoked his pipe in his favorite chair, but now it was bare of any greenery. But the Eucalyptus tree I was allergic to and that dominated the yard now towered two or three more floors above the building, as if it was standing guard over the memories of what once was home.

The beautiful old house with a garden on the corner was gone; in its place was a chic store with beautiful *objets* for your home. The large garden plot that was right next to us and provided us with a bucolic view is now a parking lot. What is not a parking lot in Beirut is a new highrise. The streets in my neighborhood seemed narrower, the old buildings I recognized shabbier. But the little grocery, Abu Taleb, a fixture in Ras Beirut, seemed untouched: same merchandise, same table, only now a younger brother in charge. There was something reassuring about finding pieces of my life, still somewhat intact. So much else had changed, including myself. As I went to sleep with the sounds of cars honking and voices drifting across balconies, I realize I was finding pieces of my Lebanese self I thought I had lost forever. Once more, everything felt familiar yet strange. I was the observer and the observed, as if I had an invisible twin who was tagging along.

We had been in Beirut a week. It was home, yet it wasn't. Both the country and I had changed. But the relatives we were staying with represented the best that Lebanon offers: welcoming you with open arms, thoughtful about your needs, and generous to a fault. On the other hand, there was the taxi driver who overcharged me since I still couldn't figure out the money. I felt angry and sad that this "trusted" driver could do this. *"I am one of you,"* I felt like screaming. But was I? I quickly got out my rusty, sharp antennae that watch for people taking advantage.

I walked all along Hamra Street, the haunt of my adolescent years. I walked past Hamra cinema looking worn, the building above it still an empty shell, a reminder that the war had ended not too long ago. The "Horseshoe Café" was still standing, filled with another generation of young people having their coffee and croissant or ice cream as they discussed their lives, the latest gossip, or just people watched. I recognized a few other buildings where shops used to be, like the store where I bought my Domtex towels for my bridal trousseau, and the Armenian hairdresser's salon where I had my hair cut. Mostly it was my memories that guided me. Stores that were once the pride of Beirut were now neglected. The action, I was told, had moved to Verdun Street, with its state of the art malls and a plethora of designer fashions from around the world.

The Lebanese are not easily outdone, you can find anything from anywhere in the world in Beirut. Unfortunately, they adopt the good and the bad along the way. Rampant consumerism has emerged as the country is still rising from the ashes of war. It created a surreal mix of devastation and chic restoration.

The pilgrimage I was making had a sweet and sour taste. Twenty five years is a long time to have been away. It was hard to recapture what was lost. Yet people maintained a sense of humor. I laughed every time I walked by a bakery in Ras Beirut that specialized in *mana'eesh*—a Lebanese pizza with *zāatar* (a wild Thyme or winter savory), sesame seeds, and olive oil. The sign above the entrance read: "Mana'eesh Bakery, Tra-lla-la!"

Walking along the streets of Beirut I felt that my face belonged, my skin belonged, my language belonged, and especially my name belonged. There is a comforting feeling of having one's name recognized and pronounced correctly by people who know what it means: halo around the moon. It was a relief to have my identity understood. My name sprouted from this land. It belonged. It carries the whole history of my family in people's memories. Here I did not have to explain where I came from. I know of many immigrants in the United States who find it tiring to constantly explain who they are, where they are from, and never know what the reaction will be. I was amazed to read in Barack Obama's book how he experienced a similar reaction when he visited Kenya. For the first time in his life, he felt, "...the comfort, the firmness of identity that a name might provide,..." and how other people there who carry his and his family's entire history in their memories, "...might nod and say knowingly, 'Oh, you are so and so's son.'"[98]

But although I was *bint al balad*, the daughter of the land, there was a glitch. I had been away for a long time. That created a bittersweet fallout. One day, while shopping in my old neighborhood, I went into a store selling dresses and other items of clothing and I chose a top. The price seemed unusually high as marked. So, I turned on my Lebanese bargaining skills—to no avail. I was intrigued and upset that the shopkeeper was not relenting or responding to the standard game played in the Middle East, or to my bargaining prowess. "Why are you not lowering your price?" I asked with some annoyance. "*Ana minel hhai.*" (I'm from the neighborhood.) "Madame, with all due respect, you are not from here anymore," he replied. I finally gave in and asked him what tipped him off. Was it my comfortable shoes? American-style clothes? No make-up? "*Yaāni*, You see, *ya madame pardon, bass ma fee sitt bi Libnène ma btossbogh shaāra.*" (Pardon me Madame, but there isn't one Lebanese woman in Lebanon who does not dye her hair.) My salt and pepper hair was a dead give-away. I laughed in a way one laughs when one hears a painful truth. Even though it was difficult to take it in, I knew what he meant. My accumulated feelings co-alesced. I could never go home again!

Images from my past continued to fill in the blanks where I felt disoriented. It was not so for the younger cousins who now live outside Lebanon. Some of them do not have the luxury of posi-tive memories from the past. They had never known the old Beirut. They grew up during the war. All they had seen was violence and destruction. Now they saw brand new roads and new buildings that meant nothing to them. There were no reference points to help them connect with a better, happier, more unified past. Peace was as alien to them as the new road system. The scars of unhealed wounds threatened to open with each new threat of violence; the sonic boom of an Israeli jet flying overhead meant to rattle the pop-ulation and the tourists. A car backfiring could and did trigger this thinly suppressed fear. The resignation I sensed in the people was tied to the nation's history of disempowerment, its status as "Grand Central Station" to all the conquering hordes and meddling nations.

Invisible Scars of War

On this visit, everywhere we went we heard how people were hurt-ing financially, but also hurting from horrific images of war im-printed in their memory. We heard stories of days and nights in the shelter, of crawling around when the fighting broke out. Some cousins reported children crying every time the sound of shelling began anew.

Physical scars were visible in shelled buildings around the city; but as a therapist I also recognized signs of the collective, invisible psychological scars of war that most Lebanese probably carried. When people are trying to get their lives back, they often suppress trauma unless they seek treatment. Perhaps Lebanon's communi-tarian culture helps mitigate those scars.

We were awed at the survival instincts of my family and the Lebanese as a whole. The fact they could walk, talk, and act so nor-mally was amazing to me. Then I remembered how in Baghdad, during the Iran-Iraq war, we too adjusted to the incoming Scud missiles that came regularly from Iran. Human beings are very adept at adjusting to a "new normal," but the Lebanese have had more practice than most.

I stopped judging what seemed to me the superficiality of a lot of Lebanese women and their obsession with beauty that included face lifts and tucks. My contemporaries, from age thirty and for the next fifteen years, lived through a horrible conflict. They spent most of those years in basements that acted as make-shift shelters, wondering if they or any loved one who left that morning would ever return. When the war ended they woke up to find themselves in their fifties. My theory is that this seemingly ridiculous need to look young was an attempt to forget the horrors of war and try to recapture those lost years and live the unlived life. In addition, they were bombarded with the same advertisements as we have in the United States that hype youth.

Everywhere we drove I strained to recognize a church or mosque or favorite haunt. My point of reference was skewed. Look at all that rebuilding, I was told. It was amazing, but not surprising to me, because the Lebanese are the epitome of the entrepreneurial spirit. But who, who was looking to heal the gaping wounds that every Lebanese carried in his soul? I asked myself. Physical reconstruction is not everything. It is as if someone had thrown a beautiful band aid over the horror of that wound. No one had taken the trouble to cleanse it. Many people wanted to forget the last fifteen years. and who could blame them?

But others needed to tell their story of pain and fear over and over again. They told of daily occurences, like taking your kid somewhere, suddenly hearing explosions, and rushing out of your car hoping you can reach shelter before the heavy shelling started again. Days spent in the crowded basements where day ran into night and fear into despair. Stories that were impossible to imagine except in our worst nightmares. Days trapped in shelters, running out of food, only a battery operated radio and lanterns to keep them informed and shed some light.

Nado's husband. Philippe, recounted, "We had been in the shelter for days, and the kids were hungry, they had not had fruit for so long. I saw a few tangerines on the street that had probably rolled off some truck, so I dashed out, grabbed them, and prayed I'd get back before I got hit as gunfire raged on." As a therapist, I could not help but recognize the signs of complex trauma and probably collective Post Traumatic Stress Disorder (PTSD). Yet I felt powerless to help my family and others. People had trouble sleeping, others were depressed, some exploded in anger. I gave a Reiki treatment to some cousins, but I felt so helpless in bringing the healing they needed.

While reconstruction was in full swing, we still came across pockets of neighborhoods that reminded us of Europe after World War II. These were reminders of a senseless war, so maybe reconstruction was a healing salve after all. The resiliency I write about was in full swing under a thin cloak of anxiety and fear. Now that the war was ended, there was finally hope, reconciliation, reinvestments, reconstruction, and thousands of tourists—the mainstay of the economy. Life had returned to this tiny beautiful country. That is why Israel's thirty-three–day bombing of Lebanon a few years later, in July of 2006, was so deeply destructive. The exhalation of a whole population, who believed they could begin their lives over again, was shattered by a disproportionate and punishing Israeli bombing campaign.

But in 2004, when I again joined Leila in Beirut, life had returned to Lebanon. When not enduring civil war and foreign invasions, streets in Lebanon are generally safe, certainly in comparison to many American cities. Well, except for crazy-but-good drivers. Lebanese joke that all the bad drivers are dead. Traffic jams are horrendous. I remember when I was a young teen, a group of Italian traffic policemen were sent to Beirut to train their Lebanese counterparts in directing traffic. These smart-looking Italians in their crisp white uniforms, large leather gloves, and fancy plumed headgear took their positions in the small roundabouts in Bab Edriss and like orchestra conductors twirled around, directing traffic. The show attracted almost the whole population, including me. They were graceful, elegant—and totally ineffective. They caused more traffic jams than before and finally gave up. Their recommendation to the Lebanese traffic force was, "We don't know how you do it, but whatever you're doing, keep doing it, it works." Having since traveled in Italy and experienced traffic there, I'm bewildered. Why were Italians asked to come and teach traffic directing to the Lebanese?

Despite all the *fawda*—chaos—there is a slower pace of life in Lebanon. As Moore points out, there's something important about being still and not constantly getting somewhere. Like the ocean, the rhythm of the ebb and flow of life is crucial.[99] Perhaps that's what keeps the Lebanese relatively sane and why long lunches, or dinners with friends and family, are so important. Along the corniche, we saw couples, young and old, jogging or strolling, taking the popular constitutional walk along the seaside promenade. There were whole families *beshemmoo al hawa*—taking in the air, picnicking and smoking a *narghileh* (hookah). Several generations shared a large blanket, and of course food. Some had brought small Hibachis to cook *kafta*. Children of all ages ran around, toddlers scampered over and around the relatives and sometimes other picnickers, who would smile and engage with the children. The sea embraced them all with its gentle breeze.

I noticed veiled women from the Gulf countries vacationing in Lebanon, and more Lebanese women in hijab, something that used to be rare.[100] Everyone was enjoying the afternoon breeze and gorgeous vistas together. I seemed to be the only one noticing the contrasts. But why was I surprised? People still coexisted as they have for millennia. Western writers have commented how Eastern cultures are more comfortable with seemingly contradictory realities. Young people looking like other young people in the world—strolling, talking, or sharing a coffee at one of the many *cafés trottoirs*, restaurants, bars, and Internet cafés. Beirut has its chic side, war or no war. Life goes on in Beirut—nothing can stop it! Once more, I felt at home, and yet a stranger. An insider, and an outsider observing. I was surprised by the gamut of outfits and the fact that no one seemed to look, stare, or find the divergence of attires in any way curious. No matter if it was a typical jogging suit, the *hijab* head scarf, or the bejeweled bared belly button and torn jeans, which at the time was popular among teens. At a café where we stopped there was a grandmother with the *hijab* sitting with her granddaughter who was in a halter top. Nobody batted an eyelash. I was the only one gawking.

An Aha Moment

On this visit, Steve had to go back to Jeddah. By now, Katie and I were exhausted, not only physically but also emotionally, trying to absorb all we had experienced in such a short time. Like Katie I also am an only child, so we both felt we needed some solitude as well as time together to process. Sharing with Katie brought up the awareness that throughout my adult life I had this gnawing feeling that I didn't know how to fit in or even that I fully belonged; that, unlike me, others knew the rules of the game. I could easily help people connect with each other, but not when it came to me. I chalked this up to part of our Foreign Service lifestyle, and perhaps even a lack of needed social skills on my part.

But several years later when I joined Katie, who was studying Arabic at the Lebanese American University (LAU), I had a life-changing realization, an aha moment that comes when one takes the time to "pause," as Tara Brach teaches: to go within and allow the soul to whisper. This time, a return visit to my land of birth had a farewell surprise gift for me.

I woke up one morning to the droning whirr of the air-conditioner and the sounds of Beirut waking up. In that state of semi-wakefulness, a clear "knowingness," "message," or "insight" dropped into my consciousness. I nudged Katie, who was still groaning with sleep. "Mom, what is it?" she asked.

"You know, *haboubti* (my love), I just realized that it was never the fact that I did not know HOW to belong, but that I CHOSE not to!" I said excitedly, like a child on Christmas morning. "Wow! How liberating!" I added. At some level, that cruel encounter of my childhood led me to assume that belonging meant having to choose between my families. There was no way I was willing to do that, I loved them both. So in my little girl's mind I unconsciously chose instead to give up fully belonging. Irrational as that may seem, it fits into the basic premise of Adlerian psychology.[101]

I sat up in bed, repeating outloud to myself this sudden understanding, as if to make sure it was real. A huge piece of my life puzzle had just fallen into place. By then, Katie was wide awake watching her mother dance around the room. I felt free, as if a weight had been lifted. I needed to return twice to Lebanon in order to discover, with the maturity of the adult, the inner child's unconscious dilemma, or "fault line" that shook her sense of belonging and identity. I was right on schedule, smack in the throes of a midlife crisis, which required me to completely dismantle myself in order to get in touch with that wounded child and reclaim the pieces that helped me create a more authentic self.

The images from my art therapy journals had forged the way for this moment to arrive. I was reclaiming my life from that tyrannical script I had unconsciously created. By making the journey back to Lebanon, I had come full circle, to a place within me that felt truly home. To see that moment reveal itself in an image sprouting from my deepest self was a wondrous thing that brought tears of relief, awe, joy, and a sense of belonging to a larger Divine presence. I have found over and over again that it is especially in times of crisis that the images in my art appear more powerful, more meaningful. They seem to knock, then pound on the door of my consciousness until I release them onto the paper.

Part of who I am is linked to the social and genetic legacy of this country that is geographically and demographically itself a bridge. Its history of seafarers and traders has created a pluralistic society, ready to embrace and synthesize aspects from East and West. The Lebanese are known among other Arabs to be more open to other ideas and worlds, and are deemed more "sophisticated," or so Arab-American friends tell me. Certainly, in our Foreign Service postings in the Arab world, I was always warmly received because I was Lebanese-born. I love both my Muslim family and my small Christian family, just as I love and respect my Lebanese culture and my adoptive American culture. This does not mean I cannot see the faults on either sides; it is just that I understand them both. Even as a child, that bridge self was already in place and as my story found me, its contours fit into my life's pattern, giving it meaning that was both unique to me and universal.

After two weeks it was time to leave. Time to go home. "This idea of home is a difficult one for us isn't it sweetheart?" I mused.

"I have learned to look at it this way, Mom," my wise ATCK daughter reassured me. "Home is where you are loved." I gave her a hug. She has much more experience than I. Unlike her, the first twenty-three years of my life were spent in one place.

We're lucky then aren't we, *haboubti?* We have many homes."

"Mom, this is what you have always taught me, to see my own bridge identity as a gift not a handicap. I cross over from my American roots to my Lebanese ones and back again just like you do."

I did not come to Lebanon to recover the memories of my life. They have always been stored in my heart. I came because I needed to find pieces of myself I left behind, and because I missed my family and wanted so much to reclaim them and introduce my daughter to them. I wanted to introduce her also to the part of her she never knew, except in telephone calls and letters. I realized also that it was important to maintain a connection for both of us, through the new and coming generations, to the very soil of my ancestral land.

On this visit to Lebanon, it was strange how the highly emotional arrival contrasted with a peaceful departure. I left, this time, having finally learned at a deep spiritual and soul level that I have always belonged to myself. The plane circled on takeoff and tipped its wings, giving us a farewell aerial view of Beirut set against the mountains rising from the blue Mediterranean. Once more I was reminded how breathtakingly beautiful this tiny, tortured country still is and I caught a lump in my throat.

These mountains and plains are a cradle and a stepping-stone.
Whenever you pass by the field where you have laid your
ancestors look well thereupon, and you shall see yourselves and
your children dancing hand in hand.

— Kahlil Gibran[102]

7

9/11—Bridge Torn Apart

A person's identity is not an assemblage of separate affiliations, nor a kind of loose patchwork; it is like a pattern drawn on a tightly stretched parchment. Touch just one part of it, just one allegiance, and the whole person will react, the whole drum will sound.
—Amin Maalouf.[103]

9/11 and its Aftermath

Back in the United States, though Steve would not retire for another three years, my life as the unpaid Foreign Service spouse thankfully came to an end. We were in the United States for good! We began the healing process in our marriage and began a new chapter in our lives. I was tired of relentlessly crossing seas and oceans, with no place to rest or put down roots. Now I was finally "home," getting settled, planting those nomadic emigrant roots, and finally, *finally* throwing away empty cartons that we had saved—just in case—(we sometimes needed them in hardship posts especially if evacuated). It was liberating to be able to look at a moving van in our neighborhood and not have my stomach jump into my throat.

Leila had launched into her theater career, and Steve was still working at the State Department. So, who was I now? I was in my fifties, but the search was really gaining momentum. Just when I felt I was getting somewhere, 9/11 happened.

That horrific act blew apart my whole concept of self. It shattered my belief that people will find ways to live peacefully together. Leila called us immediately from New York to reassure us. "Mom, Dad, I'm okay. Something terrible has happened, turn on the TV, but don't worry, I'm safe. I just wanted to call immediately before the phone lines go down. I love you." Sure enough, when we tried to call back a few minutes later, the lines were dead. She had been watching it all from the windows of New York University. Still in shock, we switched on the TV to those terrible images none of us will forget. "But how did she know the phones would go dead?" I asked Steve. Then I remembered how in Baghdad, after each Scud missile attack, the phone lines would go dead. Instinctively this ATCK child of ours made an immediate, unconscious connection. I was grateful since I would have been in major distress not knowing if she was safe.

After my initial anger, shock, and fear for Katie subsided, I prayed that whoever perpetrated those crimes not be from the Arab World. But all them were, and as expected, the backlash against Arab-Americans and Muslim communities accelerated in earnest.[104]

I braced myself as the harassment and attacks against people who looked Middle Eastern soon followed. Later with each code orange and red alert, people were reminded to continue to fear, be angry, and be ready to go to war. Like many other immigrants from that part of the world, I felt the need to explain the context and root causes of such despicable, criminal acts.

On September 11th, I felt that my bridge had been torn apart, as if those planes had crashed right through it. I remembered a similar feeling at the door of that church long ago. This time the damage was done by extremists using Islam to fulfill a political and ideological agenda. Everything I had been and done to connect the worlds I loved had collapsed under the weight of anger and violence, pulverized into a pile of dust as painful and horrific as that terrible scene. I felt now I could never fully belong anywhere and I lost the desire to be a connector. I felt I could no longer straddle the divide between the United States and the Arab World, which kept getting wider and wider.

Steve and I went to the candle vigil at the Unitarian Universalist Church trying to calm our hearts and minds, and to pray for cool heads. People all over the country seemed to be gathering, feeling the need to come together. We sat in silence, allowing our spirit to speak. One woman stood up. "I'm a multicultural educator and I know those Arabs. They are all liars!" I was speechless, but not

Steve, who shot up from his chair; "You should be ashamed of such a racist remark. You know nothing about Arabs, SIT DOWN!" I could not believe that in this open-minded congregation, of which one-third are Jews, and whose members champion social justice issues, there could be people like her. I thought that Jews, of all people, would know what's it's like to be stigmatized.

Just like anyone whose ethnicity or race is attacked, something in me was activated that day. I had this sudden need to help counter the frenzy of demonization and vilification that was sweeping the country. For the first time in my life, I started referring to myself as Arab-American instead of an American born in Lebanon or just an American. Walking to our car that night, I said to Steve, "Americans only see and hear negative things about Arabs. I need to 'show up' as one in order to give them a first-hand experience of who an Arab really is." I had never consciously thought of myself as "Arab;" Lebanese people, and probably most others, never saw me as one either. I never needed to think or talk about it before.

"I agree. I'll be right there to support you," my strong and kind husband responded. I felt the urgency of this decision. Maalouf's words came rushing back into my mind. My cultural identity drum had definitely been touched and had resonated.

In struggling to understand, I asked Steve, "What made those men want to blow up themselves and thousands of innocent people?" "Bin Laden and his people saw our troops on the ground in Saudi Arabia as sacrilegious. We had trained and supported the *mujaheddin,* meaning those struggling, including Bin Laden, to fight the Soviets in Afghanistan, so they could throw out the foreign, atheist Soviet forces from Muslim land," Steve explained. "Evidently we did a good job convincing them."

The perception in the United States of Arabs and Muslims is distorted, full of prejudicial mindsets, and far removed from the complex, diverse reality. Unsurprisingly, many Americans, angry or afraid of the "other," found an outlet in harassing and attacking anyone they thought was Muslim or Arab. Anyone "swarthy," or seemingly "Middle Eastern," even a turbaned Sikh from India, suddenly became an object of suspicion and intimidation.

But it was also heartening when Americans, reflecting the best of our values, spontaneously volunteered to hold vigils and stand guard in front of Mosques and Arab cultural centers and even homes to prevent violence and protect people. Katie's Jewish fiancé, Adam, volunteered to escort Muslim women to the market or to pick up their children from school. Anyone with a headscarf had become fair game. "Adam, I'm not sure this is a good idea since you look Semitic and could also be mistaken for an Arab," I told him. "Don't worry Hala," he assured me. "I've already been helping. I feel so bad about what's happening. I went yesterday to our local Lebanese grocer in Brooklyn, offering him a sunflower and apologizing for the ugliness against Americans of Arab or Muslim descent." Katie (Leila) volunteered at the local Arab-American cultural center to help kids with homework and reassure them that not everyone hated them.

A few days after the attack, I was at the airport on my way to teach a workshop in South Carolina. At the gate, they "suddenly" could not find my name on the passenger list. I knew that airline schedules were in disarray after 9/11, so I called my travel agent (they were still around then) and asked her what happened. "I don't understand Hala, you're right here on my screen as being confirmed on that flight." But no amount of talking changed the airline representative's mind. "You can try another airline ma'am, but we still will not be able to guarantee you a return flight," was all I got. I was getting angry when it suddenly struck me that they really didn't want me on any airplane because of my name and the fact that I looked "foreign." It was a shock for me since I don't perceive myself as such. I could pass for an Italian, Latina, or African-American. So, I stopped making a scene, called the conference organizers and told them I would not be coming. It was the first time in the United States that I felt discriminated against.

My American identity and my Lebanese-Arab identity, my Christian and my Muslim heritage, seemed unbridgeable and dangerously at odds. Would I be forced to take sides, to only condemn those three murderous acts without explaining the roots of anger, the history of occupation, betrayal, destruction and humiliation in that part of the world? For the first time in thirty-two years since I became American, I was scared of being that bridge. Now that I was happily taking root in the U.S, my kind of plant was being vilified, uprooted, and tossed into a pile of undesirables because a few of "my kind" had been destructive and had done a terrible thing. In my mind, there is never an excuse to condemn a whole people because of the act of a few. After all, all Christian white males were not suspect or condemned after the terrible Oklahoma City bombing in 1995. Timothy McVeigh, an anti-government militant, killed 168 people including 19 children and injured 500 people. Since that time other domestic terrorists are referred to as "mentally ill." The "terrorist" label seemed only to apply to Muslims.

Because a bridge gives you amazing vantage points, when horrific things happen, you also get a more spectacular and terrifying view. When you are part of two or more cultures, when you have lived among other peoples and know they are human beings just like you, with the same desire to love and protect their children, to have a decent life—food, shelter, to laugh, cry, and love just like you—you are not so quick to judge who is "good," "evil," "civilized," or—what? "Uncivilized?" These judgments come out of ignorance and fear, especially when "different" means "wrong" or "bad."

Sitting on our patio one day, I was looking up at the trees standing guard around me. "Don't let vengeance, hatred, and more violence consume people," I prayed. Thousands of people were probably pleading the same thing. As the backlash continued and the fearmongering intensified,[105] the urgency to mediate, to bring understanding and tolerance between the various elements of my rich and diversified world, again grew strong.

I realized increasingly how uncomfortable and painful this place of complex identity is. At times it felt like repairing and maintaining my bridge was an impossible task, and an overwhelming and dangerous one in view of the reversal of civil liberties and war cries. But it was my very American identity that cried out in horror as values this country stands for were being ceremoniously dismissed. It was that part of my identity that said I must voice my concern, and walk my talk. It was the patriotic thing to do. What I love about this country, and what makes us such a great nation, is not our military might, but the belief in justice for all and in our common humanness. It is our willingness to learn and open our hearts and minds if someone can give us the whole story. "Americans genuinely want to be loved. We are fair-minded people who believe in justice and want to do the right thing," I said to Steve. "Yes, but unfortunately fear, warmongering, misinformation, and lack of historical context and knowledge gets in the way," he answered.

Somehow, I regained my courage and found the resolve to ramp up my determination to once more help shrink the widening chasms between the cultures and identities I represent. I wasn't so conscious then of the process, but construction on a new bridge had just begun.

I remember shortly after 9/11, someone asked my mom where her accent was from. "Italy," she replied. I was surprised to hear my 80-year-old mother say that. She had always felt proud of her Lebanese roots. Had some fear instinctively crept in? When I asked her later she said, "Oof, I get tired of telling my life story." It also reminded me that this reaction is also endemic to TCKs, who when asked where they are from, pause and wonder, "Do they really, really want to know? Do I give them the short version, 'I'm from Virginia?,' or the long one about all the places where I have lived and left a piece of myself?"

Part of what drove my parents to emigrate, something I disliked seeing in Lebanon, was people feeling disenfranchised and powerless to effect change. I was sad to recognize it in 2004, here in the States. Marianne Williamson writes, "Out of 163 democracies in the world,…" we reportedly "…rank among the lowest in democratic participation." She argues that after 9/11, we were distracted from our collective psychic pain and grief by touting the virtue of "…endless material consumption."[106]

President Bush urged people to spend as an act of patriotism. I was shocked and saddened. After Americans had naturally reacted not only with fear but concern for others, as they rallied in houses of worship of all religions, seeking the comfort of community, they now were urged to shop?

I had seen something similar happening in Lebanon after fifteen years of violence and a long history of being attacked by outsiders and occupied. What felt like necessary coping in Lebanon, here in the United States it seemed to be a distraction that replaced the willingness to understand the motivation of those who killed themselves in that kamikaze attack on the symbol that the twin towers represented. We missed a chance as a nation to avert future violence by our unwillingeness to look at others, and understand differences.

Iraq Invasion

When the invasion of Iraq began in 2003, I had been an American citizen for thirty-four years. Leading up to it, the cries for war and the information being fed to us felt very wrong. Steve, not only an expert on the Middle East but having served as DCM/acting ambassador in Iraq said, "The premises for going into Iraq are false. The administration showed no understanding or wish to understand that part of the world. Iraq is a secular Muslim state. Al Qaeda, being an extremist group using Islam and religious fervor to further a political agenda, was a danger to Saddam's rule. He would never have allied himself with them nor did he allow them to operate in Iraq. Even though he was a ruthless dictator, invading Iraq will be catastrophic and will create more terrorists." He predicted the quagmire and the danger such a war would create. But no one wanted to listen to diplomats like him who had spent their whole careers trying to understand and communicate with other nations. "Our national interest will be threatened further by this needless war. It will turn the Arab and Muslim world against us." Steve told anyone willing to listen. Alas, no one in power did.

Frustrated, unable to counter all the false "intelligence" about "weapons of mass destruction," for the first time in our lives, Steve and I decided to march, and protest against the coming invasion. The sign I made to carry quoted Einstein: "Peace cannot be kept by force, it can only be achieved by understanding." Leila with her sign—"I lived there"—and Adam, with a sign of his own, joined us. As people gathered in Lafayette Square, I noticed two young men with crew cuts across the street, each walking a large German Shepherd along H Street. They caught my attention with their purposeful strides. They crossed the street and headed in our direction. An alarm bell went off in my head; I could sense trouble. An instant correlation happened for me. I went up to some policemen on horseback. "Do you see those men with the dogs coming here? This will cause trouble. Are they allowed to bring dogs to a demonstration like this? A lot of people here may be Muslim who don't appreciate having dogs amongst them, and some may just be afraid of dogs." "Ma'am, this is a park, they have the right to walk their dogs." "But they're not just 'walking' their dogs, look at them! They are heading straight towards the crowd. It doesn't look good. If something happens or a child is bitten, then you will be responsible. You are here to keep the peace!" They just ignored me. The guys did come straight into the densest part of the gathering. I heard dogs barking, shouts, angry sounds, then silence. A few minutes later they left. I guess the organizers and people like me who felt the same malicious intent must have sent them away. I was relieved.

A couple of years later, as Steve and I sat watching the nauseating images and reports of torture that surfaced from Abu Ghraib, it reminded me of that same strong uneasy feeling I had that day in the park. Those two men had obviously learned about Muslims, knew they would be afraid or angry about the dogs and were trying to use that knowledge to engender fear and provoke people. As Steve predicted, our disastrous invasion of Iraq diverted attention and resources from going fully after Al Qaeda in Afghanistan. Even more unsettling was the reality that it may have actually increased the danger to our national security by angering so many people around the world, making recruitment of extremists more likely, and even enabling Al Qaeda to operate, for the first time, in Iraq.

Naively transplanting "democracy" into different cultures creates a backlash. Ideals coming from a Western society need to be adjusted to be compatible and congruent with communitarian cultures, such as Iraq's. The metaphor that came to my mind was of an organ transplant. One must find an organ that is compatible with the body in need, otherwise it is rejected. People have to learn how to live in a society where everyone's rights are respected and protected. Transposing worthwhile ideas to other countries requires knowledge of, and respect for, the recipient in order for the transplant to be viable. Musicians have been able to create a vibrant fusion of East and West; why can't politicians do the same?

When we betrayed our own values with our invasion of Iraq and inhuman torture in prisons such as Abu Ghraib, the whole world reacted in anger. We lost respect and credibility as a nation. Without understanding what makes a culture tick, we are more likely to make big mistakes and worsen the problem. Steve usually explains it this way: "The U.S. was respected and liked in the Middle East because we were never a colonial power and always upheld justice and human rights. By invading and occupying Iraq, we lost that moral edge and alienated people."

Our invasion and occupation of Iraq lacked the historical understanding of and respect for this ancient civilization. Sadly, an old friendship suffered. We had known Jenn and Robert for years, sitting at dinner with them Steve and I were openly angry and agitated that we were about to invade Iraq. Steve gave them historical facts and his expert analysis, but they refused to believe we were being manipulated into supporting an unnecessary and destructive war. It all fell on deaf ears. Like many Americans consumed by fear and anger, our friends refused to let history and an understanding of Iraq stop the frenzy to invade.

While the fear generated by 9/11 was alive, it kept Americans from thinking clearly. Much later when "mission accomplished" turned out to be mission misguided, many Americans felt they had been misled on Iraq with false and cherry-picked information. Too many sons and daughters were being killed—deaths in Iraq and Afghanistan surpassed the toll of 9/11. Veterans were returning with broken spirits and bodies, families were affected. And that does not begin to speak for the staggeringly huge number of Iraqis who have died and are dying, including women and children.

And yet, Steve and I both noticed that many Americans retained a genuine desire to learn about the Middle East. As we listened to "instant experts" on the television shows who knew very little about the history and politics of the region—or worse, had a political agenda—Steve and I decided to start lecturing together. He covered foreign policy, economics, and history; I presented on the culture, women, and human rights movements.

2006—Israel Bombs Lebanon

In July 2006, Steve and I were in Germany, where I was teaching cross-cultural art therapy at ICASSI. Leila and Adam had gone to Lebanon for a friend's wedding. She had wanted so much for Adam to see Lebanon and meet the family. It was a joyous occasion, but ten days of fun rooftop dancing and celebration ended with the start of Israel's thirty-three–day bombardment of Lebanon, a retaliation for the kidnapping of two Israeli soldiers. Rather than commence the usual negotiations for prisoners, Israel told the world this collective punishment was justified.

Meanwhile in Germany, Steve and I watched with horror on CNN International the bombing not only of Hizballah strongholds, but of almost all bridges, highways, roads, gas stations, and power stations—in short, all the infrastructure that had been rebuilt in Lebanon after the civil war. Even the sole milk and yogurt factory in the country was not spared. Nor did Beirut's predominantly Christian quarter of Ashrafiyeh escape Israel's air strike. Leila and Adam were trapped in Beirut along with my family. Leila and Adam's emails told of relentless bombing and seeking safety huddled in hallways at Hanan's apartment. Leila's Baghdad experience with Scud missiles made her barricade all glass windows and doors and encourage everyone to keep clear of them, for fear of flying glass. They were living day and night with the sound of bombs and ambulance sirens, and the whole apartment building shook with every explosion. A large poster celebrating Lebanon's renaissance after the civil war, with the caption "Beirut, the city that never dies," now hung on a wall in their hiding place, a reminder of its resilience.

We and the world at large were shocked by images of dead children being pulled out from the rubble of buildings in the neighborhood of Qana, buildings gutted by American-made bunker-busting bombs sold to and dropped by Israel. Steve knew that U.S. law specifically prohibits the use of such bombs, as well as cluster bombs, in highly populated areas. There are strict limits on their use; they are meant for defensive purposes only. To crown the extensive destruction, President Bush encouraged continued bombing and refused to press for a ceasefire while American-made Israeli warplanes and American bombs—paid for with our taxpayers money—were killing Lebanese men, women, and children! This only inflamed more people, and most probably provided recruitment fodder for extremists.

Steve was on the phone with everyone he knew at the State Department, trying to find out about evacuation plans. Other embassies had sent ships to evacuate their people or arranged for buses to cross to Syria. The State Department took more than three weeks to organize evacuation of American citizens. It seems there was a problem between military commands in Europe and the Middle East trying to figure out who had jurisdiction and which one would pay for what. I was terrified and distressed because Israel had blockaded Lebanon by air and sea. The airport and all major roads and bridges had been destroyed. Katie and Adam could not escape. I don't how I managed to teach my intensive all-day classes, but it probably kept me from going crazy with worry. Between classes, Steve and I would run back to our hotel room to catch the latest news. Telephone lines were jammed and hard to get through. We were glued to CNN International, yelling at the TV, shaking our fists in anger as we watched, over and over again, the image forever imprinted in our minds of Condoleeza Rice spouting off how it was too early to call for a cease-fire. "What? Not enough Lebanese killed yet?" Steve and I screamed at the screen.

Leila and Adam spent almost three weeks with Hanan, her husband, and mother, listening to the war raging around them. They didn't want to leave the family but as my cousins kept telling them, "This is our life, we've been here before, your parents are worried, so you need to leave as soon as possible." When Leila and Adam said they didn't want to leave the family under such conditions, Hanan told them, "You can help more by going back home and letting people know what is really happening here."

Meanwhile at ICASSI, I was asking my Israeli colleagues if they thought it would be safe for Leila and Adam to leave by car. "Hala, just make sure they do not take a big car. Let them get the smallest car they can find. It's risky since Israel will bomb any moving vehicle." Some of these colleagues who were our friends were sympathetic; others could only channel the collective Israeli fear of any aggression against them. Even though Israel has the world's fourth strongest military and hundreds of nuclear warheads, and had never ratified the Nuclear Non-Proliferation Treaty, its people have never healed from the atrocities of the Holocaust, inflicted on Jews by Germany and other European countries. When one lives in a victim mentality it is hard to see one's actions as anything besides survival. "David" could not see that he had become "Goliath." So the violence went on.

Eventually, having at last relented to pressure from family in the United States and Lebanon, Adam and Leila fled to Damascus with a trusted taxi driver. It was a harrowing trip on small mountain roads. The driver tuned to the radio throughtout the trip trying to figure out the safer routes. At one point, the radio announced that Israeli planes had just destroyed a convoy of ambulances that they had seen go past them. Later, in a voice still nervous and angry, Leila recounted, "Mom, we had to keep quiet because the driver explained he had to completely focus on avoiding being strafed by Israeli jets—made in the U.S.A.!" The irony that they might have been killed by jets made in America was not lost on either of them, or us.

As we sat in Germany and absorbed the extensive, thorough reporting of the massive Israeli bombardment, Steve and I were worried that the whole Arab world would be angry. Later we learned from friends back home in the States, images of what was really happening on the ground in Lebanon—reported in full and accurately in Europe and the rest of the world—were cherry-picked and slanted towards Israel, even on CNN-USA! It was not the first time that U.S. media, fearing lost advertising revenue or because of ideology, did not televise the whole truth and context of conflicts in the Middle East.

We were not sure how Adam or Leila would be received in Syria. Thanks to their smart, diligent taxi driver, they had made it to Damascus in a little over two hours. Parents of a good friend of theirs from New York took them in and other Syrians they met were welcoming, helpful, and kind. To our relief, Adam reported in an email from Damascus, "I'm amazed how people here have been so kind, hospitable, and accepting of us, of me. I grew up being told Syria was out to eliminate all Jews. To be honest I was very nervous about going to Damascus. Everyone we met here has been friendly and open. For example, people went out of their way to walk with us to the correct bus we needed to take to Aleppo. We have had many discussions where we all voiced our anger at what is happening to Lebanon. I know you don't get to see the images of all the destruction and carnage there but we do here. We are helping pack boxes of relief supplies to send to Beirut. At least we feel we're doing something to help. Almost all the people we met still like what the United States stands for and our basic values even though they feel we have betrayed them by invading Iraq and unconditionally continuing to support Israel's occupation of Palestinians at the expense of Palestinian Human Rights, and now refusing to press Israel to stop the bombing of Lebanon."

That mini war might have ended in less than two months, but its legacy endures. Even today, unexploded cluster bombs and mines left behind by Israel in several invasions of Lebanon still injure scores of Lebanese children and innocent people. I read a report that cluster bombs look like cute colorful parachutes, so children are attracted to them and pick them. Israel has constantly refused to hand over maps of where mines were planted.[107] There is only so much that a human spirit can take before it spirals into hopelessness and helplessness. The seeds of extremism are planted in such despair.

In a country slightly smaller than Connecticut—according to an Amnesty International report and The Guardian—during Israel's "disproportionate attacks" over four weeks of bombing, "7,000 air strikes, 2,500 shells from Israeli navy" left an "estimated 1,183 Lebanese dead, mostly civilians, about a third of them children; 4,054 wounded… and 25% of a population of four million displaced…." "Around 4,000 Hozballah rockets were fired at northern Israel during the conflict, killing around 40 civilians. Up to 300,000 people in northern Israel were driven into bomb shelters by the fighting, and 117 soldiers died." The death toll among Israelis was 121 Israeli forces and 44 civilians. Also, "…large parts of the Lebanese civilian infrastructure…were destroyed, including 400 miles (640 km) of roads, 73 bridges, and 31 other targets such as Beirut's only airport, ports, water, power and sewage treatment plants, electrical facilities, 25 fuel stations, 900 commercial structures, up to 350 schools, two hospitals, and 15,000 homes. Some 130,000 more homes were damaged."[108]

As a result, the whole population was re-traumatized and its fragile government was on the brink of collapse. When Leila and Adam returned to the United States, it took them months to recover from their personal trauma. Leila's second play, In the Crossing, is about this experience.

With Leila and Adam safely home, Steve and I continued to

lecture on the Arab world in the hope that we could correct the misinformation and shed some light on the culture and politics of the region. All the news we saw lacked context. The war in Iraq and the high cost in lives made that task more urgent. As in every crisis, chaos gave us the opportunity to transform and transmute poison, to put the pieces together in a new way. I realized that now, more than ever, people like me needed to be out there working to prevent the chasm from getting wider. But first, I needed to do my own healing by working through the images and the words they engendered.

As I gathered the images and words for this book, I came to understand that this story is not only for other "human bridges," nor is it just about putting a human face on an Arab-American woman. My story is the healing journey that arises from confronting bigotry and fanaticism, whether it is a priest from long ago, or criminal militants who use Islam as a weapon, or a state that allows fear and ideology to blind its people to the suffering it inflicts as it bombs, bulldozes houses, uproots olive trees, drives people off their land, and occupies another people.

For decades, I followed the metaphoric threads of my artwork and retrieved pieces of myself strewn between continents. As a teacher, I feel deeply my inner purpose and I truly live the words "bridge between worlds." When I present another reality in a way that people can understand (and not necessarily agree with), then I feel I contribute to building new connections. I now recognize that my "differentness" has always been an asset rather than a liability.

In 2009 as I was readying this manuscript for an editor, "Arabesque: Arts of the Arab World" came to the Kennedy Center in Washington, D.C. It was a rare opportunity for Americans who had never traveled to or lived in the Arab world to experience the diversity and richness of art, music, culture—including a typical *souk* (market) from the Arab World—all in one exhibit. It provided a welcome contrast to all the disinformation and vilification of Arabs so prevalent in the United States.

As the Kennedy Center's president commented in an interview, "It provides a chance for people in the United States to see Arabs not merely as political beings but as human beings." I listened to performances such as a Syrian choir made up of Christian and

Muslim children, who sang Christian, Assyrian, Muslim, Andalusian, and Byzantine songs.

Americans attending the festival discovered how Arab musicians invite participation by the audience via the *tahyeess*—clapping, singing, and even dancing in their seats or in the aisles. Art is a matter of common life experience in Arab culture—it's the tiles on the walls, the woodwork on the Arab arched windows, the rugs, and the colorful tassels on camels and donkeys. Almost everything utilitarian in addition to being aesthetically appealing. Probably like most Arab-Americans walking through Arabesque, I felt moved, proud, and happy that Americans were finally seeing a side of the Arab world they would never have imagined. Art has a way of reaching out and touching hearts and minds.

> *True peace is not merely the absence of some negative force —tension, confusion, or war; it is the presence of some positive force—justice, good will and brotherhood.*
> —Martin Luther King[109]

8

Three Swans, a Car Alarm, and a Wedding

There was a time I used to reject those who were not of my faith. Now my heart has grown capable of taking on all forms. A pasture for gazelles, a convent for Christians. A temple for idols, a Kāaba for the pilgrim. A table for the Torah, a book of the Koran. My religion is love. Whichever the route love's caravan shall take, that path shall be the path of my faith.

—Ibn al-›Arabi [110]

The Wedding

Leila and Adam's wedding provided me with another opportunity to practice my integrative skills. I received a telephone call from them. "Mom, Adam and I have discussed this and we would like you to marry us," Leila said.

"Ha! Ha! Ha!, very funny you guys!" I said.

"But Mom, we're serious about this."

To which, now in full panic mode, I replied, "I can't marry you. I'm just your mother!"

"No problem," they volunteered. "We checked and you can get ordained on the web, many people do that."

I was unmoved. "No way. I have no desire to be ordained on the web or on anything. You know how I feel about organized religion." And that was the end of that, or so I thought.

Later I recounted this to my friends. "Hala, wow, you mean to say that your kids asked you to marry them and you refused? Do you know what an honor that is?"

My heart sank. "Yeah, I guess you're right, I never thought about it that way. I was taken by surprise."

A week later they called back. "Mom, we've talked some more and we still feel we want you to do our wedding ceremony, but we'll do whatever you ask to make you comfortable with it."

My heart bounced back: I get another chance! "Okay, I'll do the ceremony but you will have to choose an official, a justice of the peace, rabbi, minister, sheikh, someone who will pronounce you husband and wife and sign the papers. I'll do the rest."

"It's a deal!" they replied.

This was going to be an interesting wedding: a Lebanese-American woman with a Muslim and Christian heritage marrying a Jewish guy. Adam's biological mother and father are Jewish. They divorced and later, his father Rob married a Palestinian-American woman, called Mike, who was born in Colombia. Who else but a crazy human bridge would tackle all that?

Adam did not want a rabbi, and Leila did not want a random minister. They chose Ginger Luke, a Unitarian minister and a friend. She gracefully accepted and agreed to travel two hours to the Eastern Shore and limit her part to four sentences. I will always be indebted to her for her flexibility and willingness to minimize her role and let me run the show.

It was nerve racking enough to navigate through the industry that exists to meet our expectations for the "perfect" wedding. But as the mother of the bride, I agonized over the color of the tablecloths, centerpieces, the invitation, and the terror of them all, THE WEDDING LIST! But also, for nine months, I struggled to craft a ceremony that Leila and Adam would like. Steve worked on the complex seating arrangements for a very diverse guest list. The kids wanted a "simple wedding"—casual, no maids of honor, no fanfare. It was informal, but not simple, especially since it was out of town. "The kids," as I called Leila and Adam, wanted the ceremony to take place by the water, at his father's bayside home on Maryland's eastern shore.

After all the stressful visits to bridal shops, Leila chose to wear my wedding dress, which I had designed and Tante Georgette had sewn. It was a simple dress and Leila loved it and it fit her well. To make it distinctive for Leila, my mom replaced the old trim and, at Leila's request, created long, flowing sleeves that attached to Leila's upper arms. It was a wonderful blend of not only old and new, but Lebanese and American.

Together with "the kids" and Adam's family, we worked on weaving families, cultures, faiths, and beliefs. I invited close family members to participate in the ceremony. My mother read a passage from the Bible and Adam's grandfather read a Hebrew blessing from the Torah. Steve celebrated this marriage of many faiths, spoke of Katie and Adam's openness and love. He was followed by Adam's mom, who gave her blessing, and then Adam's dad, who chose my favorite joke to weave into his message. "There was this mother mouse and babies coming home after foraging in the kitchen. A huge menacing cat suddenly blocked their way. The mother mouse looked straight into the cat's eyes and barked, "WOOF–WOOF," at which point the cat quickly scrammed. The mother mouse calmly turned to her babies and said, "See children, why it's important to learn another language?"

The spot "the kids" chose in the garden for the ceremony was right on the Chesapeake Bay and was separated from a rocky beach by a fence. Rob and Mike worked very hard to complete a three-year landscaping plan in a few months. Plants and small water features created a beautiful setting, but we felt the need to create a special place for the ceremony. So after the rehearsal Leila, Adam, and I chose river stones from the beach and in the tradition of Native American spirituality, placed them in a circle. A small tent over the circle completed the "altar." We stood in the middle of the "circle of stones" holding hands to honor the moment.

I had been nervous about the weather since it had rained steadily and heavily for the whole month before, but the morning of the wedding, the sun came out and remained out until we all went to the dinner tent later. As the family scrambled to line up for the procession, I hurriedly lit some charcoal cakes in a Saudi incense burner—a gift from Saudi friends—and tossed in handfuls of frankincense crystals that I had carried back from Oman and Saudi Arabia. I was not sure how long they would last, but I wanted them for the procession at least. One of Adam's young cousins led the way, carrying the heavily-smoking incense burner. The rest of the family representing a medley of ethnic and religious origins followed the smoking incense down the imaginary aisle of grass to the music of "WE…ARE…FAMILY!" The incense burner remained on the grass in front of the stone circle and, to my delight, a gentle breeze arrived and this ancient fragrance blessed us with its cleansing smoke during the whole ceremony. It was a touch of my Middle Eastern roots and another of Native American tradition, of smudging and creating sacred space.

I began the ceremony with the words: "This beautiful place embodies all the elements of nature: water, air, earth, wood, and fire. Help us create a sacred space here where nature and intention become church, synagogue, mosque, temple, and much more—because the Divine is not limited to a particular place or a particular belief. And in the presence of the Divine there is only one human spirit that we all share."

I continued: "While we feel sadness that some loved ones are no longer with us, their presence can be felt in the most powerful earthly form, the love between Adam and Leila that brings us here today." At that moment, unbeknownst to the kids and me, three swans flew in, hovered, and landed on the water behind us. Since our backs were turned to the bay we did not see them. Adam's dad did, and kept trying to get our attention: "Psst, psst, did you see the swans?" I did not understand what he was saying and was annoyed by the distraction. Later, as Rob described what he saw, I felt tears running down my cheeks. Both of us felt as if the spirit of Rob's mother, my dad, and Teta Habouba had graced the ceremony.

But that was not the only distraction. In the midst of the ceremony, suddenly a piercing car alarm went off. Someone went to check—not only was it Adam's car causing the racket, but the trunk was open and flapping. "My car is temperamental. I'd better take care of it," he said. So off he went, leaving Leila alone at the "altar." I quickly moved to stand next to her until Adam returned. All the guests by then were laughing, and so were we. We resumed the ceremony when the groom returned. After my own blessing, Ginger gave the official pronouncement.

Later I told Rob, "You know, the car alarm reminded me how in Beirut, after a wedding, all the guests and family drive around the city honking their horns in celebration." He replied "Hala, that was your dad, letting you know he was here!"

A blend of Eastern and Western music and dancing started as soon as everyone moved under the big tent, to be interrupted only by dinner. Guests and family of all ages, faiths, and cultures poured onto the dance platform and grass sweating in the heat, but laughing and celebrating. It was heartwarming to see Adam's Jewish family dancing the *"Dabkeh,"* the Lebanese folkdance, and the belly dance, and Lebanese and Palestinian friends and cousins dancing the Jewish *hora*. The joy was tangible that night under the tent, despite the pouring rain that had returned.

Tante Paulette and my college friend, Fatima, had flown in from Beirut. There were also two cousins who lived in the States. But the rest of my family from Lebanon could not come. Watching the happiness and the love sheltered under the tent, I felt a low-grade sadness. I shook it off, but words that had poured out weeks earlier drifted back into my mind. Marrying one's daughter was emotional enough without the pain of being separated from my family in Lebanon, and missing my dad.

"Marrying My Daughter"

Nobody told me
when I married my daughter
what upheaval it would bring.
Nobody told me
that old hurt and sadness
would come flooding back.

I'm supposed to be ecstatic
and I am, so why do I keep crying?
Why does my heart feel so sad?

I know it is time to transition
once more into the new.
A new relationship with my married daughter
and her wonderful husband too.

So what are these tears about?
This emotional roller coaster that I ride?
Why am I teary
when I should be laughing all the time?

Part of it I know
is missing my family abroad.
At times like this
my support world feels small.

The familiar that comes down the ages
suddenly has a world in between.
These days the crossing is harder,
the ocean and divide too wide.

I envy the in-laws
whose families are here.
I'm marrying my daughter
and I want all my family around.

My heart feels the hands that released me
when I married and left so many years ago.
Please God have those hands of loved ones
stand behind me as I let Leila go.

Andalusia

In 2005, we took Leila and Adam on a visit to Andalusia, in southern Spain. I had always wanted to visit the place where Arab Muslims ruled for almost eight hundred years (711–1492 AD) and created a tolerant and rich blend of cultures and religions. The word Andalusia derives from its Arabic name *Al-Andalus*. In Baghdad, Damascus, and later in Andalusia, Arabs not only rescued and translated the great teachings from Greek and Roman and Eastern civilizations, they contributed their own inventions in various fields: the sciences, applied hydrology, optics, engineering, medicine where Ibn Sina or Avicenna as he was known in Europe showed how tubercolosis was contagious but sadly he was not believed in Europe. He understood the relationship between emotional and physical well-being. He wrote a 14-volume encyclopedia, the *Qanun al –Tob* (Canon of Medicine- note that the word canon comes from the Arabic) that contained Greek, Arab, Hindu and Islamic medical information. It was translated into Latin in the 12th century and became the standard medical text in Europe for almost five centuries. Ibn Nafi's diagram in 1242 CE of the human circulatory system and surgical tools surprisingly similar to those in use today. Arab physicians and scholars were centuries ahead of their Western counterparts, they were the first to use catgut to close surgical wounds. They made advances in music, (the *oud* is believed to be the precursor of the guitar), and much more. In mathematics they invented algebra (from the Arabic *al-jabr*) and—thanks to a ninth-century Arab mathematician Alkali, the algorithm (without which we might not have computers). They kept the flame of learning, art, and a peaceful, respectful, and enriching coexistence burning when the rest of Europe was in the Dark Ages. "...Arab and Islamic civilization gave an immense contribution to the development of global civilization."[111]

What moved me was the way Arab Muslim rule, based on the Ummayad interpretation of Islam, created an open, enlightened, eclectic, culturally and religiously inclusive civilization that attracted a diversity of talented people who lived and worked together. Arabs embraced and married into all religions and ethnic groups. Christians and Jews were part of this renaissance, and they were free to practice their religions. In the 10th century, the city of Cordoba boasted seventy libraries. Just the Caliphate library alone in Cordoba had 4,000 manuscripts, compared to 400 in the largest library of Christian Europe. "There was a paper factory, running water, 900 baths, but mostly intellectual wealth." I believe that Arab rule lasted as long as it did in southern Spain because of its acceptance of differences, and the "interplay between very different modes of learning, even those contradictory to each other like faith and reason."[112]

Since pre-Islamic times, Arabic had been the language of poetry and love. It was also the language in which God dictated the verses of the Qur'an to the prophet Muhammad. Being illiterate, Muhammad asked his wife, Khadijah, who was literate (and his former boss) to transcribe the words he received. That is why the Qur'an is considered the word of God and Muhammad only his messenger. It is also why the Qur'an burnings over 1300 years later in the United States were seen as sacrilegious.

At the time of Arab Muslim rule of Andalusia, no other language—

not Latin, not Hebrew—was able to move between the seemingly incompatible arenas of romantic poetry, religious discourse, liturgy, and the daily life and pathos. Arabic, and the intellectual revival it brought, attracted Christians and Jews who became "Arabized," but not necessarily "Islamized." Arabic became the catalyst for the reinvention of the Hebrew language, as described by Maimonides in the eleventh and twelfth centuries.[113]

I found myself often in tears during this visit, moved not only by the beauty and grace of Alhambra, but by what Andalusia represented for me—a peaceful, enriching co-existence that I yearned for, and that the four of us embodied. Here in this place, walking, laughing, eating with Steve, Leila, and Adam, I felt totally "at home." Perhaps it brought back that feeling as a child of belonging in my family.

The history of that period was an important piece of the puzzle for me. It was something I could take back and help counter the image of Arabs and Muslims being violent and uncivilized people. I could be proud of those ancestors who modeled mutual respect, inclusiveness, love of beauty, art, science and intellectual discourse, and who bridged so many divides and created such an enlightened society.

These days when "Muslim" is equated with "terrorist," I want to reclaim the openness, beauty, and richness of Arab and Muslim culture, which in its heyday existed in Southern Spain, just as it did first in Damascus and Baghdad. To me, the age ushered by the Catholic Spanish monarchs—the age that brought the Inquisition, the expulsion of Jews and Arabs, the burning of books—was a continuation of the Dark Ages, in which fear of otherness, of differentness, created a desire to destroy everything about that "other," even vestiges of what was good. On that visit to Andalusia, I learned more about Arab and Muslim art and science than I ever was taught in my Eurocentric college art history classes. I felt pride, marvel, anger, and sadness that this history of the Arab and Muslim civilization is mostly absent in the modern world.[114]

All four of us loved being there together. Leila and I were especially affected by this visit. "Mom, doesn't it feel like some sort of pilgrimage?" Leila asked me after another bout of tears on my part. "Yes, haboubti, Andalusia is not only a beautiful part of Spain, but it is where, during the Muslim Arab rule, all aspects of us as a family, Muslim, Christian, and Jew coexisted peacefully, respectfully, enriching each others' lives and the world around them," I answered. "And that's how the world should be!" Adam added.

God does not take sides, Jesus, Buddha, Allah all the great beings speak of compassion and inclusiveness.

—Thich Nhat Hanh[115]

9

Dropping Anchor

*Our primary relationship is with ourselves, and ultimately that's
the only one that can provide the foundation for wholeness.*
—Shakti Gawain[116]

Throughout my life I have naturally, effortlessly, and unconsciously built hundreds of bridges: every time I visited my
Christian and Muslim relatives, every time I moved countries with
my husband, every time I spoke out against exclusion and prejudice. Once you have experienced several cultural "boxes," staying in any one of them feels stifling, as most Third Culture Kids
and Global Nomads will tell you. I needed the freedom to move in,
around, and between different paradigms, such as the communitarian and the individualistic worldviews. Feeling bound to a single one takes away choice—the choice to seek my own truth unen-
cumbered by assumptions, rigid systems, cultural world views, or
religious dogmas. Ultimately, I realized I had been moving towards
what Slater calls an "integrative culture."[117]

As a child I had, subconsciously, decided not to fully belong
in either of my families because I mistakenly deduced this meant
choosing between them. As a result, I never felt that I fully belonged
in Lebanon. I left at twenty-three, and (excepting a few brief visits)
I did not return until my fifties. By then, I was reminded of many
things I did not like or agree with about my birth culture—like the
apathy and discouragement that prevent any real change. However, I rediscovered the enveloping warmth and love of my family, a
deep connection to the land, the mountains, the sea, the incredible
hospitality, the slower pace of life, the rich tradition of greetings,

the proverbs, and the ways to be with people in a respectful yet heartwarming way—all things I had not thought much about for so long. I rediscovered what tomatoes could *really* taste like, cucumbers that are crunchy, fruits that do not taste like plastic. I enjoyed the time people take for connecting on a daily basis. I had missed aromas, people, places, and things carved into my memory. I had missed being known in a way that carried my history.

As Leila and I prepared to leave Beirut at the end of our 2004 visit to Lebanon, we cried in each other's arms. She was afraid of losing the connection with family and friends that she so painstakingly had built over the summer; I realized I had never grieved when I left as a young bride so many years ago. All the accumulated losses over a lifetime converged. My daughter's soothing words still floated in my head: "Mom, home is where you are loved!" I am loved both by my family in Lebanon and by my family in the United States. I am lucky in many ways, even while destined to always live in-between. The farewell gift from that visit to Lebanon was a transformation of the narrative from my childhood, so that living between worlds was no longer a burden, but a gift.

On the plane going back to Washington D.C., there were many women and children of all ages, on their way back to Canada or to wherever they had immigrated. *Ghass albi* in Arabic means "my heart was choking," and mine was as I watched and heard a child calling out for his grandmother left behind. His anguish was met by his mother's own loss and sadness at leaving. Like many other mothers on that plane, who looked like lost children themselves, she could not truly comfort her child.

Hours later, as the plane began its descent into Dulles airport, I felt that I was "home" maybe for the first time in my life. "Home" was here in the United States, a country built on diversity and immigrants.

Family Visits Washington

A few years later, I invited Tante Paulette, her daughter, Maha, and Tante Georgette's daughter, Rita, to visit us in Washington. Tante Paulette had come twice before to see us and later she came to Jeddah with mom to visit. But this would be the first time for Maha and

Rita. With my mom getting older and beginning to lose her memory, I felt an urgency to bring them together. I realized I might have wanted to spare them the regret and pain I still harbor for having missed saying goodbye to Teta Habouba who died while we were living in Mauritania. My parents chose not to tell me she was very sick, and did not even inform me of her death. My parents meant well, but they didn't understand how being uninformed complicated my grief process and denied me closure with my beloved Teta Habouba. Many years after she passed away, I would cry at memorial services of even people I hardly knew, aware that I continued to mourn her. She had not been just a grandmother; when I was two months old, when my mom came down with jaundice, I was whisked away to live with Teta Habouba. At the time, Tante Paulette lived at home with her mom. So, from the perspective of attachment theory, I felt they were both second mothers to me. It made her loss especially difficult for me.

During the time Paulette, Maha, and Rita were with us, I was once more struck by the harmony in my family. I asked Rita, a Maronite Catholic, "How do you feel going up to Tripoli so often to visit Tante Paulette and your cousins?" (Tripoli is a mostly Sunni Muslim town in the north of Lebanon, not to be confused with Tripoli, the capital of Libya). "I need to be close to them. The closeness of family is what is sacred," she replied. Even now, family bonds enable Lebanese to look at similarities rather than differences. The centrality of family usually overrides what could be divisions between faith or politics.

Tante Paulette chipped in, *"Al deen, moāmaleh."* (Religion is about the way you treat people.) Except for those who excluded my mom and me, I'm grateful to have a family who still thinks and feels this way. It is as if each member has been an important building block of my own bridge-self.

Their visit also stirred up some unfinished issues for me. These loving family members were part of my last link to Lebanon. As each generation passes away, there will be fewer cousins with whom I have a continuous shared history. Maha was a little girl when I left as a bride so many years ago, Rita was slightly older. Their visit, which lasted a month, brought up a familiar, intimate feeling of belonging, without dispelling a sense that I was a stranger in some way. I thought I knew them, but did I? Certainly not as the adults they had become. Did they really know me? I was the one who left, and in a strange way, I had become more of a legend than a real person. It's as if my "Lola self" ended when I left, and my "Hala self" began. My relatives called out both my names, unsure which one to use—but to me it didn't matter. I am Lola *and* Hala now, and I am one of the elders in my family, hopefully a wise one. One quote I love says, "The gift of wisdom comes to you when you have walked enough pathways and found enough dead ends to truly know the forest."[118]

During their stay we all kept making adjustments. They preferred to eat the day's main meal at lunch, followed by a light supper of cheese and fruits, so we switched our routine. I wanted us to get to know each other better, and deeper, but shopping got in the way. "Everything is half of what it costs in Beirut," they would say. It was surprising to me how easily visitors get easily sucked into our shop-till-you-drop consumerism. But as I'd noticed on my first extended return in 1999, most Lebanese had adopted materialism big time, in what I guess is in an unconscious attempt to fill in that gaping wound from the civil war. I tried to explain. "Being American is not about the good bargains at the mall. Or the beautiful green lawns and trees. It is about how you find your place in a country that is so multicultural."

I felt frustrated, and didn't know why. I kept talking to them, sharing my metaphor of the American "salad," which I still championed over the "melting pot." I talked about how everyone (excepting African-Americans descended from slaves and Native Americans, who are the original inhabitants) had come for opportunity, to flee oppression and poverty, to live a better life, or just be with someone they loved. Why did I need to lecture my relatives about the immigrant experience, and take every chance to tell them what my wandering emigrant life had been like?

I couldn't stop. "It is a daunting task to start all over again building your life. Sometimes you encounter injustice and prejudice. Some newcomers are overwhelmed and hang on to traditions they remember, beliefs from their birth land. They're afraid of losing all connections to their former selves. They become frozen in a time warp while back in the birth country, the culture had moved on."

They listened politely. Arabs are taught to be courteous. But was it fair of me to try to make them understand? I wanted them to know me not as the perfect cousin they heard so much about, but as the real me. Could they understand my life? Certainly I could never fully understand what it was like to live through a civil war, through Syrian and Israeli occupation and bombings.

I gave them a copy of this manuscript to read, while I listened to their stories. They were curious about my work as an art therapist, so I invited them to play in the sand tray with me. Each of us created something in the tray of our own choosing.

Sand Tray, Sand Play

In any creative therapy, you don't "think" about what you are going to do. Just as with students and clients, I enjoined my family that we all should "let our hands and hearts lead us. Tell your left brain to get a coffee break!" They laughed. Each of us just shared what we wanted to say. Talking about their trays, the visual metaphor of what they had been through helped them shed tears, after which they said *"Moosh māa'ool, shoo rtehna!"* (Unbelievable, how peaceful and relieved we feel!) It felt as if some of the bottled-up trauma of the war was released, without any re-traumatizing.

The teacher in me could not resist. "The sand tray was so helpful because the figures are symbols that tap into our deepest selves and makes it easier to go beyond our logical mind. So, when we share our stories in the tray, our words help us make sense of art's metaphorical language."

The first title I gave my tray was "In Between." No mystery there, I thought. Later, I described what I saw in my journal.

> I am the sailboat always at sea, sailing on the currents of life between the Lebanese shore, represented by a traditional symbol of the Lebanon I grew up in, the *jurun* (stone basin) I remember Teta Habouba pounding the *kibbeh* in, and the United States, where I placed a lighthouse. I feel a certain sadness and frustration mingled with acceptance about the lingering sense of "in-betweenness." Strings of pearls representing my life's journey meander through my different

worlds. The pattern they make is beautiful to look at. The pearls start in the *jurun* and weave and wind back and forth between Lebanon's soil and the United States, perhaps symbolizing the spiral nature of life. A bear and an eagle keep watch where the feathers have floated down.

I took that as a spiritual reminder to "lighten up," and flow with the winds of life. I continued: "Both animals seem to be protecting and holding the common ground between my birth land and my adoptive country. The pearls emerge from the ocean where the lighthouse stands to guide and safeguard us. I have always loved lighthouses for their beauty and their location in or near the sea, but mostly for the light they put out to safely guide passing ships."

I added: "The lighthouse and the lighthouse keeper's house sit on a piece from the Berlin wall I bought when we visited Berlin right after the wall came down. Flowers represent growth from the seeds of understanding I have been planting in the common ground between countries and people."

"Each pearl represents a life experience, positive and negative. Each one by itself would have been lost, but strung together across the landscape of a lifetime they become a thing of beauty. The common thread that holds my pearls together is this ability to navigate between worlds and see all human beings as worthy of respect, dignity and kindness, just as the prayer hands of Namaste represents the Buddhist belief of honoring the Divine presence in each other."

Interestingly, real and cultured pearls are formed by the irritation of some piece of sand that the organism is trying to protect itself from. "Most of my pearls had started as a painful feeling, but became something precious." Looking at the tray, it seemed to hold my whole life's journey so far in one glimpse.

The family's visit clarified further the process of "coming home" for me, which began more than a decade ago. A few days later, when I went back to my sand tray, it guided me further. Looking at it I felt the *jurun* was too empty, so I filled it with little figurines dressed in traditional Lebanese garb that I had purchased on my last visit from my favorite "Artisana Libanais,"

I added butterflies, one perched on the sailboat's mast and one among the flowers. Another butterfly perched on the lighthouse keeper's house showing me more blessings. The butterflies came to symbolize the transformation that came with every crossing I ever made.

I wrote in my journal: "Flowers are now scattered and blooming, the result of seeds I planted that now attract more butterflies, more transformation. The lighthouse is like a bridge, it sends its beacon all the way around. But instead of connecting, it lights the way. The piece from the Berlin wall was like my life's work, just as people hammered at that wall and broke it down, I have tried to break down what separates people—prejudice, ignorance, and fear—and worked to create a bridge of understanding out of the rubble of walls." O'Donohue's words resonated with me: "Where you are understood, you are home. Understanding nourishes belonging."[119] This struck me as central to my newfound self.

After the family left and throughout the next week I kept changing my tray. I added an Arabic coffee pot next to the *jurun,* which symbolized Lebanese hospitality, food, and community. On the U.S. side, I added a cozy house and a transplanted cedar tree behind it, guarding its back, and a butterfly on top, plus two fruit trees—gifts from nature and from nurturing others. I piled rocks around the lighthouse to reinforce its foundation, because the piece from the Berlin wall no longer felt strong enough to withstand the storms. Lastly, I beached the sailboat next to the lighthouse.

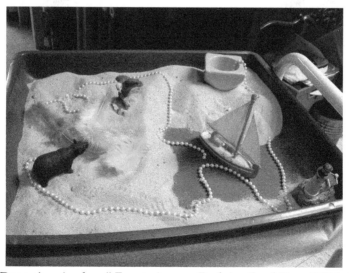

59. "Dropping Anchor." Empty jurun. *Evolving Sand Tray.* ©Hala Buck

60. "Dropping Anchor." Full view. *Sand Tray ©Hala Buck*

61. "Dropping Anchor." Reinforcing lighthouse. *Sand Tray ©Hala Buck*

I shared this with Steve. "I am no longer traveling in between, but now have anchored at my 'home port.' Even though I know that here, too, I will probably not be fully understood." Something within me released and the tears came. As Steve held me I cried about this existential sense of being alone. "When my mother dies," I said, "I will have no one close by from my childhood, except my cousin Mona, who lives in another state." I felt the deep sadness of un-grieved losses: mine, my ancestors', and even my current family's. I cried for all of them and for Lebanon. After two wars, continued instability, and unhealed trauma, I saw how my family—probably like so many Lebanese—are afraid of getting in touch with their feelings. It is frustrating to be a therapist and not be able to heal your family's wounds. But I was glad to give them the opportunity to experience the healing power of their creative expressions.

The latest Syrian crisis, which is spilling over into Lebanon, reminded me of what another cousin, Reem, had told me after she visited her parents in Lebanon after the Hizballah/Israel month-long war in 2006. As an immigrant herself, she noticed how changed the country was after Israel's aerial bombing. It is as if all the old trauma resurfaced and was tearing the fabric of its pluralistic culture. "Prior to this punishing bombardment, people had regained hope and energy; they had rebuilt all the infrastructure, they could breath in life without danger. They were beginning to mend wounds and hearts, until that summer." She added that values we both cherished and carried from our childhoods, such as being there for each other, were fraying as people struggled to survive once more. Rampant materialism and spending beyond one's means continues. "Why does Lebanon need McDonalds when it has the best and healthiest food?" we both railed.

Wars and conflict leave residual damage, some of it not easy to spot or understand. The tray seemed to remind me: "Stop agonizing about everyone, Lebanon, the family, the world, and stop feeling sorry for yourself. Look, you have a home port now!"

I took a deep breath and smiled. The lighthouse had come to represent the guiding light within me, a divine source that is within all of us. Having lived the transient life of the Foreign Service for so long, being uprooted so many times, I liked the idea of being anchored in one place and also in the ocean. It suggested freedom to continue exploring, connecting, and being connected. I changed the title of the tray to "Dropping Anchor."

Family Constellation

Throughout the family's visit I became even more aware of intergenerational factors, especially regarding goodbyes and grief. Iversen writes about the "web of connection lost when our ancestors emigrated from the home countries," and how those countries have a place in the American soul.[120] As a therapist, I have explored how we all carry what I call "ancestral baggage," which contains a multitude of unresolved issues passed down through the generations. This reflects the new science of "epigenetics," which, if I understand it correctly, shows how our DNA carries our ancestral genes and how those genes may have been changed by our ancestors' experiences. Thus began my exploration of ways to help myself and clients heal intergenerational wounds.

After my family went back to Lebanon, I decided to join a "Family Constellation" workshop to sort out what reconnecting with my family had brought up. Like me, the facilitator, Susan, integrates many healing practices. She reminded me that even though I stand here on American soil *as* an American, all my direct ancestors are standing behind me, providing the loving energy that runs through the generations. I had not yet told her about the sand tray. "So those people I felt I needed in and around the *jurun* were my ancestors. Wow, I did feel forlorn with it empty in the beginning." It was also what those strings of pearls were trying to show me," I remembered the feeling of peace that the sand tray brought to that lonely place of "in-betweenness." Having watched my father slip into depression and death, I learned to be thankful for the loving family I always had and still do despite the distance.

Art and sand tray therapy have a spiritual way of providing guidance, and can even show you the solution to a problem. Intuitively, I felt the need to place all those little ancestral figures in that *jurun*. At the time, I did not understand why, but later it became clear to me. Other cultures have rituals honoring their ancestors, perhaps the sand tray was my way of doing that. Even though I left my birth country, I was not bereft of a history, of timeless guidance, and love that pours out of Teta Habouba's *jurun*. My family and ancestors will always be part of who I am, and I will always be part of them. I never had to choose as a child between my parents' religions; nor do I now, as an elder, need to choose between the two countries I love. Nor do I need, in my professional work, to choose only one way of helping people pierce the fog of separateness. Instead, I can help guide them towards the interconnectedness of all beings.

A week after my family left I was called in for jury duty. Sitting in the waiting room with people looking as diverse and as American as me, I was grateful my sailboat had brought me "home." I was back in my American life, at peace, and grateful for it. Everything around me looked clearer, sharper. The trees were dropping their leaves early that year; everything looked beautiful and, like my sand tray, continuously changing.

Several months after the family's visit, I received a phone call telling me that my cousin Maha, who we thought had terrible fibromyalgia, died. I learned then that she had been in stage-four cancer and didn't want to tell her mother, or me. I'm glad she was able to come for what turned out to be her first and last visit here. I cannot begin to imagine what it must be like for Tante Paulette to lose her daughter like that.

Towards the end of writing of this book, something began to percolate into a clear insight that I had formerly only touched upon. When I married Steve and left Lebanon, I never thought of myself as an immigrant. I had stepped off one piece of land, but did not step onto U.S. soil permanently for another thirty-one years. Accompanying my husband, I landed and soon after took off for and from nine different places. My life was about creating a feeling of safety, belonging, and "home" for whatever time we had in each country—one year, or two, or four. Even the five U.S. assignments and "home leave" vacations concluded with yet another move. I remember always feeling the pressure of finishing a degree, or taking a course before our "tour of duty" in the United States was over.

Even after we returned for good, it took me a while to realize there was no longer any time constraint on my life. "Wow," I said to Steve one day. "I believe that I am experiencing what a newly arrived immigrant experiences. It is as if I had just gotten off the boat so to speak!" "What do you mean?" he asked, rather perplexed. "Well, while we were still in the active transient life of the Foreign Service, I did not have to deal with the permanence of leaving my birth culture because we were assigned to the Arab World so often." The strangeness and uniqueness of that situation was confusing.

While in 2000 I had been a U.S. citizen for thirty years, I was just beginning to feel the pangs of separation, and the need to permanently plant my roots here. One drawing in my art journal shows a figure carrying a large tree with its roots dangling. It was a perfect visual metaphor of my nomadic life. I had been in transit for so long that I did not fully realize that I had truly landed; the delayed jet lag of this long journey finally hit me.

An intensifying need to explore one's identity usually comes early in the acculturation process of an immigrant. I identified with so much that is part of being American, so why was I experiencing bouts of isolation? The phrase "hidden immigrant," from the TCK literature, seemed to apply to me even after all those years—no one saw me as an immigrant, and I certainly did not perceive myself as one either. Like many other immigrants, I know I can no longer live back in my birth country; but here, sometimes I feel that the way I see things, the wide angle I use, is different from most people, and that brings out this sense of being an outsider again. It was ironic that my parents, who immigrated to the United States in 1975 and remained for the rest of their lives, had actually lived here longer here than I had. I was the new kid on the block. I loved staying put in the United States. I was learning to adjust to a more rooted life, something I had missed while on the move for so long. Unfortunately the ongoing vilification of Arabs, Muslims, and Arab-Americans made me—and still makes me—feel sad and frustrated.

My story is finding me as I write this. It has been tracking me for over sixty years. "We find our stories in the dark, and share them in the light."[121] These synchronistic messages boosted my courage to pursue publishing my manuscript. By "storying" my life, as Stone says, I was able to revisit mistaken conclusions and life scripts that I constructed long ago. In so doing I uncovered a new and empowering story of myself and my search for belonging. If we never revisit conclusions made in our past, they "...become frozen in time and our present and future may become extensions of this cold reality."

We risk being "... caught forever in an endless replay of old and often painful narratives."[122]

In response to fearful experiences, we physically develop what Tara Brach calls a "character suit of armor," and "spacesuit strategies."[123] Adlerians call it "lifestyle strategies." We are unaware of this process until it starts creating problems for us, physically and otherwise. "Dropping anchor" further clarified my problematic life pattern. I had convinced myself that I did not need to belong anywhere. That worked for a while and taught me much. But this most recent creative dialogue in the sand tray revealed a self-imposed exile and a feeling of condemning myself to forever live in-between. At some point in writing my story I reconnected with the wounded child within and gently coaxed her out of that limiting shield that had become a prison. What the creative process did was to gently present the reality that, once and for all, I belong simultaneously in both worlds and in all spiritual practices of the world that I have encountered.

My own therapy and my work with clients helped me understand personal and intergenerational armoring. As we move through and out of childhood, we all unconsciously create protective mechanisms to keep us safe. That spacesuit model can be passed down to the next generations. But it also occurred to me that there is what I call "cultural armor" that is forged and shared among a group of people when they perceive threats to their collective culture's survival. This could be what Slater refers to as "control culture," in contrast to "integrative culture" that embraces diversity and continuous integration.[124] For me those strings of pearls that meander through the sand tray represented the latter, since my life is woven into both cultures crossing land and oceans.

My journey had brought me to a new place. This book seemed to be telling me what it wants to be: multidimensional and not beholden to any one category. "I am you; I can, and will, go in these different directions. I will be something different for each person who picks me up to read." It refused to be limited to a "genre." It is memoir, history, exploration of the immigrant history, and a teaching story. I remember reading somewhere that Americans from different heritages write their stories in ways that reflect where they are coming from. Not surprisingly, I recognized myself in several categories. I was committed to tell my truth. At the same time I come from a culture that honors the collective and elders. Therefore my story needed to include my tribe's stories (so-to-speak) that reflect the oral tradition of storytelling that passes from one generation to the next.

If, as a bridge, I was meant to help people understand my birth culture, I had to tell the story of my Semitic Lebanese and Arab roots. I had to fully explore the reality of being this person living in and between worlds. I consciously accepted that destiny and am grateful for its gifts. I often wondered: Do people who *seem* to belong feel fully understood and accepted all the time? Do they ever wonder if—or when—they will be rejected? Reflecting on and making sense of my life enabled me to come home to myself, to find a deep sense of belonging with other human beings and every aspect of nature.

That summer, standing ankle deep in the Atlantic Ocean, I felt a bittersweet warmth course through my body. A thought crossed my mind. By the ocean there are no "aliens." The ocean touches so many shores bringing people together. This water lapping at my feet also laps at the feet of my family in Lebanon and friends we have made around the world. We share its beauty and strength, no matter what name we give the land.

The sand tray not only showed me my sense of in-betweenness, but gently guided me to an understanding that I had finally arrived and planted my symbolic cedar tree in American soil. I am as "home" here as I will ever be. Perhaps that's why my mom planted *nāa'nāa* (mint,) in every house they lived in, even at the retirement home she moved into. Planting those little roots was her way of anchoring, of coming home. My mini-journey around the sand tray led me towards more healing that I didn't know I needed.

In telling my story I am saying, "This is me: now you can know me and the culture I came from and in being known perhaps I can finally belong." My home is now in the United States. This is where I have planted myself and bloomed. All my life I was a master at doing my best to bloom wherever I was transplanted. At the end of my nomadic life I finally found a lovely cove to drop my anchor.

"Belonging to Places"

Belonging to one old land
so much by birth
I learn each day now
what it means
to be born into a new land and new people...

...Let my history then
be a gate unfastened
to new life
and not a barrier
to my becoming...
...and let me now have
the innocence to grow
just as well in shadow or light
by what is gifted
in this land
as the one to which I was born.

—David Whyte[125]

10

Zaātar, Love, and *Mazaher*

*We live between worlds, sometimes comfortable in one, sometimes
in the other, but only truly comfortable in the space between.
This is our conflict and the heart of our story.*
                                            —Marilyn R. Gardner [126]

While I had finally found a peaceful cove, it was not without its
tribulations. For ten years, I was my mom's caregiver as she
slipped away slowly into the fog of dementia, then Alzheimer's. I
wrote most of this book during the middle part of her transition
from this world. She passed away before I had finished the final
edit.

Witnessing her dying process was an unexpected gift. During
the last few weeks, for a few lucid minutes, I got my mother back—
the loving, funny mom I had lost to this terrible disease. I learned
later that this phenomenom is called "terminal lucidity" and there
is a word for it in Arabic as well *sihwat al mawt* (the waking of death).
During the thirty-eight days that my mom lay dying, Leila and I
sang to her, and told her about all the wonderful things she taught
us, did for us and for others, and what she meant to us. So many
memories bubbled up—and they provided the title for this chapter.

Zaātar, a wild herb in the thyme family, is harvested in the
mountains of Lebanon as well as in Palestine and Jordan. It is the
main ingredient in Lebanese *mana'eesh*, which also contains *summac*
(a lemony spice), sesame seeds, and olive oil and is spread on a
large pita dough. This is a beloved breakfast for most Lebanese.
Its tangy taste and the feel of holding a rolled-up, warm piece of
"man'ooshi"—usually wrapped in a paper napkin—is the equivalent

perhaps of holding a comforting cup of tea or coffee. Mom was always using *zaātar*, "because it is good for ze brrain." Even today, I spread it every morning on toast with *labneh*, or kefir cheese, as it's known here. It's just yogurt that is strained overnight through a cheesecloth.

Recently in Washington, a young man came to our house to pick up furniture for a charity organization. He walked into our kitchen, saw the bowl of *zaātar* and olive oil I always have on my counter, and exclaimed "*Zaātar!!!*" with a huge smile and enthusiastic gesture. He did not look Lebanese, so I asked him how come he knew what it was. "My grandmother is Lebanese and she always has a dish of it ready in her kitchen like you have here." His delight was a reminder that *Zaātar* travels with people and transcends borders. Recently *Zaātar* was featured in a National Public Radio program with a food guru who grew up in an Israeli Kibbutz.[127]

Mazaher (also known as *café blanc*, or white coffee) is the distilled essence of orange blossoms in hot water that Teta Habouba or my mom would give me to soothe a stomach ache, or just for comfort. Even now, I make sure I always have a bottle of it. It always brings a whiff of a Beirut spring, pregnant with the smell of orange blossoms, and the image of colorful poppies (coquelicots) and cyclamen dotting the mountainsides, and with that, memories of being loved and nurtured. Even today, *Zaātar* and *Mazaher* transport me to a place within me that I can call "home."

My 2014 visit to Lebanon was not planned. That summer I was teaching at ICASSI's summer institute in the U.K. At that time, the Gaza war was in full swing, and ISIS (or Dāesh, the Arabic acronym for it) was poised near the Lebanese border, so I had not intended to go to Beirut.

But as fate would have it, Leila was offered a residency for two months with a theater company in Beirut (Zoukak) and was invited to perform her latest play, *Hkeelee* ("Tell Me"). This, Leila's third play, began with her recording her *teta's* stories and became an exploration of memory loss and what it means to be(come) American—what we choose to hold unto or let go, and how those decisions come to shape who we are. I decided I wanted to witness and share this important journey, so after my work in the U.K. was done, I joined Leila in Beirut. For years, I had watched her forging and nurturing her own connections with family, friends, and now professional colleagues in Beirut. I felt as if I was passing the generational baton. She was completing a bridge of her own.

Bridging in Transit

En route to Beirut in Heathrow Airport's transit lounge, I found myself mediating between the staff at the passengers' assistance office and an older Palestinian couple traveling with their adult daughter. She wore a bright, fuchsia headscarf or hijab and fashionable tight jeans with matching top. I had overheard her on the cell phone earlier, chatting away in a flawless British accent. We were all waiting for the cartmobile to take us to our respective gates.

I chatted with the desk clerk who turned out to be Romanian, and since I had taught there a few years before, we had a pleasant conversation. "I loved my Lebanese friends," she said. "But when I went to Beirut the waiters were rude, and I hated it." She said it with such anger I was taken aback. It was the first time someone had told me they hated their visit to Lebanon. Later, I witnessed this clerk being nasty and rude to the Palestinian couple. Their daughter had left for a few minutes when their cartmobile arrived. The desk clerk and driver—who turned out to be Polish—both berated the father for putting the hand luggage in the back of the empty cart, instead of his lap, although no one had given any instructions. The father became angry and distressed. That's when I felt I had to step in.

I wondered if the disrespectul tone of the attendant with the parents was triggered by her unpleasant experience in Beirut. It certainly alerted my prejudice antenna. Once more I found myself in that "in between" place—straddling worlds, intervening, and calming tempers (including mine). I helped the father move their hand luggage while firmly asking the attendant and driver to speak respectfully to him, and recognize that they hadn't explained any rules about what luggage went where. I was sure had the couple been European, neither the attendant nor driver would have dared yell at them. Having heard all the shouting, their daughter came running back. Just then my cartmobile arrived, and I gladly climbed in to go to my departure gate.

I arrived at my gate still shaken by the altercation I witnessed.

The staff of the Lebanese air carrier, Middle East Airlines (MEA) were kind and courteous and accustomed to intercultural exchange. The waiting room was full of people speaking a mixture of Arabic, English, and French, and some women wore hijabs. One young Arab girl was walking about in very short shorts, at which even I couldn't help but stare. I had stepped into the diverse Arab world I knew. I dreaded the mad dash to board and the usual *fawda*, or chaos, but actually, all went well. The MEA staff were efficient and polite, the boarding process was smooth, and soon we were on our way.

The MEA Airbus was full of the summer crop of immigrants returning to visit family. These were people from the Arab Diaspora: Lebanese and Palestinian families with children, some itching to show their newborns off to grandparents eagerly anticipating their arrival. They all looked calm; for most, it was probably an annual trip.

I, on the other hand, was a little nervous. Somehow, another ten years had passed since my last visit and I wondered would I feel more at ease if I too had returned every summer?

I also found myself reliving some of the trauma that occurred when Leila and Adam were trapped in Beirut in 2006 during the Israeli-Hizbollah war.[128] Now, Israel was winding down its most recent round of bombings of Gaza, and ISIS was gaining strength next door in Syria, so I worried that violence might erupt again.

Luckily for me, there is always something comforting about airplanes. For our Foreign Service family, they were our secondary transient homes. It usually meant that something had ended and we were on our way to something new. We were once more in transition mode with its different stages; its ending, its neutral zone and heading towards new beginnings.[129]

I took a deep breath and settled into my seat. Hassan, the young man in the seat next to me, was a Canadian citizen, but a Palestinian by birth who grew up in Sidon, in Southern Lebanon. He told me he was a nurse practioner. We enjoyed sharing our commitment to help people in our respective specialties. "I love working with the native people in North Canada," he told me. "I provide the only medical care they have. I respect them and their connection to nature."

Two things struck me on this flight. First, I noticed how helpful and attentive the impeccably made-up MEA crew was. They
helped the passengers without being asked. On many Western airlines, such service is reserved for business or first class passengers.
The meals were delicious and filling, unlike what I remembered
from long flights with United Airlines, and even Air France. The
flight attendant delivered my lunch with a smile and a *"taffaddali
Madame Hala,"* and *"tikrami madame"*—hard to translate, but basically a courteous way to say "here you are, please enjoy." Arabic is
a flowery language and therefore rich in these "feel-good" phrases
that reflect the value its speakers place on respect and hospitality.
Later, while walking up and down the aisle, I saw one flight attendant sitting in the galley kitchen, rocking a baby and feeding her a
bottle while the mom was in the bathroom.

I also noticed how easily passengers struck up conversation
with others across aisles and with people in front or back of them.
All these perfect strangers connecting with ease provided quite a
contrast to the quiet, detached atmosphere I had gotten used to on
other airlines. I realized I had missed these niceties—the warmth
and comfort of being seen and heard.

Along with Hassan, I talked with a young woman with a six-
week-old baby sitting across the aisle, the same age as Leila on her
first transatlantic flight. The mother could hardly contain her excitement. She was eagerly anticipating her parents meeting their
first grandchild. During the five-hour plus flight, she fell into a
deep sleep holding her baby in her lap. We all dozed on and off
and at one point, I looked and saw that the baby had slid down the
mom's knees and now its head was much lower than its body. Almost simultaneously, Nadia, the woman in front of me, and I both
reached out to wake the mom up, but to no avail. The poor thing
was completely zonked out. So we gently repositioned the baby so
its head was up and was more securely held. Just then the mother
woke up, appalled and scared for what could have happened, and
thanked us profusely.

Next I chatted with Nadia, who turned out to be Lebanese-Ca-
nadian, originally from Zahleh, a beautiful town nestled in the
Bekaa valley. I told her I remembered having dinner with my family there at the popular outdoor cafés with small streams running

between the tables. We shared our experiences with yoga and she said she had just brought an Indian guru and his family to Beirut to establish a yoga center that offered Ayurvedic medicine. There were, it seemed, quite a few holistic centers already there. Amazing, I thought. Even with the regional tensions stuck on high, the Lebanese still sought out new and avant-garde things. Between my conversations with Nadia and Hassan, time passed quickly and soon we were beginning our descent into Beirut.

"Home" Here and There

At passport control I decided to go to the "foreign passports" line. I had my American passport, my Lebanese ID card, and my expired Lebanese passport, which I had kept in the event of a family emergency (as the U.S. State Department had often forbidden Foreign Service employees and their families from visiting Lebanon during the civil war.)

I showed both passports and the ID to the officer, who smiled. *"Ahlan wa sahlan!"* he said (Welcome!) as he stamped my U.S. passport. And I knew that when I went home, the U.S. passport officer would also tell me, "Welcome back!" Seeing I was coming back from a Middle Eastern country, he would usually add, "I bet you're glad you're home." I felt blessed to call both countries "home."

My cousin Rita and Leila were waiting for me in the arrival hall, despite the late hour. There was an unusual extra baggage security re-check at the exit, which fueled the anxiety I felt. It was very late when Rita dropped us off at the apartment building that housed the Zoukak theatre company's office and performance space. The private room that came with Leila's residency provided us with a little mother-daughter retreat in this city where my roots, and Leila's will always remain. We both felt we were here to continue nurturing these roots.

Daily Life in Beirut

The next morning, I awoke to the familiar cacophony of car honking, dogs barking, children playing, construction noise, and some occasional vendor loudly promoting his wares. From the window I saw buildings, all in close proximity, balconies overlooking others and all the ground floor verandas and gardens. The buildings in this neighborhood were typical of the houses I remembered, but most were in dire need of repair—concrete chipped from balcony edges and shutters that had not been painted for years.

The sun streamed in through the windows. I showed Leila how to partially close the shutters to keep things cool and still allow the breeze in, as I'd learned in childhood. You can always count on the sun in Lebanon; there are close to 300 days of sunshine to enjoy. But in hot and humid July, you need to keep the sun out of your living quarters, and the shutters, dilapidated as they were, did the trick. As we prepared breakfast in the small kitchen, we would hear a siren that pierced through the other noise. Seeing my face, Leila reassured me, "Mom, it's just like New York City."

The neighborhood had everything one needs: an ATM, pharmacy, a store to buy Sim cards, and grocers stocking all kinds of products—from Charmin toilet paper to every kind of food and amenities one would want from around the world. The one thing not as easily available or reliable was electricity. This was now eight years after the 2006 Israeli bombing, which destroyed the primary power station along with most other infrastructure. Yet electricity was not fully restored; a hobbled government, corruption, ongoing turmoil in neighboring countries, and the influx of one million-plus Syrian refugees all meant that when the power goes off, you're at the mercy of the generator, just like Lebanon is at the mercy of regional conflicts and other kinds of power plays. Lebanese pay the municipality for electricity, and those who can afford it pay for a generator for the hours with no power. People seem resigned to this, although there is plenty of grumbling, fuming, and disgust with the ineptness of the government or, more accurately, the lack thereof. What offsets that is plenty of cathartic collective humor, a key survival skill.

In our little studio, the window unit A/C, thank God, was functioning, except when the power was out—this was for three hours at a time, rotated daily throughout different parts of the city to conserve electricity and help prevent outages. On my first day there, noon was our neighborhood's turn. Before it went out, we had to make sure the hot water heater and A/C were switched off, so as not to overload the generator (or *moteur*, as it is called). Besides a few lights and the refrigerator, the generator could only support a fan in our bedroom. Luckily the residual cool we had prepared for before by putting the A/C on max kept us comfortable.

The studio was in a different neighborhood from Ras Beirut, where I grew up. I felt disoriented, totally dependent on Leila to help me navigate. She was so much more confident and at ease, as if *she* had grown up in Beirut and *I* was the visitor. I still couldn't figure out the exchange rate for Lebanese pounds, the value of which had dropped dramatically since my youth. A taxi now cost what a year's tuition at A.U.B did forty years ago.[130]

Luckily one could use dollars in most situations. Besides the money, I couldn't figure out which *servees* to take. I was constantly reminded that life in Lebanon, as I knew it, was no more. I felt disconnected except for family, food, and the landscape. I didn't like feeling like a stranger, an "alien," in a city that should feel like home.

Leila's Play

On the morning of Leila's play, I sketched my morning random scribble in my trusted art journal. The words it inspired were reassuring. I titled it, "Guardian angel of us all."

> A woman, perhaps embodying all the women in my ancestral line, sits peacefully in front of a guardian angel, wings outstretched to embrace us all. The outline of a figure behind her may represent my parents and the ancestral line of men standing guard as Leila is about to present *Hkeelee*, her play and gift to all of them, thus replanting us both in the land of these ancestors. 8/9/14

Leila and I helped a staff member of Zoukak to set up the classic Lebanese living room that doubled up as a theater. This created an intimate space that was perfect for her play. *Hkeelee* is a personal, moving, and funny performance about memories lost, retrieved, and released—a journey through time and place and back again. As she told the stories of her *teta* and *jeddo*, many in the audience were reminded of their own grandparents. It was a moving experience for Leila and me to have the audience not only understand the words and stories in three languages (French, Arabic, and English), but also spontaneously respond to her. It was particularly touching for both of us when the whole audience joined Leila with gusto as she began singing an Edith Piaf song that my mother especially loved, *"NON!, rien de rien, NON! je ne regrette rien...."* (No, nothing of nothing, no, I regret nothing). They even knew the old Rahbani Lebanese children's song, *"Fi Īndna Shajra Iddam el Beit...,"* It's a song about having a tree in front the house in whose shade children play and build a house.

As Leila transposed these songs and stories, she was connecting the pieces of her life with mine. She recounted how my father, her *jeddo*, had tried to teach her to write Arabic letters when she was little, but she had not been interested. Years later, after Papi died, when Leila decided to learn to write Arabic script she said, "I could feel my *jeddo's* hand on mine." There wasn't a dry eye in the house.

At one point, Leila stopped and passed around index cards and pencils to the audience. She asked them to write down which memories they would want to hold onto and which would they want to let go. For a Lebanese audience, some with memories of the 1975-1990 war and others of the most recent Israeli bombings, this was a very loaded question, and I wasn't sure it would go over well. To my surprise, those gathered found it healing and this simple invitation created a community out of strangers.[131]

Suddenly we heard what sounded like explosions. Leila and I jumped, but the audience was unperturbed. With amused smiles they reassured us, "These are just fireworks, don't worry. It's the late prime minister Hariri's son, coming back today." The Lebanese had become so adept at distinguishing various sounds of exploding ammunition. "You see," they joked, "when we have no bombs, we need to have noisy fireworks." Humor is a great equalizer and healer, and essential to the Lebanese psyche as they endure the uncertainties and tensions of geopolitics around and between them.

Scenes from Our Balcony

A lot of rooftops and balconies in Beirut are like hanging gardens, providing a green respite to a city that has lost so much to the ravages of war and greed. Jasmine was in full bloom, wafting its special scent throughout the neighborhood. From our balcony, I couldn't help but follow the daily life of our neighbors; proximity of buildings made invasion of privacy inevitable and totally normal. I watched as the ground floor neighbor patiently taught a little boy and his sister how to stroke her two cats draped over the small concrete wall. Squeals of delight filled the neighborhood as the cats purred contently.

Another morning it was her husband and adult son playing *tawleh* (backgammon),[132] which Steve and I also like to play. Conversation and comments on the game drifted up. The cat lady came out with a tray of Turkish coffee. She poured it from the *rakwi* (Arabic coffee pot) into small demitasse cups that she passed around. One of the men offered her a cigarette as she sipped her coffee while watching the game. It was beastly hot outside, but they seemed unconcerned.

The next day I woke up to a dog barking. I looked for our neighbors below. The old couple were sitting contently on the veranda, for their morning *sobhiyeh* together—feet up on the parapet, sipping their coffee and smoking cigarettes. That day, the power was off between 6 and 9 a.m. and on their small patio they could enjoy what little coolness the morning provided.

These scenes from our balcony reminded me of my childhood and how different and slower the pace is in Lebanon. There is no frenzy in going about life. Earning a living is important, but balanced by the centrality of family and socializing with friends and neighbors. I realized that's why I had instinctively explained to Richard in Mauritania (the lawyer from New York) why the three cups of tea, a terrible waste of time to him, were so essential in that culture. I had grown up with the same cultural value. No matter how important his job was, Papi always gave top priority to family, friends, and even some of his staff.

On our last morning at the Zoukak apartment, I woke up at 6 a.m. and sat on the balcony, drinking my tea. It was still cool enough to sit comfortably and listen to the sounds of Beirut waking up. A pigeon was cooing, a car alarm went off, voices drifted from various other balconies and, slowly, the sound of the city coming to life filled in the background. By seven, the humidity crept in and tiny gnats found me. Not wanting to be their breakfast, I moved back indoors to finish packing.

Before I arrived in Beirut, I had endured a heatwave in the UK with no air- conditioning. The stress of power outages in Beirut's hot and humid summer built up until Leila and I decided to move to a hotel in Ras Beirut. The hotel had twenty-four-hour electricity, thanks to a powerful generator, and was a stone's throw from the A.U.B campus and my old haunts. The hotel offered a good discount for A.U.B alumni, so the next day I got my alumni card. Another root recovered.

That week, Leila and I noticed more army presence on the streets. It was the result of an earlier kidnapping by *Jabhat-al-Nusra* (a Jihadist opposition group in Syria formerly allied with Al-Qaeda) of Lebanese soldiers in Arsal (a town in Northeast Lebanon close to the Syrian border). That news had stirred people's angst, but somehow life went on. We continued to marvel at how people in Lebanon survive year after year of uncertainty, intermittent flaring up of conflicts, and power cuts. This tiny country is full of contradictions, warmth, beauty, suspicion, and unhealed, collective trauma. And then there are the refugees. In just the past seventy years Lebanon has taken in Palestinians and others. Some, like my best friend Jeanny and her family who were forced out of their homes in Haifa by the creation of Israel in 1948 were given Lebanese citizenship. There was a second wave of Palestinian refugees following Israel's takeover of the West Bank, East Jerusalem, and the Gaza strip in 1967. The majority of them still live in camps hoping to return one day to Palestine. In addition there was also a large number of Iraqis after our invasion of their country and since 2011, a huge influx of Syrian refugees as well.

Lebanon's infrastructure, already inadequate, could hardly keep up with the continuing influx of at least 1.5 million Syrians fleeing for their lives.[133] It was heartwrenching to see some of these refugees begging on the street in Beirut. And it was heartening to see many individuals and non-governmental organizations (including from my alma mater, the American University of Beirut, and the Lebanese American University setting up schools, clinics, and help stations for those fleeing the war next door. Even Zoukak, the theatre group that sponsored Leila, had a traveling troupe that created a safe place for refugee kids and their parents, along with Lebanese children by engaging them in something positive and healing. Many Syrian and Lebanese artists, and even the government, had set up similar programs throughout the country since.

As in any country that has gone through war itself, and now living with another one raging next door, people inevitably carried some tension; but most Lebanese had learned to brush it to the back of their conscious awareness, while at some level ready to go into survival mode at any moment. This is an ability honed over millenia given the history of invasions and occupations. Of course, some people worried overtly, like a friend who said, "We're waiting. When is it our turn for things to go bad?"

Other friends and family said that the collective memory of fifteen years of civil war was like a vaccine that made Lebanon more resistant to outside pressures from Syria and elsewhere. Even with the government staggering under the weight of the refugees, people carried on without making their country the latest vicitim of the violent wolf stalking the Middle East. Not even an occasional car bomb detonation could push them back to the brink of civil war.

Family and Friends — Our Root System

When Leila and I arrived at Samir and Sano's apartment, hugging Samir felt like embracing my dad. We both choked up. I cried as I hugged Sano as well. These are the people I grew up with, who know me, my parents, and our history. Though we all had aged since my last visit, Samir still had a twinkle in his eyes, just like my papi. Sano was still as sharp and witty as ever and a terrific hostess. It felt like a reunion of our shrinking family, with Sano's sister, Salwa, and Samir's sister, Fadwa, with whom I grew up. As usual, the lunch table was laden with *kibbeh*, beef stroganoff, chicken curry, *tabbouleh, loubiye bizayt,* and more.

After lunch, Fadwa noticing that my hip had started to hurt

(a remnant of Lyme Disease), insisted on driving Leila and me to get Sim cards for our phones, waiting for us as we negotiated rates and service providers, and then dropping us off at the hotel.

My cousin Rita picked us up later to have lunch at her house with Maroun, her husband. Tante Paulette, her daughter May, and three granddaughters, Rasha, Rana, and Rima, all came from Tripoli to join us. They had been nervous about us driving the hour-and-a-half north to see them since there had been some fighting recently with pro-Assad groups in the Alawite area north of Tripoli. May's daughters were teenagers now—smart, loving, and curious. It didn't take long for the house to warm up during the three-hour, rolling power cut, but we didn't care. A powerful fan kept some air circulating as we sat down to lunch.

Since these family members had missed Leila's play, Leila gave them their own private performance. As her stories triggered theirs, we all laughed, cried, and sang along with her creating the heartwarming intimacy of love that my family so easily gives us.

I watched my daughter weave her story with theirs, I felt my mother's presence among us, and I realized I would never forget this evening. Finally, it was getting dark and the Tripoli contingent had to drive back home.[134] No one wanted to break the spell of this special gathering.

The next day we lunch with another cousin, Hanan, after which she kindly offered her car and driver to take us around Āin Mreissi. Leila had wanted to visit all my old haunts and her dad's old apartment there, and so we did. It was nostalgic and slightly disorienting because Steve's apartment building, which used to be right on the Mediterranean, was now one block inland because of the extensive landfill from war debris. But the Italian Trattoria where Steve and I had our second date was still there, and the mosque next door as well. We continued along the sea promenade affectionately called the Corniche. We passed by the site where the U.S. Embassy used to be before a car bomb destroyed it in 1983. Steve and I lost several Lebanese and American colleagues who were working there that day. As we drove by, I flashed back to June 1967 when I was working at the Embassy. During a demonstration against the U.S. Embassy, protesting its unilateral support of Israel in the 1967 war. I remembered how we all huddled in the hallways of the Embassy—

away from the windows. It was a little scary, but measured against things to come, not too serious. When the demonstration was over and I returned to my desk by the window, with the beautiful view of the Mediterranean, I found a rock on top of it. Now, it was eerie to drive by a new, non-descript high-rise apartment building that occupied that lot. Gleaming skyscrapers created a glitzy picture, but I missed the buildings that were more in character with traditional Lebanese architecture. We continued our visits. Rita took us to see her sister Nado and her family. Nado and I grew up together and had a lot of catching up to do. It would be the last time we saw Nado's oldest daughter, who died two years later from cancer.

A few days later, we decided it was safe to drive to Tripoli for a day and see Tante Paulette and the rest of her grandchildren and great-grandchildren. Rita again volunteered to drive us and we visited another granddaughter and her family at a trendy beach club outside Tripoli. I felt so much at home with Tante Paulette and her family; and I loved watching the bond Leila had forged and nurtured with May and her daughters that continues to blossom.

I also loved summoning all the skills I had learned as a counselor and art therapist to help my cousins in whatever way seemed appropriate for them and had fun teaching them Energy Medicine as well.

Then it was off to make the rounds with A.U.B classmates. My classmate, Fatima, invited us to dinner at *Al-Ajami*, a well-known traditional Lebanese restaurant overlooking the sea. Richard (pronounced in the French way: *Rich-aar*), our driver, was in his late twenties—a computer programmer by day, he had just recently joined the taxi company to supplement his income. He looked European, with a crop of blonde hair and features that I could not place. He told us his grandmother was Armenian Lebanese, his dad a mixture of French and Turkish. So, he spoke all those languages plus English and Arabic. He was the prototype for so many Lebanese always straddling worlds and languages.[135]

We arrived a little late, which is a cultural norm and not a problem. It was great reuniting with Fatima and her kids, who were Leila's friends and playmates when we all lived in Baghdad in the eighties. Fatima was her usual effervescent self and a great hostess. She had invited Shafika, a classmate from A.U.B and before that the

American School for Girls (A.S.G). We had reconnected in Jeddah, Saudi Arabia where her husband had been working while we were posted there. Sampling and sharing a *mezzé* echoed the friendship we were savoring after so many years. It was special for Leila to reconnect with May and Ramzi. They reminisced about Baghdad days and the time we had together there. It was like putting back together chapters of our lives and it reminded me of Steve's metaphor for our transient life—"It's like slices of salami scattered here and there."

On another night, Leila and I were invited by more A.U.B classmates to a rooftop restaurant in the Christian neighborhood of Beirut, *Ashrafiyeh*. I had not seen some of them since I left Lebanon. Leila came along, looking very much at home. Back in our room that night, I felt a warm feeling and with it a surprising realization. I do have a place here, one always held for me by family and friends. I do belong here in spite of my chosen exile.

Then it was off to Fatima's summer home in Beit Mery. As the taxi climbed up into the mountains, we left the hot, humid air of Beirut and took in the cool, crisp air with the scent of umbrella pines my mom loved so much. The view from Fatima's balcony took in valleys and more mountains dotted with apartments and houses—some with the traditional red-tiled roofs. In the distance we could see the Mediterranean.

On the last few days of my visit, at Samir and Sano's apartment, there were spontaneous outpourings of family stories, things I had never heard before. Out came photo albums, a book about old Beirut showing the *petit Serail*, where my father and Samir had had their offices. I was glad to be the recipient of this legacy to fill in the blanks from years away from Lebanon. I felt I had become the bridge between Samir and Sano's generation and their children's and grandchildren's, as if they were passing the bâton to a new elder. This reconnection to friends and family continued to shore up my bridge foundation that will always be planted deeply both in Lebanese soil and firmly anchored in the United States. That summer, I witnessed Leila putting the finishing touches on her bridge—one that will continue enriching both families in both countries, even long after I'm gone.

Immigrants and Those Left Behind

Lebanon also has a long history of emigration. Every time there is turmoil and conflict, a new exodus begins and more Lebanese leave the country. While currently Lebanon has around six million people, an estimated 16 million of Lebanese ancestry live outside the country, scattered across almost every continent. Perhaps it's a legacy of the ancient Phoenicians, who were highly accomplished, curious about the world, powerful and enterprising seafaring traders, always looking westward. Phoenician DNA has been found as far North as Ireland, the British Isles, and even some parts of Scandinavia.[136]

My family is no different. Like many Lebanese, Samir and Sano have children and grandchildren scattered throughout the world. Since they no longer are able to make the long trips they now enjoy the rotating visits from all three kids and their children. That is the other face of immigration—those one leaves behind—disrupting age-old patterns of multi-generational support.

This was something that I heard both in our family and even from strangers. One experience in particular stayed with me. We were looking for "Papa Choux"—a restaurant we were told had the best *mlukhiyyeh* (a green like spinach that's cooked to a soupy consistency and served with lamb or chicken, toasted pita, and a wonderful vinegar and chopped onion sauce). All I knew was that it was somewhere near Rue Badaro; addresses are meaningless in Lebanon, you need landmarks as reference points.

We flagged down a *servees*. Hearing that we were Lebanese emigrants, the driver recounted, "My brother left fifty years ago. He lives in Chicago. I saw him only once during all these years for a few hours when he was in transit at the airport." He added sadly, *"al Hinniyeh raahhit."* (*Hinniyeh* is gone.) *Hinniyeh* is hard to translate. It's at once a complex feeling of love and compassion, and heartfelt desire to nurture and help. This is not just between parent and children but a much revered quality in a person. It is central to the communitarian culture to which Lebanon belongs. This nurturing bond makes life bearable in the midst of whatever uncertainty and hardship exists. I understood that he felt that this bond, on his emigrant brother's side, had untangled. What was left unsaid is, "why else would my brother not come to visit?"

As he shared his story our driver went off his normal route, stopping at a shop to get further directions. I was surprised that he would take the time to help us, despite a slight resentment he might have been feeling towards people like us, who had left the motherland. But there was no bitterness in his voice, no begrudging, just sadness. He told us his story like a rotund, good papa proudly pointing out landmarks along the way: a new shopping mall and a health spa with adjoining store carrying organic products and supplements with a homeopathic doctor on staff. He was proud that Lebanon always keeps abreast of the latest world trends. But he was silent when we passed some buildings still carrying the scars of war.

I tried to explain to him what life was like as an immigrant in an effort to mitigate his sadness, but I realized there was no way he could really relate to that. I could feel his loss and pain, and I could also imagine his brother at that time arriving in the new world, looking for a job, working hard to make a new life for himself. Some emigrés fled conflict, some sought a better life for themselves and especially their children. In the days when phone calls were astronomically expensive and one sent all the money one could back to the family, it was close to impossible to afford to go back to Lebanon. I remembered that two of Teta Habouba's brothers had emigrated to Brazil and were never heard from again. On opposite sides of the world, those who left and those left behind could not possibly understand how life had evolved for the other.

Sometimes, the loss for the émigré is so strong that he blocks out everything that reminds him of the past, even his family. It reminded me of how even my dad did not want to talk about Lebanon and the life he left behind. "That's in the past," he would say with a twinge of sadness. I always felt that even though he had left voluntarily, it was too painful for him to remember the life he left behind. Other Lebanese emigrants passed down the values and traditions they brought from the birth country "traditions they refined and adapted to the ... culture to which they had emigrated."[137]

Lebanese immigrants, like others, have worked hard to integrate into their adoptive cultures and make new lives for their families. The earliest Lebanese who came to the United States in the early 19th century were referred to as Syrians since Lebanon was then part of Greater Syria. They were mostly Christians, but there were also Muslims. Little Syria in New York City now has an exhibit on Ellis Island. Those from rural areas of Lebanon started off peddling cloth and souvenirs from the Holy Land (Palestine at the time)[138] throughout the United States. Different waves of Lebanese immigrants brought different talents, education, and resources and made great entrepreneurs. They assimilated quickly and sometimes to the degree of changing their names—much like Jews, Germans, and other new immigrants did—trying to blend in and avoid discrimination. Some famous Lebanese-Americans include Khalil or Kahlil Jibran, Ralph Nader (an attorney, noted for his involvement in consumer protection, environmentalism, and government reform causes), Dr. Michael DeBakey (who invented the heart pump and was the first doctor to do a successful heart transplant), Salma Hayek (the daughter of a Lebanese who immigrated to Mexico), Danny Thomas (who established St Jude Hospital for Children that is still run by his daughter, Marlo Thomas), Jamie Farr who acted in *M*A*S*H*, and many others. Steve Jobs's biological father was a Syrian political refugee. Steve was adopted by an American family.

> *I believe that you have inherited from your forefathers an ancient dream, a song, a prophecy, which you can proudly lay as a gift of gratitude upon the lap of America.*
>
> —Kahlil Gibran[139]

I remember that for most Lebanese and other emigrants, the United States has always sounded like a place where the roads are paved with gold. That's partly thanks to Hollywood fantasies, and also to early immigrants who sent letters to their families embellishing their descriptions of their new life, perhaps in the hope that their leaving was deemed worth the losses on both sides—as if painting this rosy picture might ease the sadness and pain of having left "everything and everybody behind."

In addition, before email and the internet, immigrants arrived in the United States and their cultural norms often became frozen in that time capsule, while their birth country moved on.

I remember a young Syrian-American lawyer I had invited to a panel on the diversity of Arab-American women. She told us how her Syrian-American parents had always been strict about sleepovers and dating, so she grew up feeling torn between the world at home and the one outside. Years later, when the family went back to Syria for her first visit, she was surprised and angry at her parents—because her Syrian cousins were not as restricted as she was back in the United States! Life had gone on in Damascus, and mores had changed, but her immigrant parents wanted to pass on and maintain traditions and beliefs they brought with them frozen in a time capsule of yesteryears. Like other immigrants, they were terrified of losing their children to a totally new set of cultural beliefs and behaviors thus losing their own cultural values. But as with many immigrant parents, the irony is the more they tightened the rules, the more rebellious their children became. Each generation saw the world through their own distinct lenses. The immigrant parents' mores were often ossified.

Today, thanks to more affordable air travel, more immigrants are able to return regularly to visit. The rest of the time, new technology keeps them well-connected. My cousin Sano talks daily on Skype with her daughters and son, who live on three different continents. With the world shrinking, it now seems normal to be able to connect so easily. There are even some returning immigrants who decide to stay, perhaps to start a new business, and not just in Lebanon. I imagine those who return most often have an easier time with this insider/outsider feeling—the more trips back and forth, the more familiar things remain.

Identity Pilgrimage—Reviving Ancestral Roots

I had the feeling that summer that Leila and I were making a sort of pilgrimage to Lebanon. We were saying goodbye for my mom, who would never see her birthland again, and allowing the family who adored her to say goodbye to her vicariously, through us. It felt to me as if we were completing the circle of my parents' immigrant journey.

On this visit, I found myself straddling the generations, listening to the stories rarely told now but vividly remembered by the remaining older family members. Elders in many countries have little opportunity anymore to practice their traditional role of storytellers, carriers of the family history, yet they are desperate to hand it down. For my family, thankfully, some young grandchildren are still there to listen and eventually pass it on.

This trip to Beirut solidified what I had not fully acknowledged all these years: I had a yearning to be fully "known" by family, friends, colleagues, and acquaintances.

These family members and friends knew and loved my mom and dad. They knew me up to my young adulthood; they carried my parents' stories as well as mine. Sitting in Sano and Samir's living room, drinking Turkish coffee *mazboot* ("just right"—meaning the right amount of sugar) and munching on a yummy delicacy, I knew I belonged here, even if only just for the short time I was with them. Memories of my Lebanese life flooded back triggered by a word, a joke, a recollection. *"Btitzakkaree...?"* (Do you remember...?) Ah yes! I did. Stories that inherently carried my mixed identity—stories that are embedded in my roots there.

Yet there was the part of who I had become that naturally eluded them, just as my formative years in Lebanon elude friends and even family in the United States. It remains important to me that people in the West do not villify, demonize, or paint with one single brush stroke this rich, vibrant, and ancient culture. This visit reinforced my passion for the cross-cultural work and storytelling that both Leila and I do and love.

I went back to Maalouf and re-read what he had to say about complex identities like Leila's and mine. "The more ties I have, the rarer and more particular my own identity becomes," he writes about himself.[140] For Leila and me, the more ingredients in our identity salad, the less likely we are to find a name for the distinctive heritage and history that defines us.

Those of us who carry multiple identities can feel both connected to many peoples, places, cultures, and communities—and at times feel very alone. This chameleon-like characteristic is natural. In crossing back and forth, we each can be both "us" and "them," declaring and feeling ties and connections with Americans, Lebanese, other Arabs, Arab-Americans, Muslims, Buddhists, Christians, ATCKs, CCKs, and many more and yet reveling in our unique identities.

I remember reading in Steve's Harvard Alumni magazine about

a valedictorian who happened to be Arab-American. The speech he delivered about being both "us" and "them" landed him in trouble. But the reality of this dual identity is not "unpatriotic," nor a betrayal of either, but a beautiful, peaceful acceptance with respect, love, and dignity, regardless of religion or political affiliation. If all people could say "us" and "them" in that spirit, we would not have violence and wars. It's when we get hung up over who is "them" and who is "us" that hatred and violence erupt driven by our fear of the "other," which is really fear of the "unknown."

What I find interesting in this pluralistic nation is that the majority of my fellow Americans do carry multiple allegiances from the ancestors who were here originally and those who came later. Even the forgotten ancestral past can nevertheless affect the way each of us perceives the "other." We fail to see our common humanity and focus only on the differences. By virtue of being a human bridge I feel a huge need, indeed a responsibility, to forge connections, correct misinformation, and clear misunderstandings between cultures, communities, and peoples. By accepting our composite identity—what I have referred to as "in-betweeness"—I feel Leila and I have been enriched and freed to go with what life offers us. Neither of us needs to hyphenate ourselves, but it is helpful to get people thinking in these times of division about the "other" and find we are not as different as we imagine. Perhaps the hyphen is itself a bridge.

Language, Maalouf writes, is a tool for bridging the gap because it is both a crucial "component of identity" and a means of communication. The Lebanese are adept at mixing languages even in the same sentence. For them it is a source of pride and shows their openness to the world. Referring to himself, Maalouf, a Christian Lebanese, goes on to talk about the paradox of being Christian and speaking Arabic, which became the holy language of Islam. In speaking that language, he says bonds him with all those who use it everyday in prayer.

For Leila, being fluent in the Lebanese dialect put the finishing touches on the Lebanese side of her bridge. Leila had always been frustrated that Lebanese citizenship could only be passed down through the father.[141] So I told her, "*Habibti,* your Lebanese citizenship is what you carry in your blood. You don't need a piece of paper for that. Just as I have never felt that by giving up my passport forty-five years ago meant I had lost my Lebaneseness." Soon after that she told me: "Mom, one of the reasons I have worked so hard to perfect my Lebanese dialect is that the language is my citizenship." "Wow, I had never thought about it that way," I replied. But when I joined her in Beirut, I saw what she meant. I was amazed at how fluent her Lebanese dialect had become. Other than a few pronounciation corrections, she was following every conversation and no one was stopping to make sure she "got it." It was as if she had always been there speaking Arabic with them—I sensed she was reclaiming and creating the connection and kinship the civil war had denied her. I felt that she was now at peace with the unique individual she is, knowing she belongs in so many relationships in her life and work, and can naturally integrate the best of both worlds.

Language is not only about culture but also "about recognizable affiliations to heritage ... bridges to the other."[142] I could understand how the language really was a key part of our daughter's connection to family and culture—her own living, growing passport to identity and belonging.

On our last visit with Samir and Sano, I glanced over at Leila. Was she feeling it too? This refurbishing of our roots during this visit? Roots she thought she never had in Lebanon, roots I thought I had left behind even, perhaps lost forever, when I left physically so many years ago. Roots my extended family tended for us, and now their children do—because we are family—even if ten or twenty-five years go by without setting eyes on each other. These family members knew and understood my origins. They had helped nurture my beginnings, and they continue now to provide a sense of "home" for Leila and me. Together with the breezes of the Mediterranean, the Cedar, and the pine trees, they are my anchor on this side of the world. Because of my ancestral roots firmly planted in this land, I could grow and reach up and out like the cedar. Or perhaps my life was like the plant whose roots the gardener divides, in order to plant new ones in different places.

Flying "Home"

On our way back to the United States, while waiting for the plane to take off from Beirut I reflected on how I had left Lebanon as a young adult and returned as one of the elders. This made me regret not having asked my dad for his story: *"Hkeelee Papi"* like Leila did with my mom. I realized how this trip reinforced the fact that I remain Lola, the person my family knew and still love. I'll also always be Kamal and Jeanne's daughter, and Leila their granddaughter.

I was seated next to a young Lebanese-American woman who worked as a pharmacist in Boston. "I love it in Boston," she said "but I'm always thinking of Lebanon and being there. But when I'm in Lebanon, I'm always thinking of Boston. If only we could merge both." "I know what you mean," I said. "My mom always told Leila (who lives in New York, and mom in Washington): "I want to shrink the land between us." In this case we would have to shrink oceans. Here was another person learning to live in that "in-betweeness." I was guessing she missed the warmth of family and familiar surroundings in Beirut. Merging it with her happy, daily life in Boston would have been utopia for her. We both fell silent as we looked out the window to see Lebanon receding further as the plane turned and headed west.

I fluffed my little MEA pillow with a small cedar imprinted on its cover. The last verse of the Lebanese national anthem popped into my head: *"Majduhu arzuhu ramzuhu Lilkhulud...."* (Our nation's grandeur is the cedar as it is its symbol till the end of time....)

"Cedrus Libani" is the Latin name for the Lebanese Cedar. Its saplings have been planted all over the world. Cedars of Lebanon have thrived in various climates and provided hardy wood and healing oils wherever they put down roots. From the Pharaohs of Egypt to Napoleon's wife, who is reported to have planted one in the Malmaison Park to celebrate her husband's victory at Marengo.[143] Recently, I even spied quite a few in the gardens of PBS's "Downton Abbey" series.

Back home in the United States, I often drive along "Cedar Lane." After this visit, I began looking for the cedars that gave the road its name. I looked for the unique silhouette they carve in the sky. I found only one. Everytime I pass by this lone, hardy, beautiful cedar, I smile and say hello. "You and I have the same origins, yet we thrive wherever we are planted."

As I write this, I'm reminded of the storekeeper's words during my visit in 2004. "Madame, with all due respect, you're not from here anymore." Fourteen years later, I know at last how to answer him. "Like the transplanted cedar, I may not live here anymore, but I am from here and that will never change. Lebanon is where I was raised and nurtured and where my ancestral roots are. Yes, I've been transplanted to the United States and I thrive there too."

I have come to accept that I can never be one hundred percent home anywhere, anymore. It is both a blessing and a burden. Yes, there are things in both cultures and societies I dislike or disagree with. And there are so many things from each that I embrace tightly. Most of the time I'm at peace with this; "at peace" being the key phrase here. Sadly, right now peace is lacking in both of my "homes" — divisions and gridlock are intertwined with bad policies and disturbing world events. After 9/11, I realized my purpose in life is to work hard to help my fellow Americans understand and hopefully be able to see my Lebanese-Arab culture through the lens of compassion, and not through the biased, misinformed, and distorted lens of fear. That's the way I can feel at home in both cultures and work to keep the bridge between them peaceful and open. So, if I can lend a hand by sharing my story, then I can feel grounded in both of my homes.

Back in the United States, it took some time for Leila and I to process this visit to Lebanon. It was both jet lag and life lag — a feeling of random pieces of ourselves floating in our head and heart. Discovering that I still had a "place" in Lebanon was hugely healing, because losing that physical and emotional grounding when I left so hurriedly decades ago was something I had not fully grieved. This trip back was another opportunity for me to finally and fully mourn. For Leila it was poignant to know she is the one who will be keeping the connection with the younger generation, and those to come long after I'm gone.

As someone on PBS's "Finding Your Roots" once said, "You have to go back to your ancestry to find yourself!" This reminded me of the "Family Constellation" I participated in several years ago, in which a facilitator asked another group member to stand in for "Lebanon" at the back of my family constellation line. As that "representative" took her assigned place, I remember taking a deep breath, relieved that she did. I suddenly felt a deep peace, a sense of grounding and completeness. This reclaiming of my birth country is what this summer in Lebanon gifted me, a key healing piece of this part of my journey towards wholeness. I felt that the land that is Lebanon and I share the same duality of being. Our roots are deeply planted even as we cross constantly from one identity to another. We are just like the ancient Phoenicians and caravan drivers—constantly on the move, yet our center holds.

Back in the United States

The Christmas after our 2014 summer visit, my Muslim family in Tripoli told me that that year the trees in the city were decorated for Christmas even more fully than usual, and there were more festivals as well. It was a message to ISIS, or Dāesh as it is called in Arabic, and also to remind themselves and the world that in a Sunni Muslim city, people respect each others' religion. My Muslim family joined in celebrating with their Christian neighbors and friends.

I was very moved to hear not only the words, but the defiant and happy tone in my cousins' voices, who live in an area in North Lebanon that is more vulnerable to extremists. Tante Paulette and her daughter had bought a turkey for Christmas and were preparing the *hashweh*—Lebanese rice stuffing that I love so much. So they took the time to give me the recipe which I had lost. "You toast the almonds and pine nuts, you cook the turkey and with its juices, prepare the rice with all the special Lebanese spices, then add the browned chopped lamb or beef and mix everything together. The home-made *Bûche de Nöel* (Yule Log) that my mom was famous for, topped their holiday meal. They added with nostalgia, "*Ya rayt kun ma'na.*" (How we wish you were with us.)

As I child, I loved how my Lebanese family and others melded tradition and memories; now I was homesick for them. We were all thinking of my mother, and sad at being so far apart, knowing she was slipping away from us all. She passed away in March 2015. With her, one connection to my childhood disappeared. A year after that, my cousin Marianna died after fighting cancer for many years. Even though I really did not know her well, having left Lebanon so long ago, I had seen her on recent visits. She was a tall, graceful woman. She left her three children, her mom, sisters, and husband behind. One of her sisters, Nicole, lives in Canada and I knew she would be devastated. So I called her and we talked about how difficult it is to be so far away from family, and how painful it can be to not comfort and be comforted physically, in person, in real time, rather than via Skype, WhatsApp, or Viber. When the computer screen goes dark, or the cell phone is off, the physical distance between you and your family remains.

I also called Tante Paulette, and I mentioned how hard it is when you lose a loved one while you are living so far away. In typical comforting fashion, just like my mom would have done, she responded with an Arabic proverb: *"Matrahh ma btirzak ilzak"* — literally, "Wherever your good fortune is, glue yourself there." It was just what I needed to be reminded of. I chose to plant myself here in the United States where I bloom best, even though I always miss my family in Lebanon. After hanging up, I went and made myself some *mazaher*; its aroma and taste brought me a tiny bit closer to my homeland and family. It continues to transport me to a place within that I call "home."

A few months after mom's passing I experienced a burst of energy. This didn't mean I was not grieving; but somehow the pale, sad figures in my images for the last ten years were being transformed. The deep, vibrant colors that emerged in my art journal lifted my heart. Looking at the finished image, I felt a joy knocking at my consciousness. Mami would approve; she was always full of enthusiasm, and uplifting to everyone she met. Perhaps she is doing that right now in the scribble, "Boomerang," and the words that flowed.

"Boomerang"

Today I show up in deep purple, a smile on my face.
Everything is vivid, clear, crisp, colorful and vibrant,
even the angels, especially the one with the flamboyant wings.

What's that shape hovering above?
A boomerang that wanted to be pink.
What does it mean?

I know that when thrown it always comes back to you.
I realize it's shaped like a bridge, upside down.
The fact that it's pink indicates a gentle roundtrip.

A big heart appears encircling me, touching the boomerang.
Then words emerge insisting on being included.
All clamoring to be put "out there?"

And when they're "out into the world"
What will come back to me? I often wonder.
The self-portrait I've created will never be finished.

For now, I am grounded, visible and fully present,
every aspect of myself within the other, perfect Yin-Yang,
as the next chapter of my life begins!

*And could you keep your heart in wonder at the daily miracles of
your life, your pain would not seem less wondrous than your joy.*

—Kahlil Gibran[144]

11

2015—Outsider and Insider

Being an outsider…makes life difficult, but it also…forces you out of unconsciousness.

—Eckart Tolle[145]

My Fiftieth College Reunion

I thought I had finished my book when (after much urging from Steve, Leila, and my classmates) I decided to go to my fiftieth college reunion at the American University of Beirut in the summer of 2015. Mom had passed away a few months before, and I felt the need to see the family again. Unfortunately, Leila had an accident and was laid up with major foot surgery and rehabilitation, so Steve and I ended up going without her. But this allowed for other memories to come to the fore. Steve and I found ourselves revisiting the places where we met and fell in love.

In addition to the ongoing worry about ISIS and the unrelenting violence next door in Syria, I felt nervous going without Leila, who had been my guide the summer before. Navigating modern Beirut, the money, and other things would be stressful. Heartbroken as she was to not be coming with us, Leila said, "Mom, maybe this is an opportunity to regain your own footing in Beirut, and be your own guide." She was right.

As it turned out, my new iPhone proved to be the most frustrating challenge as I dealt with the local sim card, Viber, WhatsApp, and the rest of its functions. But everyone was helpful, even Hassan, the concierge at the hotel, who patiently explained things to me. Another time, when my pre-paid plan finished, on a weekend, the pool attendant at the hotel transferred money into my phone, which prompted Steve to remark how he had forgotten how much people in Lebanon will go out of their way to help you.

We took taxis everywhere because Steve had torn his calf muscle a few days before we left the United States; he was in a special boot up to his knee and couldn't walk much. Family, friends, and even sisters of friends took turns picking us up and wining and dining us as usual.

The family was ecstatic seeing Steve again, and it was poignant to talk about my mom, share our memories of her, and their recollections of both my parents in Lebanon. I had prepared photos of Mami in little albums for my aunt and cousins—all of the photos taken during the years she had been in the United States and far away from them. Symbolically, we brought her home to her birth country and back to her family.

My classmate Fatima had already planned a pre-reunion lunch in Beit Mery. She had a classmate's sister and her husband, who lived not far from our hotel, pick us up and drive us up the mountains to her summer place. Steve got to meet other classmates of mine, and get reacquainted with those he had first met during our courtship.

For the first few days, besides jet lag, I lived with jumble of roiling feelings I couldn't fully decipher or untangle. A little fragment of anxiety felt familiar. I knew it was that "outsider" feeling that had lurked behind an invisible door all my life, despite the fact that the "insider" waited on the other side. I thought I had made peace with this reality. Obviously there was more journeying inward I needed to do.

Syrian Refugees

It was a tense time to be in Lebanon. Since my visit the year before, the number of Syrian refugees had continued to grow. According to the UN High Commissioner for Refugees (UNHCR), in 2015 there were 1,172,753 registered Syrian refugees in Lebanon. When those who are not registered are considered, the number is estimated between 1.6 and 1.9 million and climbing. One report in 2015 said that there were "...more Syrian school-age children in Lebanon than

Lebanese school-age children...."[146] The government in some areas had schools on a rotating class schedule to accommodate all the children. Syrian refugees in Lebanon now accounted for between a quarter and half the Lebanese population, and that excludes refugees from other neighboring conflicts, such as Palestinians and Iraqis. Lebanon has the highest per capita number of refugees according to recent UN estimates, and has the smallest land mass of all the neighboring countries harboring refugees. There are 5.9 million Lebanese in Lebanon; an equivalent refugee population in the United States would number between 80 and 160 million people.

Because Lebanon is the closest neighbor geographically, culturally, and linguistically to Syria, Syrian refugees continued to pour in. A large number of them have Lebanese relatives, which made it easy for them to integrate and find safety with their families. Most hoped they would be able to go back to their homes as soon as the conflict was resolved. Alas, since 2011 the devastation, violence, and destruction in Syria has worsened. The UN, World Food Program, and other aid and relief agencies have seen their donations falling drastically and according to a report, "...the per-capita food allowance was less than $14 a month for many Syrians..."[147] Lebanon's already overwhelmed resources could barely keep up. The nation's hospitality was fraying fast, and compassion fatigue set in as the years dragged on and this human tragedy showed no signs of ending. Compassion gave way to frustration and resentment, and people were more vocal about it.

Taxi drivers we encountered grumbled about Syrian refugees who had taken to driving around and illegally picking up passengers. "They're taking our livelihood away and besides, they don't know the city so the people have to tell *them* where to go." There was also the fear that extremists would infiltrate refugee neighborhoods and create danger for Lebanese citzens. ISIS and *Jabhat-al-nusra* were poised at Lebanon's northern and eastern borders, only forty miles from Beirut, and a year before kidnapped thirty or more Lebanese soldiers. A few were killed and others were still missing.

A grocer we talked to was also very angry about the Syrian influx. He feared yet another large group of refugees could throw off the delicate balance of pluralistic Lebanon, as had happened after a huge influx of Palestinian refugees in 1948 and 1967. Those refugee camps formed their own militias creating a backlash. People believe it created conflict and eventually triggered the civil war. I imagined that the bitter taste of all that still lingered for many people. The fear of becoming a theatre for proxy wars again was real. Besides, there were touchy domestic issues—not the least being that parliament had not been able to agree on a president. The confessional political system—designed to ensure equal representation for all religious groups—was showing signs of paralysis and it affected people's lives directly.

I felt terrible for Lebanon and its people, and for the Syrian refugees who continue to live in a hellish limbo of increasingly deteriorating circumstances. I heard of more NGOs that had set up makeshift schools, activists who were continuing to use art to help the children, university outreach programs still offering programs to alleviate suffering, but it felt like so many band-aids applied to a gaping wound. Steve reminded me that America's responsibility for these problems could not be denied. "By invading Iraq, dismantling its army and police, we created a vacuum which ISIS/Daēsh could fill. Our invasion of Iraq and drawn out military presence— some would call it occupation—has destabilized the whole region." It was something he and other knowledgeable State Department veterans had predicted and tried to warn about before the invasion began.

I marveled again how in the midst of all this uncertainty and hardship, the Lebanese continued to demonstrate an uncanny ability and determination to get on with life. The war had taught them the painful lesson that anything could happen, so they embraced life in the moment. Family, friends, and food are the rallying point for this resiliency. Even in the midst of economic downturn, political dysfunction, and threats of violence, they seemed to be able to put all that on the back burner and savor the little joys. Restaurants everywhere were just as full as they had been in 1999, or 2004. The new Zeytouni yacht club, new restaurants, and the promenade stayed alive late into the night. People of every faith, and in everything from hijab to the latest fashion mingled, enjoying the balmy nights. In contrast, back home in the United States, people seem to be constantly on edge. Maalouf says, one can get to the point of being afraid of fear itself.

But resiliency has a downside too—a certain resignation, especially among the older generation. During the last few days of our visit, the Ministry of Environment closed the Naameh landfill, south of the capital Beirut, without having first identified a replacement site. Residents of that area had finally had enough and blocked access to the landfill. This brought all garbage collection services in Beirut and Mount Lebanon to a standstill. Trash quickly piled up, clogging streets in the July heat. The stench and fear of vermin and disease scared away tourists—a mainstay of the economy. People were fed up. They wrote seething articles in all the papers. Complaints and grumbling were not bringing any change. In addition, the news that a group of activists were killed by ISIS probably dampened people's courage and willingness to act, and reinforced the belief in some that they could not change things.

To add to the misery, power cuts were lasting even longer due to ongoing (and worsening) problems at the electric power plant. What was infuriating people was that in Sidon, a city in the South of Lebanon, the municipality there had built a state of the art trash processing and recycling plant, which had the capacity to take half of Beirut's garbage; and it was even making money. But greedy politicians were still vying for a larger cut from the trash collecting companies for Beirut and Mt. Lebanon. Finally, tired of looking the other way, the trash fiasco became a flash point—the last straw for people long suffering from a greedy, corrupt, inept (at best) parliament, which couldn't even come together to elect a new president.

Before we left Beirut, trash had started to disappear from the streets, although there were rumors that it was just being dumped in the dry Beirut river bed and in some *wadis*, or valleys. Environmnetal activists moved the trash out of the river to prevent an ecological disaster before the rains came. After we left Lebanon, the anger and fear exploded and people from all walks of life, religions, and ages took to the streets. These were peaceful demonstrations with the rallying message in English and Arabic—"You Stink!"— directed at the politicians who had once more failed them. They dumped garbage in front of Parliament, chanting demands that the politial elite come up with a sustainable solution, or resign.

Thankfully, before all this erupted, my college reunion went off without a glitch. I not only reconnected with classmates I knew well, but also got to know others with whom I had not been close. I found an amazing group of like-minded women and men who have accomplished so much—not just in Lebanon, but around the world. A lot of them also straddle worlds; a few live part-time in Lebanon and part-time in the United States. Some split their time in Europe. It made me feel even more "at home."

Since Steve could not walk much, I took a solitary stroll around part of AUB's 61-acre campus, which sits on a hill overlooking the Mediterranean. The buildings with the red tile roofs and warm ochre stone were a comforting presence in an otherwise new and changing city. There were many modern buildings, but mostly on the lower campus surrounding the athletic field—where I had participated in basketball and track, and had placed second in long jump events. I found the great banyan trees were still there, together with the cypresses, oleander, lantana, and other flowering bushes I remembered so well. I felt a deep peace of recognition of it and it of me. It brought back such happy memories of the four years I had spent here, walking these same paths. I walked by A.U.B's Archeological Museum, the third oldest in the whole Middle East. It had just been renovated. I had to circumvent a few of the campus cat residents in order to get in. One was curled up around an ancient stela,[148] others were draped on the museum steps. I took a guided tour and marveled at the rich history of this area and beyond. I felt proud, nostalgic, and glad that all this was part of my heritage.

At the entrance of the museum there was a cross section of a cedar that was 28.5 feet (9.5 meters) in diameter. It was identified as the largest known single piece of prehistoric *Cedrus Libani* tree. It died around 7760 years ago. Its tree rings indicated it had lived for about 300 years. I stood there feeling proud of this symbol of Lebanon.

A few days later, Steve and I went on the A.U.B alumni trip to the Cedar Reserve in Tannourine. The park ranger explained why cedars take a long time to grow to full maturity. First, the fruit seed drops to the ground and takes three years just to germinate. It then takes it one hundred years to grow vertically to its maximum height; after that, it begins to fill out horizontally—up to 150 feet (50 meters). We were glad to find out that ecotourism allows only guided visits, and that although only seventeen forests were fully protected by the government at the time, environmentalists are working hard to preserve the remaining thirty-one cedar reserves in Lebanon.

The cedar's graceful silhouette, lush greenery, and horizontal branching system distinguishes it from other conifer evergreens.[149] According to several sources, the Cedar of Lebanon is mentioned seventy times in the Bible. For thousands of years, these magnificent trees have been prized for their high-quality timber, resin, and healing oil—including Egyptian Pharaohs who used it to build their tombs and used the oil for embalming. Solomon's Temple in Jerusalem was built from ancient Lebanon Cedars, as were the Phoenicians' famous ships.

My reunion included a panel about the future of the UN, where we also learned that nineteen A.U.B alumni were delegates to the signing of the UN charter in 1945—more than any other university in the world. A dinner dance concluded the reunion and lasted into the night, complete with well-known entertainers performing in several languages. My classmates and I were the first ones on the dance floor and the last to leave.

During our two weeks in Lebanon, as usual, we were invited out for just about every lunch and dinner. Besides the hospitality, I realized that food also carries sensory memories for me. Eating *kibbeh* could transport me back to *Teta* Habouba, and watching her pound the *jurun* as she prepared it. The *bizri* and *sultan Ibrahim* fish reminded me of the wonderful *mézzés* I had with my family in beautiful settings, from Zahle's café in the Bekaā valley to restaurants on the Mediterranean. It also occurred to me that food permeates many endearment phrases in Arabic such as *shoo taybeh* or *tayyib* (she or he is so delicious). *Btittakal akil* or *byitakal akil* (one can eat her/him up, i.e. so cute—usually referring to babies and kids). *Mahdoomeh or mahdooom* (digestible, i.e. funny and easygoing).

Rita took us to visit her paternal cousins who lived in a traditional Lebanese house in the *yaoos'iya*, the Jesuit quarter in Ashrafieh. Next door to them used to be their uncle Joseph and Tante Georgette's house where Rita and her sisters grew up—a traditional Lebanese house with the same marble floors and Arab-arched windows with beautiful wooden carvings as our first house in *Burj Abu Haydar*.

As we sat in Elie and Tony's lush garden, where the shade kept the heat at bay, I asked what happened to Tante Georgette's house. "For a while someone had bought it and turned it into a very chic discothêque, but the monks from the Jesuit monastery across the street complained. Now there's a huge hole waiting for some high rise to be built," Tony said sadly. Despite the presence of a wall that had been built to separate the two properties, in my mind's eye I could vizualize the old steps leading from their garden down to Tante Georgette's, the grape arbor that was on the right where, as children, we used to pick grapes before they were even ripe. I recalled the chicken coop across the yard with the aggressive rooster we were careful to stay away from because he took his role very seriously.

It is funny how my inner eye and memories could go right through the wall that blocked access to what had been part of my childhood. Every visit back to Lebanon had felt like another "re-entry"—Foreign Service lingo for coming back to the passport country and feeling somewhat disoriented, yet expecting to fit right back in. It felt with each visit that I was building a bridge back to myself.

Lebanon's contradictions, always familiar, could still surprise me. On the one hand, there was the *servees* drivers who, on my visit the year before with Leila, went out of his way to find the restaurant we wanted. On the other, there was the grumpy and dishonest one trying to convince two women in *hijab* that it would be better for them if he drove them to *Jounieh* instead of the bus stop. The women had heavy accents, not like any I had heard before. I intervened and told them they were right to take the bus instead, which is where they had asked him to drop them off. Both extremes seemed acceptable to Lebanese. Like many other old cultures, they accept those complexities of life. The more I saw of Lebanese traditions and history, the more I had to admire the Lebanese traits of being open to the world, blending East and West in all sectors of society, and being a refuge for so many over the centuries.

But like my dad, I felt frustrated and angry that the Lebanese government couldn't get its act together. When Papi emigrated to the United States, he was deeply disappointed that in America, where he'd hoped for perfection, there was also dysfunction in government and corrupt financing of politicians. As for me being an insider and outsider in both places, I could chalk it up to the fact that human beings in any adoptive country will surprise and disappoint just like those back home.

Later that summer, on a trip to Ireland where I was teaching for a week, I shared those thoughts with Steve. "Yes," he agreed. "I was reminded how kind, courteous people are in the Arab world." Since he needed a wheelchair at the airport, the assistance at Beirut's airport was efficient and caring. The only helpful and caring people at Charles de Gaulle airport were the Moroccan or Algerian immigrants who wheeled Steve from our arrival terminal to the van for Air France's terminal.

But once we were in that terminal we had a maddening experience. We waited four hours for the wheelchair we had requested weeks and days in advance to take Steve to the small plane below. Air France personnel at the desk kept reassuring me that the wheelchair would be arriving shortly. "Ça arrive, Madame." (It's coming Madam.)

It was only when all the passengers boarded and there was still no sign of the wheelchair that I lost my temper. "What kind of incompetent service is this!? We've been waiting for four hours!"

The response was, *"Pourquoi êtes-vous stréssée madame?L'avion ne quittera pas sans vous."* (Why are you so stressed madame? The plane will not leave without you.) Finally, my enraged spouting paid off, and the wheelchair arrived. But when Steve was wheeled to the elevator by the top of the stairs, we found that the elevator only went up. True Story!

So after four-plus hours of waiting, Steve still had to slowly walk down the stairs, out to the small plane, and up the steps to a plane full of irate passengers who had been waiting for us. "So much for the civilized world," I said loudly as we made our way to our seats. "And to think that they exported this bureaucracy to Lebanon and other colonies!" I fumed.

Later when I recounted this to my longtime French friend, she said. " Knowing French bureaucracy, I'm not surprised. And you know Hala, that if this was in a Middle Eastern country, someone would have found a way to carry Steve down the stairs if they had to."

News from Lebanon

Back home in the United States, I checked on the family in Lebanon as the garbage crisis got more serious and one demonstration turned violent. They assured me that the police arrested the group of troublemakers and instigators who had aimed to turn the peaceful and inclusive popular expressions of frustration and anger into a dangerous confrontation. On the phone, an older relative said, "We're in a cold war, it's very disturbing. During the civil war you could stay out of the danger and the bombs, but now we're all touched." The power cuts and garbage crisis had not occurred even at the height of the civil war. These elders felt they had to put up with it and be patient: "*Bidna ntawwil balnah.*" It's hard to translate *bal.* Basically it means, "We need to expand our reserve of patience." When I asked my cousin about her sister, she said, "These days because the streets are full of garbage and it's beastly hot we stay home, and do visits on Skype. We make our *Ziyarats* online so to speak. Thank God for that."

When I asked my younger cousin, Rita, who lives in the center of the city, she had a different outlook. "We watched the demonstrations from our house. They were okay—people from all walks of life, faiths, genders were chanting and excited to be able to express how they feel, to shatter the apathy and do that among such a diverse group of fellow Lebanese."

I thought Tante Paulette, eighty-four that year, exemplified the wry humor that enables the Lebanese to survive and even thrive. When I called to inquire how things were, she said with a chuckle, "As usual, neither the garbage nor the president is resolved." Then she laughed at her juxtaposition of two unrelated, but inseparable issues—and their similarities.

I followed several articles in The Washington Post and The New York Times about the situation in Lebanon. Most focused on the uncertainty. One even predicted Lebanon was heading for a breakdown. But another headline really caught my attention: "As Chaos Swirls in the Region, the Shawarma at this Restaurant Keeps Spinning."[150] The article depicted Barbar's—a simple, no-frills restaurant that takes up an entire block in Hamra, Ras Beirut. It caters to the "poor, rich and famous." Its founder is a Lebanese, now retired, who in the 1960s, at age seventeen, worked on a Greek shipping vessel, and toured the world and its restaurants. Upon returning to Lebanon he opened a small *man'oosheh* shop. He tried a few times to turn it into a fine dining place, but that didn't work. So he went back "to his roots," his son said, which meant catering to people from all walks of life and religions, and keeping it a "tad gritty." Barbar's has never closed its doors since its founding in 1979, staying open 24/7 even during the civil war, Israel's bombardment, and occupation. During the war, the only thing the owner did was to "erect a ten-foot high sandbag wall between the entrance and the adjacent street to protect patrons." Such is the resilience and entrepreneurial spirit of the Lebanese. A Foreign Service friend told me recently that the State Department has considered sending a delegation to teach the Lebanese about entrepreneurship. We both laughed at the thought.

In Lebanon, food bridges religion, ethnicity, and politics. It remains an equalizer and an anchor, especially in turbulent times. During violent periods, the Barbar's article went on to say, feuding groups would stop fighting and take breaks to fill up on the restaurant's famous grilled meats, salads, and pizzas. People seemed to come from around the world to eat there; two years ago, the article said, "CNN ranked Barbar's first in a list of the world's best kebab places, coming ahead of restaurants in Israel, Iran, and Greece." The culture writer Amal Andary declared, "Barbar's resonates on a deeper level, symbolizing stability in a place so often shaken by unrest."

There's a word in Lebanese that encapsulates the important role that food plays in the society—*sahtayn*—meaning double health, and usually said with a satisfied smile to someone, a sort of *bon appetit* before, during, and after a meal. The response is —*ala albik or albak*—meaning double health for your heart.

Lebanon is a country whose cuisine is an integral part of its identity. But even there, in the last few years western fast food chains have gained ground, contributing to a rise in obesity and other health issues. Thankfully, there is resistance to this trend. One can find a revival of the country's healthy culinary heritage and a new focus on organic and locally grown food. Because, as the restaurateur being interviewed put it, "We don't become modern by throwing away the treasures and traditions we have."[151]

Pope Francis's Healing Salve

Back in the United States, it was the usual gridlock and infighting in Congress. There was mud-slinging between competing presidential candidates and toxic "Trumpeting"—all of which reminded me of the garbage crisis in Lebanon. Threatening to shut-down the U.S.government also sounded strangely familiar.

Since I have been visiting Lebanon more often, the transition as a bridge between my two cultures became easier, less fraught with anxiety. I realized that the insider-outsider dichotomy I had been writing about was changing. Although disconcerting and sad at times, it no longer felt painful to me. I could see the benefits of each vantage point. As an insider, I could appreciate the positive elements of my birth culture. As an outsider, I could clearly see what has kept Lebanon so vulnerable.

I will always have a dual identity. Even though I know I won't live in Lebanon again, it remains so much a part of who I am. When I'm in the United States I am also "at home" and I also see things as both an insider and outsider. A human bridge is suspended between two worlds, while remaining anchored in both encompassing what is wounded with what is healthy and vibrant. That's what makes us strong and able to weather the storms that inevitably cross our paths.

Growing up in Lebanon, I was well aware of all the drawbacks and problems the country faced. More problems have arrived since I left to marry Steve and call the Foreign Service and the United States "home." Despite all this, there is something special about Lebanon and its people that one can only fathom by living there. There are things I miss in my life in the United States: the *joie de vivre*, a more relaxed pace of life, the interconnectedness of people, and the safety net of my extended family and friends. And as Papi painfully discovered, there is no perfect country, government, or people. By our very nature, we are all imperfect, doing what we can and sometimes our best. I've been blessed with the ability to cross back and forth between many cultures and integrate what I felt was worthwhile and congruent with who I am. That openness is part of my Lebanese heritage as well as my American values: both, in their way, are pluralistic countries and historically, at least, open to newcomers. I came to understand that this feeling of being connected to "a place" depended a great deal on my reconnecting with myself, where I came from, and who I am today.

The conclusion of my 2015 visit brought one more unexpected experience. As we left Rita's cousins in the quarter where Tante Georgette used to live, I came face to face with the actual church building, the *yasoo'iya*, or Jesuit church, where that early encounter with the priest occurred. It was being renovated. I took a photo of it from across the street, not wanting to get any closer than that. It was if an invisible hand was holding me back.

When Steve asked me if I would like him to take a picture of me in front of it I immediately and fiercely said, "NO!" Every cell in my body refused to have me in that picture.

The power of that feeling surprised me. I had already found so much peace and wholeness since that little girl turned around and walked down the steps I was now looking at. They seemed smaller than I remembered, but the large iron gates were still there, and just as forbidding as in that early memory. My cousin Rita said she would take a photo of it once the scaffolding came down. "Okay," I said, not sure what I would do with it.

Later that year when Pope Francis came to the United States, I marveled at how this compassionate, inclusive Jesuit priest could belong to the same religious order as the one who denied me a place inside a house of God. Perhaps Pope Francis was the final healing salve for me. Now, I could truly close that chapter.

Life can only be understood backwards but must be lived forwards.
—Soren Kierkegaard[152]

12

Epilogue—Reflections on a Journey

The task of the unfinished woman is to acknowledge her life as a work in progress, allowing each passage, evolution, experience to offer wisdom for her soul. .... And at some point realise she has "recovered herself."

—Joan Anderson [153]

Reflections

At the time I was revising this chapter, I was co-leading an art therapy support group for eight Arab-American women of different ages, religions, and countries. One directive I gave them involved making a picture of their name, one in English and one in Arabic. I created this directive many years ago for "at-risk" immigrant high schoolers and found it very helpful with most multicultural clients. I now teach it to other therapists and counselors. It is powerful and illuminating because one's name is an essential part of one's identity. Each woman's drawing brought to light a struggle to integrate the different aspects of her present and past self with memories from a childhood and country left behind. The creative process gave each of them an insight into ungrieved and unresolved losses and, for some, a sense of existential "aloneness" that immigrants can feel.

Watching and listening to each of them delve deeply into themselves reminded me of how I have made the same journey, and how excavating and piecing together disparate pieces of myself had helped me feel whole. I was grateful that I am now at peace with my "differentness," and the fact that I will always belong simultaneously in two worlds.

My journey began long before I was born, when my parents bridged the gap between Muslim and Christian. But the toxic dregs of fanaticism hung on and contaminated my life. At age six, the circumstances of my interfaith identity, seen through another's bigoted eyes, damaged my inner child's innocence. Unbeknownst to me, my "prejudice detector" was born, and no doubt it went on to propel me to fight injustice, inequality, and intolerance. I grew up wanting, needing to help people connect and find commonalities instead of focusing on differences. This was perhaps the inner child's way of making sense of her world.

In hindsight, I wonder if the cruel encounter with the Jesuit priest was especially traumatic because I grew up in a communitarian culture, where the individual's identity is tied to one's social and religious group. One doesn't see oneself as a separate individual, but always as part of the social web of extended family and friends. Did feeling "different" in a society that is interdependent and interconnected make the incident more distressing? As confusing and painful as that was, the safety net of my immediate family helped create a loving shield, which attenuated and tempered the damage. In family- centered societies such as Lebanon and other Arab countries, the fact that you are born means you totally belong, unless you bring dishonor to the family. Had I been born and raised in a very individualistic culture like the United States, would that have been any less traumatic?

As a result of the priest's rejection, I've been wary of any organized religion or ideology, especially when it shuts people out or proclaims to have the only path to God or a Higher Power, the only way to "salvation." We love and maintain dogmas because they give us a feeling of security and "a false sense of 'I know.'"[154] "Fear of others closes our heart. We get caught in our own self-centered drama, everyone else then becomes "other" to us, different and unreal. Thus we lose sight of the the fact that they hurt, and it becomes easy to inflict pain."[155]

Something in my child's mind and immature, private logic led me to reach the mistaken conclusion that I could not belong because I was different. I rejected any search for a full sense of belonging. I unconsciously gave it up in one painful moment, and never looked back. Hence my never wanting to join any group, always having one foot in and one foot out, and being ready to leave if I felt a twinge of this "outsider" feeling. It may also be why I could marry someone from outside my culture. Along the way, I discovered the gift in this reality. It freed me to be who I am, to follow my inner compass, to be curious and open, to see the positive and the negative in other worlds, beliefs and to make my own choices. True, at times it was a lonely journey, but I wouldn't have wanted it any other way.

The inward pilgrimage I started many years ago allowed me to create over the years my own integrative, professional, cross-cultural model of art therapy. Creativity is not only everyone's birthright, but also an integral part of our spirituality; I am grateful for mine every day of my life. Combining the clinician in me, based in Adlerian Psychology and art therapy, with the artist that I am, reinforced my conviction that creativity and art are essential to helping people uncover unhelpful patterns in their life, and find the courage to change. Art makes visible what was hitherto in our subconscious, and it speaks with the body and all our senses. In this way, art helped me discover who I am, thus helping me heal the child within. In the process, I have drawn from other disciplines—Body Psychotherapy, neuroscience, cross-cultural training, Energy Medicine, Energy Psychology, mindfulness meditation, and Family Constellation—thus creating a holistic model that works for me, my clients, and students. It is a blessing and a curse, in some way, that being beholden to one thing feels too confining. It is a curse because it is more complex; it is a blessing because it enables me to use my creativity to help others, just as it has enlightened and enriched my life.

Even though on each return visit I found a Lebanon a bit different from the one I grew up in, I still felt deeply that I was touching my roots. Feelings I had not completely resolved surfaced again; but as I tell my clients, "Don't be discouraged; when an issue you thought you had worked on resurfaces, our psyche knows to bring these up when we're ready to work through them at a deeper level."

It was during my visit to Beirut in 2004 that I had an important insight and realized my inner little girl's central false premise. In fact, I never needed to choose between my Muslim and Christian family. I was and will always be both, and more. By refusing to divide myself up to fit anyone's narrow perception, my perceived "differentness" was painful at times. But it freed me to create my own spirituality—open, embracing, inclusive, and integrating a variety of beliefs, traditions, and worldviews. Although I was kept out by closed human minds, I always felt the caring hands of a Higher Power. Along with my father's words, these acted as a healing salve for my soul. I may have lost faith in organized religion, but I never lost my faith—a knowledge that we are all interconnected, that an entity larger than us is in each of us regardless of what name we choose to use. This Higher Power, God, *Allah, Dieu, Dios*, Great Spirit, the Universe, Great Mother, Great Mystery, is larger than that petty priest or any religious extremist.

As an adult I was able to see how my "story" of not belonging had become what Tara Brach calls a "false refuge." By exploring that narrative in this book, I discovered how I had been enriched and freed to explore, unfettered by the binding ropes of religion, groups, or theory. This nascent insight helped determine the path my life would take. Along the way I integrated the best of many teachings.

From Islam, I adopted the importance of generosity and helping others less fortunate, of connecting often with God, of learning to surrender to a larger purpose. From Native American spirituality I learned about the connection to Mother Earth and all living things. From Christianity, its essence of forgiveness (and yes, I have asked Saint Anthony to help me find things ever since I had to deal with my mother's tendency to hide things as she journeyed through dementia; Saint Anthony has always come through helping me locate mom's dentures, keys, or earrings). From Tara Brach's Buddhist teachings, the importance of mindfulness: pausing to go within, be present with oneself, to accept and befriend all that is, and the importance of compassion and lovingkindness for oneself and for others. Over the years I'm grateful for my father's teachings as I observe how religions do not practice what they preach, nor live up to their essence.

The large number of my paintings of bridges in Ottawa made me see that I had been moving through life building bridges. When I began exploring and reflecting on this theme in therapy and in my art, I became aware of the choices I had made in the past, was still making in the present, and how I might want to move forward. As I reached inward, art became the bridge connecting me with my authentic self. Throughout this journey of self-discovery, the images and words showed me where I was stuck and how to move on.

After being constantly uprooted, starting my life over again and again during our three decades in the Foreign Service, now my paintings on our walls tell the story of our lives, enrich our memories of people we met, stories we gathered, and hearts we were touched by and touched. Metaphors in my artwork acted like beacons lighting my path when it was dark and foggy, encouraging me, teaching me to trust the images, to dialogue with them and uncover my own spiritual journey. The images, together with the words they engendered, have been travel guides helping me find those scattered fragments of self and in the process provided meaning to my life experiences. Using my creativity as a catalyst enabled me to share my narrative with you, the readers, and by so doing come home to myself.

> *As the mind explores the symbol it is led to ideas that lie beyond the grasp of reason.*
>
> —Carl Jung[156]

Belonging vs. Fitting In

Yet, I felt there was still a piece that needed more healing. Just as my mother was disowned and shut out from her father's family, I was shut out of a house of God because of my father's religion. I asked myself, as her only child, had I carried mom's pain as well as mine, even though she never told me about it? Were there other ancestors who experienced rejection as well?

According to Hellinger's "Family Constellation" and other intergenerational energy work, whenever any member is excluded from the family and the feelings associated with that event are repressed, subsequent generations will share a similar fate. The "family conscience" does not allow for excluded members to be forgotten.[157]

We know that we carry our ancestors' genes; but how they

experienced their lives may have affected and even altered those genes. Ancestral fears and trauma then get replayed down the generations unless they are consciously brought out into the open, accepted, integrated with love into the family consciousness, and put to rest—thus saving descendants the burden of repeating the past, or worse, perpetrating more injustice. I hoped that bringing my mom's and my own trauma of rejection out into the open, and examining it, I might put an end to the pain that was buried, and prevent it from being transmitted to Leila and her descendants.

I decided to explore these themes and joined another "Family Constellation" workshop, which is somewhat similar to Psychodrama (creative role play to work through problems). Replaying my family's drama in a group setting, my mom— figuratively represented by a protagonist—could assert her place in that family and take back the birthright she deserved. I was then able to release my own fury and sadness for having been robbed of the chance to be loved and nurtured and known by my maternal Christian grandfather's family.

I believe it is very important to get in touch with our roots, re- connect with our past, explore the positives and the negatives, and listen to the stories of our family. Doing so helped me embrace the things that give me strength and meaning to life, and it helped me understand and put an end to destructive intergenerational pat- terns. Thus my feeling rejected and ostracized, as my mother also was, had to be unmasked, the trauma healed, and the whole story integrated into the "family soul." Writing my book helped me real- ize that we are the stories we tell, and it's only by telling them that we come to know ourselves.

This work helped me understand why, whenever I didn't feel accepted or understood, I would leave—just like the little girl did so many years ago. I turned around and walked away—away from prejudice, bigotry, and hatred. Later, I discovered the part of me that wasn't afraid to fight, which was nurtured by Papi's encour- agement, the grounding of my family, and, in adulthood, Steve's support. At some point, I had learned to turn around and confront people—to confront with words, art, and truth what I saw was dis- criminatory and unjust.

When 9/11 blew apart my old self construct as a predestined

bridge, I felt engulfed in the blinding dust and debris that I watched with horror on TV. It left me adrift in a new, yet familiar place where my "people" were being subjected to rejection, harrassment, and even violence by my "other people." As the two worlds I worked so hard to connect drifted further and further apart, it rekindled my own fear, sadness, anger, and probably the collective angst of most Arab and Muslim-Americans. I was caught in between the atmosphere of anger and fear I shared with my fellow Americans. Confronted with discrimination and violence against a group I belonged to, I felt the need to "show up" for our shared humanity. I began referring to myself as Arab-American, even though all my life I have shunned labels.

Eventually, this crisis gave me the opportunity to discover my deepest self. Yes, I was born a bridge, but the most important crossing I was making was the journey back to myself. Despite the pain and sadness I felt listening to the fear mongering and Islamophobia (spreading misinformation and hateful propaganda about Muslims and Islam),[158] the visual metaphors in the images that emerged from deep within me brought me a new sense of interconnectedness and grace. This part of my journey was not about putting myself back together. Rather, it was a spiritual journey that transmuted the poison of rejection and transcended my search for identity.

Being in a mixed marriage, and spending thirty-one years moving every two or three years was an interesting, though stressful adventure. I understood later how, during those years, my precarious sense of belonging was being tested over and over again. The incident with the nurse in Baghdad was especially painful, and the inequities I experienced as a Foreign Service spouse grated on me. Raising Leila, a "Third Culture Kid" and a child of a mixed marriage, added another layer to the experience. It was only when we finally "landed" on terra firma in the United States that I felt what I call the "wandering emigrant" blues. As relieved and happy as I was to finally put down roots, I felt as if I had just disembarked from a very long Foreign Service cruise ship, and still had my sea legs. I had to adjust to the permanency of remaining in one place and finding a new purpose and meaning in this reality. This was a new chapter in my life as an "immigrant" who has come to live for good in the United States, even though I had already been a citizen for over thirty years.

By the time "we" retired from the Foreign Service, the United States was no longer a welcoming place for "visible minorities," as Canadians refer to immigrants of non-European origins. That was especially the case for Muslims and Arab-Americans. The mood was definitely anti-"other." Unlike the six-year-old who chose to opt out of fully belonging and left, I had nowhere to run. There was no place for me to go to anymore that I could call home. The United States, being a salad of cultures, was the only country I had dropped anchor in, and this was where I could see planting myself for good. This is the home I know I can live in and want to live in; as an immigrant, I am "American by choice."[159] But I also needed to have the part of me that is Lebanese and Arab understood and respected. Along with Steve, I continued giving talks to help facilitate mutual understanding between the American and Arab worlds. Being both the "us" and the "them," I culled my Foreign Service experience in the Arab World and my Lebanese upbringing to help people learn about my birth culture. It was no easy task.

On a cruise to Tunisia and Libya, where Steve and I were lecturing, I learned another lesson. During my talk, the fact that one woman refused to even consider that all Arab women are not totally oppressed and that all Arab men are not monsters left me frustrated and angry. When I returned to our cabin almost in tears, art and journaling helped me face my obsession with changing the world one person at a time. I understood that my job is to plant seeds of tolerance and understanding. But it was not my role to stand there and make sure those seeds germinate and grow. Some just shrivel up and die.

By rewinding my life story to write this book, I came to understand the root of this outsider/insider feeling that has nagged me all my life. It was not about one or even several experiences. It is related to my whole identity. My first-hand-knowledge of different religions, languages, countries, and professions meant I could relate to every one of those connections, but none of them has "absolute supremacy" in my life.[160] Unlike the little girl who thought something was wrong with her, I now understand it is just the nature of anyone with a composite personality to be integrative and inclusive. The fact that I am the offspring of an interfaith marriage means I carry both Muslim and Christian "affiliations."[161] Being married to a white Anglo-Saxon Protestant American, and having spent three decades representing the United States, I have a strong affinity to and a soft spot for my adoptive country. Every additional "element" of my identity has created this "human bridge," adding to the complexity of defining who I am. I chose not to fit in any social peg hole, but I discovered my sense of belonging was always there. I could, and did, embrace the best of my Lebanese heritage and my American culture.

As my journey unfolded in these pages, I discovered that I do belong "here" and "there," even though I may not "fit in" one hundred percent—something that my inner child decided so long ago not to do. By the very nature of who I am, fitting-in was not an option. But I was never rootless nor lost between worlds. Rather, I reveled in my ability to navigate many different worlds and in the process helped bridge some gaps. My parents taught me, not so much in words as by how they loved and treated each other, that differences could only enrich our lives—if we let them. For a long time, I was trapped in that "outsider-insider" identity. I had confused feeling I don't "fit in" with feeling "I don't belong." Within my story, however, lived the awareness that belonging has always been my birthright. My parents' love and protection made sure of that.

In mining my cache of memories and putting them on paper, I was able to grieve the losses along the way. I believe that without allowing myself the process of "going to pieces without falling apart,"[162] I might not have been able to puzzle out the layers of my identity and reassemble them into a coherent whole. By releasing the traumas of the past, I could make sense of my life's journey.

Our last posting in Saudi Arabia coupled with a midlife crisis, triggered a release of all the anger, hurt, and sadness that I had been holding onto for a long time. These feelings coalesced with my sense of being trapped in the Foreign Service, needing to find a permanent home and put down roots. At the end, the catharsis of images and words that exploded allowed the healing to begin.

Years later, the image from a random scribble turned into "Beautiful Chrysalis," and brought more understanding of the transformation that had been taking place. I remembered years ago going to a butterfly farm and being mesmerized by the stages those

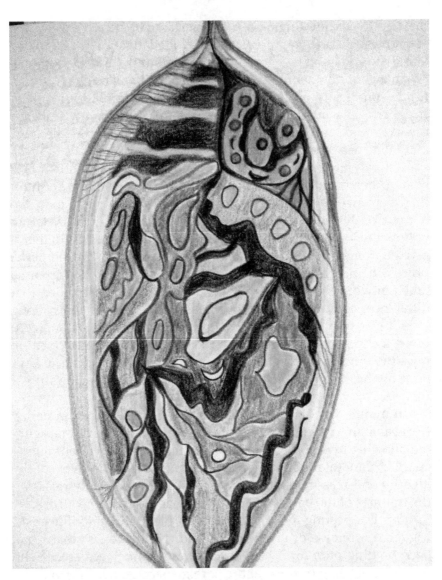

62. "Beautiful chrysalis." *Colored pencils ©Hala Buck*

beautiful, winged creatures must go through to emerge—and then the pause necessary to dry out their wings—before taking flight. "Beautiful Chrysalis" conveyed the full understanding of the transformation I was feeling.

"Beautiful Chrysalis"

Beautiful chrysalis
you're strong and vibrant.
Within you lies the power of metamorphosis.

Everything that is meant to be
lies waiting within you,
like folded wings gaining strength.

Your beauty like a stained glass window
in some sacred chapel
makes you glow from within.

Within you are roots and rivers, ,
movement and change
with every passing moment.

Moment by moment, day by day, ever shifting,
contained within the strong membrane
created by ancestral weavings.

They are all here
creating a humming, energizing sanctuary
for the beautiful unfolding destined to occur.

Butterfly woman is all in there
waiting
for the right time to emerge.

Intrigued by this image, I researched further the life cycle of the butterfly. How does a green caterpillar turn into a chrysalis, and then into a butterfly? I learned that within the chrysalis, a scary, messy metamorphosis occurs, which requires an almost complete disassembling of the caterpillar's original self. Its deconstructed essence churns inside the chrysalis and eventually, when the time is right, this mass coalesces and emerges as... a butterfly. But throughout this painful and scary process, the caterpillar doesn't know it will be a butterfly.[163] It is a great metaphor for how pain and suffering can transform into compassion and understanding, and a new way of being.

As it is for the chrysalis, the emotional upheaval our last posting unleashed was the catalyst for repacking and restructuring my life suitcase. It revealed the gift of recognizing the beauty and value in seemingly different and sometimes conflicting world views and bringing them together in a way that maintains their essential nature while creating a larger meaning.

This is a natural by-product of being a connector. When I looked back at my life, I saw that I have been bridging and integrating almost from the beginning. I had continually chosen what I value most from every culture and belief system I encountered. From my Lebanese culture, I embraced the hospitality, the caring for family and community, generosity, and *joie de vivre* and of course, the food. From my adoptive American culture, I adopted the importance of the individual, the fierce fight for equality, the ideals of human rights, freedom with responsibility, and opportunity to bring about change. And from both I took the thirst for knowledge and the openness to new ideas and worlds.

A month before "Chrysalis," in a strangely reversed, predictive order, the image of a butterfly woman emerged. I was journaling through a difficult transition time exploring the concept of that scary, uncomfortable feeling of leaving something, but not yet being ready to move towards what may be awaiting. Perhaps it showed me what can happen if we allow the process of change and transformation to take its course.

"Butterfly Woman"

Butterfly woman
resplendant in your new wings.
You stand with them unfurled
smiling at your good fortune.

63. "Butterfly woman." *Colored pencils ©Hala Buck*

You sprouted multicolored wings
matching the colors of your dress,
and stand like a gentle flower
in all her glory.
The wings you needed
were transformation wings,
it wasn't enough that you could fly.

You needed to dance around
the garden of life
nourishing yourself and others.

Your wings are so striking
that even when closed
you will no longer be invisible.

Your flowing gown
melds into the earth
like the roots of a beautiful tree.

You can fly and connect with sky
then land on a beautiful flower,
a gift from mother nature.

The last few lines above echoed the earlier collage "Waiting to dip my pen" (Figure 1).

At the time I was writing this, I was exhausted, struggling with Lyme Disease, and caring for my ailing mom. For a while I had to shelve this manuscript and focus on my health. But watching my mom slip further and further into the hell that is Alzheimer's, losing her sense of meaning and purpose, reactivated the desire to finish this book. In addition to bearing witness to my truth, it was also a way of saying "I matter. This life I have lived has meaning!" I'm grateful that Leila and I began collecting my mother's stories before she was completely engulfed in the fog of her handicapped brain. I hope that those stories will keep the essence of who she was alive for the next generations. Leila's play, *Hkeelee*, continues to do that.

As a therapist, I encourage my clients to tell their children and grandchildren their own story, and to ask their own parents theirs. Sometimes that lost piece of history is just what is needed at some point for people to make sense of their own lives. Weaving my personal history around the metaphor of a human bridge helped me accept and honor the complex layers of my identity, and guided me to articulate who I am beyond that paradigm.

Rainer's observation that writing is a process of self-discovery "rather than self-promotion" came to mind and deeply resonated with me.[164] My narrative evolved and culminated in the sand tray, which made me realize that I had indeed come "home" to myself, to who I am and to this land where I bloom best. I had finally dropped anchor where I could plant new roots that thrive and still be able to travel and visit my other home, the one I left behind so long ago.

It is not a coincidence that so much personal integration happened in my fifties and sixties—the stage of life when one can harvest experiences and, if lucky, enter the role of wise elder. Sadly, in American society, we no longer seem to have a role for the elderly. As someone said recently, we have many elderly people in the United States but not so many true elders. Nonetheless, my story had become an elder's story. I come from a culture that values and respects the older generation and maintains a meaningful role for them in the family and community. So, is this story I am sharing a synthesis of that heritage and aging baby boomers in the United States? Instead of looking into the future, anticipating uselessness and helplessness, are baby-boomers going through their own initiation to bring elder wisdom to a society intoxicated with youth—brainwashed to believe that hair coloring, cosmetic surgery, and Viagra will fend off aging and death? As one author's title says, "Don't Call me Old. I'm Just Awakening!" What counts, she writes, is the sense that our life's journey has helped us fulfill our spiritual destiny.[165]

While there is no template for how to be an elder in American society, and as some communitarian cultures also lose touch with their traditions, each one of us may have to create that path for ourselves. Teta Habouba passed down her wisdom to me in person. What about my daughter, grandchildren, and their children? Will this book help my descendants know who I was, and what lessons I learned?

Life as a human bridge may have been exciting, but it was also exhausting. Just think of an actual bridge: it's constantly buffeted by wind and water, internal and external pressures, yet it must always remain strong and flexible as it spans the divide. Lyme disease forced me to undertake a re-evaluation of my life. In addition to the effects of this debilitating disease, growing social divisions, anti-immigrant and increased hate rhetoric and actions were taking their toll on me. I needed a break so I could reassess my life.

A New Integrated Bridge

As I was putting the final touch on this manuscript, the image of an awkward-looking composite suspension bridge came up in my daily art journal. I was somewhat surprised but, as usual, I trusted that, together with journaling about it I would be able to understand its message. This bridge looked strange—it was partly the familiar stone arch bridge from before and a nascent suspension bridge. It seemed to signal that another transition was occurring, one where my old self, the stone arch bridge, had become an anchor for the evolving new suspension bridge. So I researched how such a bridge is constructed. The engineering alone was impressive and building it requires time and labor. I knew I was in another transition point in my life, but that was all. I realized that after 9/11 and the damage sixteen years ago to my former bridge-self, I had been gradually not just repairing and rebuilding, but building a new, stronger, larger, and more flexible bridge that can span wider and bigger chasms and separation. But it was no easy task.

As if to confirm this new aha moment, on the plane back from teaching in Vancouver, the flight attendant handed cocktail napkins to everyone in our row. Mine had a partial picture of a suspension bridge. Fellow passengers received ones with the Statue of Liberty or the Eiffel Tower, all with the airline logo. I saw those two noticeable things as synchronicities that I could not ignore. According to Carl Jung, synchronicities are "meaningful coincidences" if they occur with no causal relationship, yet seem to be meaningfully related. Both the drawing and the napkin having occurred within two weeks of each other, I felt this had to be important.

I have always admired and loved crossing suspension bridges I have encountered on our travels, such as the Golden Gate Bridge. Their tall towers are well secured in piers that are deeply anchored in the bedrock beneath the water. Steel-supporting suspension cables drape gracefully and attach at either end to solid anchorages that ground the bridge. The whole bridge must carry its own weight and that of those crossing it. Just like my stone arch bridge, it provides a way for people and traffic to cross over to the "other" side.

So I decided to take a workshop to further explore this new transition.[166] I had had my share of those during our years in the Foreign Service. We were asked to create a picture of the "transition" process we were in. Once more, I found myself drawing a suspension bridge; but even though I had learned about its construction, I could only draw half the bridge. Surprisingly I was not frustrated, just curious as to why?

Something was holding me back. I felt I needed to stop and wait for things to unfold. I have been "suspended" between worlds for so many years. That is why sharing my story may have been the way I hoped people would understand, through me and my birth culture, that we all have the universal and basic need to belong with

64. New unfinished suspension bridge. *Markers and pastels* ©Hala Buck

dignity. I see now how every word I have put down has helped me continue building my bridge-self. Perhaps what it was telling me is that only when I finally launch *Bridge between Worlds* will I be able to complete this new bridge.

Soon after sharing the drawing and story with our "Third Agers" group (as we call ourselves), my friend John said, "Hala, perhaps what this is telling you is that your daughter and her descendants will be the ones to finish it." That resonated with me and helped me see this new suspension bridge in a new light. I realized that, actually, my parents had started the stone arch bridge, which I then completed. The fact that, in this new picture, the stone bridge had become anchorage for this new suspension bridge now made a lot of sense. So all along, Leila had not just been building her own separate bridge, but participating, with her husband Adam, in continuing to build our intergenerational one.

Duerk encourages women to weave the threads of their lives into a fabric that needs to be named and then shared.[167] As I slowly untangled the yarn of my past through old stories that had kept me trapped, art showed me how I could reweave them into a rich new pattern. With compassion for my family, the United States, Lebanon, and myself I was creating a new tapestry of meaning—a new sense of wholeness. Each experience and each memory retrieved was a steppingstone that guided me towards my purpose in life. Learning to pause and reflect every now and then made me aware of the gifts strewn in my path, and reminded me that the journey itself is a "present."

My journey however doesn't end here as this new bridge showed me. I have learned that life does not unfold in a linear fashion but is rather circular, and at times confusing. It made me realize that the ladder in "Waiting to dip my pen" (Figure 1) was itself a vertical bridge that reached into my past to connect me to my future. The word journey entails a lifelong process, one in which, if we are lucky, we can come home to a sense of wholeness.

Madeleine L'Engle is quoted saying, "The author and reader 'know' each other; they meet on a bridge of words." For now, you, the readers, and I have met on this bridge of words, storytelling, and images.

May you have the commitment to harvest your life,
to heal what has hurt you, to allow it
to come closer to you and become one with you.

—John O'Donohue[168]

Notes

Prologue

1. Dag Hammarskjold, Second U.N. Secretary General, Nobel Prize Winner, Author. 1905–1961, www.en.wikiquote.org.
2. Hala Buck, *Dialoguing Soul* (Unpublished copyrighted manuscript, in the author's possession), Sequel II, 85.
3. Tara Brach, *True Refuge: Finding Peace and Freedom in Your Own Awakened Heart* (New York: Bantam Books, 2012), 154.

Chapter 1

4. Tristine Rainer, *Your Life as Story: Discovering the "New Autobiography" and Writing Memoir as Literature* (New York: Jeremy P. Tarcher/Putnam Inc, 1998), 98.
5. Munir Nasr, *Lebanon through the Lens of Munir Nasr* (Beirut, Lebanon: Arab Printing Press).
6. Ian Johnston, @montaukian, http://www.independent.co.uk. Independent, accessed 07/27/2017. Using remains found in the former Canaanite city-state of Sidon and dated to about 3,700 years ago, scientists managed to extract enough DNA to sequence their entire genome. They compared this to 99 modern Lebanese people and discovered these modern Lebanese had inherited about 90 percent of their genetic ancestry from their ancient Canaanite forebears.
7. Fouad Debbas, *Our Memory: Beirut, an Illustrated Tour of the Old City from 1880-1930* (Beirut, Lebanon: Naufal Group Editions, 1986), 178.
8. Marco Bonechi (Ed), *Lebanon: The Golden Book* (Florence, Italy: Casa Editrice Bonechi, 2000), 5.
9. Much has been written about the Sykes-Picot Agreement, and it continues to be a subject of extensive historical analysis. For two examples, see https://interactive.aljazeera.com/aje/2016/sykes-picot-100-years-middle-east-map/index.html, A Century On: Why Arabs Resent Sykes-Picot; and Robin Wright, newyorker.com. *The New Yorker.* "How the Curse of Sykes-Picot Still Haunts the Middle East," April 30, 2016.

10. For example, in the government crisis and reshuffling of 2009–2010, General Aoun, a Christian, allied himself with Hizballah, a Lebanese Shia Muslim group, and against another coalition of Lebanese Sunni Muslims and another Lebanese Christian group.

11. Dawn Chatty, *Syria: The Making and Unmaking of a Refuge State* (London, UK, C. Hurst & Co. 2017).

12. news,bbc.co.uk/2/hi/middleeast/6932786.stm. Accessed 06/08/2007. *Who are the Maronites.* Maronites were formed by Syriac Christians who have followed their patron Saint Maroun since the 5th Century AD. They are affiliated to the Roman Catholic Church but retain their own Eastern Christian traditions and practices. Most still use Aramaic in their liturgy.

13. Albert H. Hourani, *Syria and Lebanon: A Political Essay* (London: Oxford University Press,1954), 25.

14. This is further proof that Muslims and Eastern Christians coexisted in the Middle East for millennia and had not been killing each other without interruption. Muslim rulers allowed Christians and Jews to practice their faith as people of the book. Ironically, it was when the crusaders invaded the Middle East that Christians, Muslims, and Jews were indiscriminately massacred. "It is said that rivers of blood filled the streets of Jerusalem." Amin Maalouf, *The Crusades through Arab Eyes* (Transl. Jon Rothschild. New York: Schocken Books), 18.

15. The French "Security Administration" governed Lebanon under the French 'Mandate' from 1920 to 1943.

16. Rosina-Fawzia Al-Rawi, *Grandmother's Secrets: The Ancient Rituals and Healing Power of Belly Dance* (Transl. Arav M. Northampton, MA: Interlink Books, 2003), viii.

17. Ibid.

18. For more on Orientalism and its effect up to the present see Edward Said, *Orientalism* (New York: Vintage Books, 1979).

19. Ilan Pappe, *The Ethnic Cleansing of Palestine* (Oxford, England: Oneworld Publications Limited, 2007), 40–41, 90–91, 196–97, 258. And Phyllis Bennis, *Understanding the Palestinian-Israeli Conflict: A Primer* (Northampton: MA Olive Branch Press, 2019), 122–125, and 284-288. [Also: en.wikipedia.org. The Irgun was a right-wing Zionist underground paramilitary militia that operated in Palestine between 1931 and 1948 when Palestine was under British mandate. During the 1936–39 Arab revolt in Palestine against the British Mandate, the militant Zionist group Irgun carried out 60 attacks against Palestinian people and the British Army. Irgun was described as a terrorist organization by *The New York Times*, the Anglo-American Committee of Enquiry, prominent world figures such as Winston Churchill, and

Jewish figures such as Hannah Arendt, Albert Einstein, and many others. The Israeli Ministry of Foreign Affairs describes it as "an underground organization." *The New York Times* at the time cited sources ... which linked the Haganah paramilitary group to Irgun attacks such as the King David Hotel bombing. Irgun launched a series of attacks which lasted until the founding of Israel. Irgun attacks against Arab villages and consequent massacres in many villages included the infamous massacre of Deyr Yasseen.

20. Kamal S. Salibi, *Crossroads to Civil War: Lebanon 1958–1976* (London: Ithaca Press, 1976).
21. Alasdair Soussi, aljazeera.com. Al Jazeera. *Legacy of U.S.' 1958 Lebanon Invasion,* July 15, 2013.
22. Karen Armstrong, *The Battle for God* (New York: The Ballantine Publishing Group, 2000), 123.
23. Graham Fuller, *A World without Islam* (New York: Little, Brown and Company, 2010), 249.
24. *"I-Site"* consisted of vignettes from Katie's life growing up as a globally mobile Foreign Service kid who was also the offspring of a mixed marriage. The title itself is a play on words about place and identity.
25. Maggie Callahan & Patricia Kelley, *Final Gifts: Understanding the Special Awareness, Needs, and Communications of the Dying* (New York: Simon and Schuster, 2012).
26. John O'Donohue, *Anam Cara: A book of Celtic Wisdom* (New York: Harper Perennial, 1997), 83.

Chapter 2

27. Amin Maalouf, *In the Name of Identity: Violence and the Need to Belong* (Trans: Barbra Bray. New York: Arcade Publishing, 1996), 25.
28. Tabitha Petran, *The Struggle over Lebanon* (New York: Monthly Review Press, 1987). 34, 275.
29. Shibley Telhami, *The World through Arab Eye,* (New York: Basic Books, 2013). 32.
30. The U.S. State Department renamed it Cedar Revolution because of the meaning of it in relation to the Palestinian *Intifada*.
31. John O'Donohue, *Eternal Echoes: Celtic Reflections on Our Yearning to Belong,* (New York: Harper Perennial, 2002), xxii.
32. Bessel A.Van der Kolk, *The Body Keeps the Score: Brain, Mind and Body in the Healing of Trauma* (New York: Penguin Books, 2014). And Peter A. Levine, *In an Unspoken Voice: How the Body Releases Trauma and Restores Goodness* (Berkeley, CA: North Atlantic Books, 2010).

33. The emphasis on classical Arabic demonstrated the understanding and respect that American missionaries had for the local culture and language, which made them greatly loved in Lebanon and other Middle Eastern countries. This respect contributed to the good feeling towards Americans for over fifty years. It was only later, when Israel was created and Palestinians were displaced that disenchantment with the United States began. The 2003 invasion of Iraq and ensuing occupation—including the torture scandal of Abu Ghraib—exacerbated the anger towards and distrust of the United States in that part of the world.

34. When I was checking the spelling, I found out that *chutzpah* is Yiddish, but it originally came from Aramaic—the language of the first group of Semitic people that includes Jews and Arabs.

35. Amin Maalouf, *In the Name of Identity: Violence and the Need to Belong* (New York: Transl. Bray B, Arcade Publishing 2000), 22.

Chapter 3

36. Marcel Khalifeh.

37. State Department rules have changed since then, and such a nerve-racking step is no longer necessary.

38. Frederica Marsi, "It's all Relative," *Lebanese American University Alumni Bulletin* 17, no, 3 (Fall 2015): 7.

39. During the June 1967 Arab-Israeli war many Arab nations broke diplomatic relations with the United States because of its support of Israel. South Yemen was still under British rule, so they were not able to break relations. South Yemen gained independence on Nov. 1, 1967 and belatedly followed the rest of the Arab world by breaking relations a few years later.

40. Katherine L. Hughes, *The Accidental Diplomat: Dilemmas of the Trailing Spouse* (Putnam Valley, NY: Aletheia Publications, 1999), 36–37.

41. Ibid.

42. TCK is an acronym for "Third-Culture Kids," a concept discussed at length in Chapter 4.

43. HRH Prince Charles, "Islam and the West" (Oxford, UK: Ref. National Geographic Society, Al-Hassani chief editor), October 27, 1993.

44. Nuha Al-Radi, *Baghdad Diaries: A Woman's Chronicle of War and Exile* (New York: Vintage Books, 2003).

45. Rami Zurayk, *War Diary: Lebanon 2006* (www.justworldbooks.com, 2012).

46. Shankar Vedantam, *Social Network's Healing Power Is Borne Out in Poorer Nations* (www.washingtonpostcom.health, June 27, 2005).

47. Daniel Siegel, *The Mindful Brain: Reflection and Attunement in the Cultivation of Well-Being* (New York: W.W. Norton & Company Inc., 2007), 169–70.

48. J. M. Bumsted in Paul Magocsi, ed. *Encyclopedia of Canada's Peoples* (Toronto: University of Toronto Press, 1999), 197.

49. Dennis Jett, "Psst! Hey, Buddy, Wanna Buy an Ambassadorship?" *Foreign Service Journal* (Nov. 2012) 18–23.

50. John O'Donohue, *Eternal Echoes: Celtic Reflections on Our Yearning to Belong* (New York: Harper Perrenial), 7.

Chapter 4

51. Paula Reeves, *Heart Sense: Unlocking Your Highest Purpose and Deepest Desires* (Boston, MA: Conari Press, 2002), 131.

52. Amin Maalouf, *In the Name of Identity: Violence and the Need to Belong,* trans. Bray B (New York: Arcade Publishing, 2000), 1.

53. Ibid., 2, 46.

54. Tara Brach, *True Refuge: Finding Peace and Freedom in Your Own Awakened Heart* (New York: Bantam Books, 2012), 16, 20.

55. David C.Pollock & Ruth E.Van Reken Rev. Ed. *Third Culture Kids: Growing Up among Worlds* (Boston, MA: Nicholas Brealey Publishing, 2009), 21–23.

56. Ibid.

57. Ibid., xii.

58. Norma McCaig, Founder of Global Nomads International, passed away November 10, 2008.   third-culture-kid.com/tag/global-nomads-international-gni/.

59. Pollock, & Van Reken, *Third Culture Kids.*

60. Linda Bell, *Hidden Immigrants: Legacies of Growing Up Abroad* (Notre Dame: IND. Cross Cultural Publications Inc., 1997), xviii.

61. Michael Najjar M., Ed., *Four Arab American Plays: Works by Leila Buck, Jamil Khoury, Yussef El Guindi, Lamees Issaq & Jacob Kader* (N.C. and London: McFarland & Co, 2014), 21–44.

62. Pollock & Van Reken, *Third Culture Kids,* 246.

63. Ibid.

64. Mary Edwards Wertsch, in Faith Eidse & Nina Sichel (Eds.), *Unrooted Childhoods: Memoirs of Growing Up Global* (Yarmouth, MA: Intercultural Press, 2004), 127.

65. Lois J.Bushong, *Belonging Everywhere and Nowhere: Insights into Counseling the Globally Mobile* (Indianapolis, IND: Mango Tree Intercultural Services, 2014), 125.

66. Pollock & Van Reken, *Third Culture Kids*, xii.
67. Pollock & Van Reken, *Third Culture Kids,*146.
68. Pollock & Van Reken, *Third Culture Kids*, 126–129.
69. Ruth E. Van Reken, *Letters Never Sent: One Woman's Journey from Hurt to Wholeness* (Indianapolis, IN: Letters, 1995).
70. Linda Bell, *Hidden Immigrants: Legacies of Growing up Abroad* (Notre Dame: IND: Cross-cultural Publication, Inc. Cross Roads Books, 1997), 2.
71. www.qalqilyathefilm.com and www.skateqilya.org
72. Lisa Majaj in Eidse & Sichel (Eds.), *Unrooted Childhoods*, 5, 246.

Chapter 5

73. Sydney Barbara Metrick, *Crossing the Bridge: Creating Ceremonies for Grieving and Healing from Life's Losses* (Berkeley, CA: Celestial Arts, 1994), 29.
74. Mona Al Munajjed, *Women in Saudi Arabia Today* (New York: St Martin's Press, Inc., 1997), 105.
    Also See WETA/PBS *Frontline* and en.wikipedia.org.
75. Daniel J. Siegel, "Mindful Awareness, Mindsight, and Neural Integration," in *The Humanistic Psychologist*, 37:2, (2009), 137–58.
76. Margaret Coker, https://www.nytimes.com/2017/09/26/world/middleeast/saudi-arabia-women-drive.html. "Saudi Arabian Women Can Drive: But Here's the Real Roadblock," June 22, 2018.
77. Maalouf, *In the Name of Identity,*
78. Karen Armstrong, *The Battle for God* (New York: Ballantine Books, 2001).
79. Al Munajjed, *Women in Saudi Arabia Today*, 47.
80. Dona Lee Bowen (Ed.), *Everyday Life in the Middle East* (Bloomington, Indiana: Indiana University Press, 2014), 228.
81. Leila Ahmed, *A Quiet Revolution: The Veil's Resurgence from the Middle East to America* (New Haven, CT: Yale University Press, 2011).
82. Al Munajjed, *Women in Saudi Arabia Today*, 105.
83. Jean Baker Miller, *Toward a New Psychology of Women* (Boston, MA: Bacon Press,1986); & Carol Gilligan, *In a Different Voice: Psychological Theory and Women's Development* (Cambridge, MA: Harvard University Press, 1994). Both revolutionized the world of psychology.
84. Elizabeth Warnock Fernea, *In Search of Islamic Feminism: One Woman's Global Journey* (New York: Anchor Books, Doubleday, 1998), 421.
85. Warnock Fernea, *In Search of Islamic Feminism*, 415.
86. "Women Deserve Equal Pay," National Organization for Women. now.org. According to the Shriver Report, released in 2014, wom-

en's average annual paychecks reflected only 77 cents for every $1.00 earned by men. For women of color, the gap is even wider: In comparison to a white, non-Hispanic man's dollar, African American women earn only 64 cents, and Latinas just 55 cents. Even in 2019 it is only up to 80 cents.

87. In the interest of not feeding persistent stereotypes about Muslims, let me share some observations. I have found positives and negatives in every culture I have explored, and for every choice a community makes there is a price to be paid. For example, Middle Eastern families place less emphasis on the individual. Although I'm told even this is changing with the technology revolution, the family and the group still take precedence, as does the tradition of reciprocity. On the other end of the spectrum is the hyper-individualistic culture of the West, particularly of the United States, where we treasure individuality, at the expense of community. I believe the world needs to find a balance that will lead us to a place of interconnectedness. Historically the pendulum usually swings to one extreme before it finally reaches equilibrium.

88. As I prepared this manuscript for publication in the fall of 2017, an uprising by women in the United States against the sexual harassment and power wielding they have endured from men in many sectors of life was taking place. The #metoo movement was spreading around the world.

89. Clarissa Pinkola Estés, *Women Who Run with Wolves: Myths and Stories of Wild Woman Archetype* (New York: Ballantine Books, 1992), 367.

90. Hala Buck, *Dialoguing Soul,* Sequel, Part II, 100.

91. Kahlil Gibran, *The Prophet* (London: Heinemann, 1971), 61.

Chapter 6

92. Robert Fulghum, *All I Really Need to Know, I Learned in Kindergarten* (New York: Ivy Books, 1986).

93. Thomas Moore, *Dark Nights of the Soul: A Guide to Finding Your Way through Life's Ordeals* (New York: Gotham Books, 2004), 60.

94. Nina Jidejian, *Beirut through the Ages* (Beirut, Lebanon: Librairie Orientale. Imprimerie Catholique, 1997), 141.

95. Jidejian, *Beirut through the Ages.* During Emperor Justinian's reign in the sixth century it was in Beirut that law professors worked on commisions for the official revision of the entire legal system of the Roman Empire that culminated in the Code of Justinian, a judicial code that contributed much to the principles that underlie modern municipal

law. In addition law professor Dorotheos of the Beirut School of Law together with his counterpart in Constantinople, Theopilus, were commissioned to compile a handbook of civil law.

96. John Murchison Munro, *Giesen's Lebanon* (Beirut, Lebanon: Rihani House Publishing, 1984).

97. Munro, *Giesen's Lebanon*.

98. Barack Obama, *Dreams from My Father* (New York: Three Rivers Press, 2004), 305.

99. Moore, *Dark Nights of the Soul*, 57.

100. Growing up, I remember hardly any women in *hijabs*, the elderly like Teta Hajjeh just draped a scarf loosely when they went out, but the political and social scene had changed. Wearing the hijab had become a reaction to the West's cultural, military, political, and social intrusions. One theory is that whenever the West interferes, invades, and tries to dictate to the Muslim world, the women—mostly of their own choice (although not so much in Saudi Arabia), don the hijab as a way of asserting or reaffirming an identity. Paradoxically this feels like an act of defiance and liberation. Tradition became overlaid with adherence to religion, which provided an anchor for an identity tossed around in the storm of global politics.

101. Eva Dreikurs Ferguson, *Adlerian Theory: An Introduction* (Canada: Adlerian Psychology Association of British Columbia, 1984).

102. Kahlil Gibran, *The Prophet*. 104.

Chapter 7

103. Amin Maalouf, *In the Name of Identity*, 26.

104. Department of Justice, https://www.justice.gov/crt/combating-post-911-discriminatory-backlash-6, updated August 6, 2015.
https://aflcio.org/2016/4/6/backlash-post-911-america-extends-workplace-too.
https://www.huffingtonpost.com/.../911-15-years-muslims-middle-east_b_11938494.

105. "The Islamophobia Network's Effort to Manufacture Hate in America," Center for American Progress, Fear, Inc. 2.0: February 2015.

106. Marianne Williamson, *Healing the Soul of America: Reclaiming Our Voices as Spiritual Citizens* (New York: Touchstone, Simon & Schuster, 2000), 28, 31.

107. George W. Ball, *Error and Betrayal in Lebanon: An Analysis of Israel's Invasion of Lebanon and the Implications of U.S.-Israeli Relations* (Washington, D.C.: Foundation for Middle East Peace, 1984), 47–49; and Al

Jazeera, "Life among Israeli Cluster Bombs in Lebanon," Aljazeera. com, August 2015.

108. Amnesty International, "Israel/Lebanon: All Out of Proportion—Civilians Bear the Brunt of the War," November 21, 2006, Index number: MDE 02/033/2006; and David Fickling's article "Amnesty report accuses Israel of war crimes," *The Guardian,* Wednesday August 23, 2016. According to a *Haaretz* article of September 12, 2006 an Israeli IDF commander reported Israel's use of a million phosphorus shells and cluster bombs against civilian concentrations in South Lebanon and in West Beirut despite International Law and U.S. prohibition of using such munitions among civilians. At least 40% of those still litter the Lebanese countryside and continue to kill unsuspecting civilians, especially children.

109. Martin Luther King, Jr., in Marianne Williamson, *Healing the Soul of America: Reclaiming Our Voices as Spiritual Citizens* (New York: Touchstone, Simon& Schuster, 2000), 141.

Chapter 8

110. Ibn al-›Arabi (1165 C.E.–1240 C.E.) was a Muslim mystic, philosopher, poet, and writer who came to be acknowledged as one of the most important spiritual teachers within Sufism, the mystical tradition of Islam. *New World Encyclopedia.*

111. S. Halilović, "Islamic Civilization in Spain – a Magnificent Example of Interaction and Unity of Religion and Science," https://www.ncbi.nlm.nih.gov/pubmed/28468023 Psychiatr Danub, 201.

112. Maria Rosa Menocal, *The Ornament of the World: How Muslims, Jews and Christians Created a Culture of Tolerance in Medieval Spain* (New York: Back Bay Books, 2002), 33.

113. Ibid.

114. https://www.ncbi.nlm.nih.gov/pubmed/28468023. Accessed April 29, 2017

115. Thich Nhat Hanh, *Calming the Fearful Mind: Peace Has to Start in Our Hearts* (Berkeley, CA: Parallax Press, 2005), 23.

Chapter 9

116. Shakti Gawain, *"Awakening: A Daily Guide to Conscious Living"* (San Rafael CA: New World Library, 1991).

117. Philip Slater, *The Chrysalis Effect: The Metamorphosis of Global Culture* (Portland OR.: Sussex Academic Press, 2010), 15–25.

118. Jamie Sams & David Carson, *Medicine Cards* (Santa Fe, NM: Bear and Co.).

119. John O'Donohue, *Anam Cara: A Book of Celtic Wisdom* (New York: Cliff St. Harper Perennial, 1997), 14.

120. Lisa. B. Iversen, *Ancestral Blueprints: Revealing Invisible Truths in America's Soul* (Canada: Hignell Book Printing, 2009) 12, 36.

121. Susan Tiberghian, *One Year in the Writing Life* (Boston, MA: De Capo Press, 2007), 36.

122. Richard Stone, *The Healing Art of Storytelling: A Sacred Journey of Personal Discovery* (Lincoln, NE: Author's Choice Press, 2005).

123. Tara Brach, *Radical Acceptance: Embracing Your Life with the Heart of a Buddha* (New York: Bantam Books, 2003), 169, and *True Refuge: Finding Peace and Freedom in Your Own Awakened Heart* (New York: Bantam Books, 2012), 17.

124. Slater, *The Chrysalis Effect.*

125. David Whyte, *The House of Belonging* (WA: Many Rivers Press, 2006), 45, 46.

Chapter 10

126. Marilyn R. Gardner, *Between Worlds: Essays on Culture and Belonging* (Doorlight Publications, 2014), 29, www.doorlightpubs.com.

127. Recently on a National Public Radio show the food guru was enthusiastic about this great new food discovery from a chef who had grown up in a Kibbutz in Israel. One was *Zaātar or Zaa'tar* and the other was *bharat,* or as she pronounced it *baharat*—a favorite spice mix used widely in Lebanese, Palestinian, and some other Arab countries' cuisine and which the Israelis also have learned to use.

128. English transliteration of Hizballah, also as Hezbollah, or Hozballah.

129. William Bridges, *The Way of Transition: Embracing Life's Most Difficult Moments* (Cambridge, MA: Perseus, 2001), 2.

130. One U.S. Dollar in 1963 was the equivalent of .77 Lebanese Piasters. In June 2018 one U.S. Dollar is the equivalent of 1,516 Lebanese Liras.

131. Leila's performance was well received, with a great write-up in a prominent newspaper, *L'Orient Le Jour.*

132. *Mahhboosi* is the Middle Eastern version of backgammon.

133. The number of Syrian refugees has risen and now is the equivalent of half the Lebanese population. According to a recent European Commission report Lebanon has the highest per capita number of Syrian refugees. https://ec.europa.eu/echo/files/aid/countries/factsheets/lebanon_syrian_crisis_en.pdf.

134. Tripoli, Lebanon is 52 miles (85 Kms) north of Beirut and the largest city in the north of Lebanon. Its rich history dates back to the 9th century B.C. Ref: *Lebanon, through the Lens of Munir Nasr* (Arab Printing Press), 68.

135. Armenians fled Armenia and Turkey for Lebanon during World War I. One estimate before the civil war said that Armenians comprised 40 percent of the Lebanese population.

136. Louisa Ajami, *DNA of the Ancient Mariners*, Beirut, *Lebanese American University Magazine & Alumni Bulletin*, Vol. 29, Issue No.1, Spring 2018, https://magazine.lau.edu.lb/20-1/dna-of-the-ancient-mariners.php.

137. Ralph Nader, *The Seventeen Traditions* (New York: Harper Collins, 2007), 4.

138. Nawar Shora, *The Arab-American Handbook. A Guide to the Arab, Arab-American and Muslim Worlds* (Seattle, WA: Cune Press, 2009).

139. Kahlil Gibran, *I Believe in You* (to Americans of Syrian origin).

140. Maalouf, *In the Name of Identity,*18

141. The issue is a complicated political one given the number of intermarriages with Palestinians and Syrians in the country. Even though many groups are fighting to change that law, to date those efforts have failed.

142. Maalouf , *In the Name of Identity*, 120.

143. Youmna Jazzar Medrej, *Le Cèdre du Liban* (Beirut, Lebanon: Anis Commercial Printing Press s.a.l, 2009), 16.

144. Kahlil Gibran.

Chapter 11

145. Eckart Tolle, *The Power of Now: A Guide to Spiritual Enlightenment* (Novato, CA: New World Library,1999), 144.

146. Michael Gerson, "The Children among Syria's ruins." *Washington Post*, 10/15/15, https://www.washingtonpost.com/.../8d0510de-7360-11e5-8d93- 0af317ed58c9_story...

147. Hugh Naylor and Taylor Luck, *Washington Post*, 9-22-15, A11.

148. Stela: An archeological term for an ancient upright stone slab or column.

149. Conifers are evergreens that bear cones and have needlelike leaves. Anne Barnard, https://www.nytimes.com/interactive/2018/07/18/climate/lebanon-climate-change-environment-cedars.html.

150. *Washington Post*, September 28, 2015.

151. *Lebanese American University Magazine & Alumni Bulletin,* Vol. 15, issue 1 (2014): 44.

152. Søren Kierkegaard.

Chapter 12

153. Joan Anderson, *A Year by the Sea* (New York: Broadway Books, 2000), 170, 146.

154. Tolle, *The Power of Now,* 16.

155. Tara Brach, *Radical Acceptance,* 229.

156. Carl G Jung was a Swiss psychiatrist and founder of Analytical Psychology. He is best known for his theories of the Collective Unconscious, including the concept of archetypes, and the use of synchronicity in psychotherapy. https://en.wikipedia.org/wiki/Carl_Jung

157. Mark Wolynn, *It Didn't Start with You: How Inherited Family Trauma Shapes Who We Are and How to End the Cycle* (New York: Viking, 2016), 40.

158. https://www.americanprogress.org/issues/religion/reports/2015/02/11/106394/fear-inc-2-0/.

159. Ralph Nader, *The Seventeen Traditions* (New York: Harper Collins, 2007), 124.

160. Maalouf, *In the Name of Identity,*13.

161. Ibid., 19–20.

162. Mark Epstein, *Going to Pieces Without Falling Apart: A Buddhist Perspective on Wholeness* (New York: Broadway Books, 1999).

163. Bill Plotkin, *Soulcraft: Crossing into the Mysteries of Nature and Psyche* (CA: Novato, New World Library, 2003), 77–78.

164. Rainer Maria Rilke. *Letters to a Young Poet* (NY: Norton, 1962).

165. Marsha Sinetar, *Don't Call Me Old I'm Just Awakening! Spiritual Encouragement for Later Life* (Mahwah, N.J: Paulist Press, 2002), 133.

166. William Bridges, *The Way of Transition.*

167. Judith Duerk, *Circle of Stones: A Woman's Journey to Herself* (Philadelphia, PA: Innisfree Press, Inc, 1999), 53.

168. John O'Donohue, *Anam Cara,*198.

CPSIA information can be obtained
at www.ICGtesting.com
Printed in the USA
BVHW012234151019
561225BV00005B/89/P